D0354364

THE BIRTH OF HEAD START

THE BIRTH of

HEAD START

Preschool Education Policies in the Kennedy
and Johnson Administrations

MARIS A. VINOVSKIS

THE UNIVERSITY OF CHICAGO PRESS
CHICAGO AND LONDON

MARIS A. VINOVSKIS is the Bentley Professor of History at the University of Michigan, where he is also a member of the faculty of the Gerald R. Ford School of Public Policy and the Institute for Social Research. His books include *Education, Society, and Economic Opportunity* (1995) and *History and Educational Policymaking* (1999).

The University of Chicago Press, Chicago 60637
The University of Chicago Press, Ltd., London
© 2005 by The University of Chicago
All rights reserved. Published 2005
Printed in the United States of America

14 13 12 11 10 09 08 07 06 05   1 2 3 4 5

ISBN: 0-226-85671-2 (cloth)

Library of Congress Cataloging-in-Publication Data

Vinovskis, Maris.
    The birth of Head Start : preschool education policies in the Kennedy and Johnson administrations / Maris A. Vinovskis.
        p.   cm.
    Includes bibliographical references and index.
    ISBN 0-226-85671-2 (cloth : alk. paper)
    1. Head Start Program (U.S.)—History.   2. Project Head Start (U.S.)—History.   I. Title.
    LC4091.V56 2005
    372.21'0973—dc22

                                                    2004021033

⊗ The paper used in this publication meets the minimum requirements of the American National Standard for Information Sciences—Permanence of Paper for Printed Library Materials, ANSI Z39.48-1992.

For Daila Kuhr and Edward Vinovskis

CONTENTS

Acknowledgments / ix
List of Abbreviations / xi
Introduction / 1

1 Changing Views of Poverty
   and Early Child Development / 5

2 Education, Poverty, and Early Schooling
   in the Kennedy Administration / 12

3 Education Policy, the War on Poverty,
   and the 1964 Election / 35

4 Organizing OEO and Passing ESEA / 60

5 Implementing, Evaluating, and Improving
   Head Start Programs / 87

6 Congressional and Administration Debates
   about Transferring Head Start / 119

Conclusion / 145
Notes / 157
Index / 195

ACKNOWLEDGMENTS

My interest in the history of early childhood education began with the study of infant schools in early nineteenth-century America and continued with an investigation of the ways Puritans educated their young. Many individuals, including Carl Kaestle, Dean May, and Gerald Moran, have been instrumental in helping me pursue those interests over the years.

The present study builds on my earlier interest in the changing patterns of childhood education and merges it with my increased involvement with national education policy since the early 1990s. As the research adviser to the Office of Education and Research Improvement under Assistant Secretary Diane Ravitch in the administration of George H. W. Bush and Assistant Secretary Sharon Robinson in the Clinton administration, I had the opportunity to research and write about early childhood education and the National Education Goals. Subsequently, the Center for the Improvement of Early Reading Achievement at the University of Michigan under the leadership of Susan Neuman commissioned me to write an analysis of the Carter administration's attempts to transfer Head Start to the U.S. Department of Education in the late 1970s.

I am deeply grateful to the Spencer Foundation's Small Grant Program for funding this investigation of Head Start's origins. The grant provided funds for extensive travel and photocopying at archives and for the hiring of Tanya Hart and Elizabeth Leimbach, who provided invaluable editorial assistance in the early phases of the project. Archivists at various libraries were extremely generous and helpful throughout the entire project.

The University of Chicago Press was exemplary in expediting the publication of the manuscript. As an editor, Robert Devens provided enthusiastic and thoughtful assistance in meeting the challenges of writing a scholarly monograph for both policymakers and general readers. Jane Zanichkowsky was a superb copyeditor, and Bonny McLaughlin ably indexed the volume. I was especially fortunate to have two outstanding outside readers. Edward Zigler, one of the most astute analysts of and active participants in the early years of Head Start, made excellent suggestions for improving the manuscript. Barbara Beatty not only drew on her own expertise in the history of early childhood education but suggested the title for the book. And my colleague and good friend Jeff Mirel read the entire manuscript and made excellent substantive and editorial suggestions.

As always, the love and support I continue to receive from my wife, Mary, and my son, Andy, have made the writing of the volume much easier. During respites from research we have managed to watch the reruns of the first five seasons of *Buffy the Vampire Slayer*. Competition from Gerry Moran on the tennis court has reminded me of my limitations. And the weekly bridge games Mary and I play with Barbara and Jeff Mirel have added a source of pleasure and frustration to our lives.

The book is dedicated to my older sister, Daila Kuhr, and my younger brother, Edward Vinovskis. As we age together we are drawn more to each other, not only as siblings but as increasingly close friends with the same heritage and many of the same interests.

AFL-CIO	American Federation of Labor-Congress of Industrial Organizations
BOB	Bureau of the Budget
CAA	Community Action Agency
CAP	Community Action Program
CCAP	Citizens' Crusade against Poverty
CDGM	Child Development Group of Mississippi
CEA	Council of Economic Advisers
EOA	Economic Opportunity Act
ESEA	Elementary and Secondary Education Act
FAP	Family Assistance Plan
FERA	Federal Emergency Relief Administration
GAO	General Accounting Office
HEW	Department of Health, Education, and Welfare
HUD	Department of Housing and Urban Development
IQ	Intellectual Quotient
MAP	Mississippi Action for Progress
NDEA	National Defense Education Act
NEA	National Education Association

OCD	Office of Child Development
OE	Office of Education
OEO	Office of Economic Opportunity
OPED	Office of Programs for Education of the Disadvantaged
PPB	Planning-Programming-Budgeting System
RFP	Request for Proposal
RPP&E	Office of Research, Planning, Programs, and Evaluation
SRS	Social Rehabilitation Service
VISTA	Volunteers in Service to America
WPA	Works Progress Administration

Project Head Start has been one of the most popular and enduring legacies of President Lyndon B. Johnson's Great Society. Although questions remain about the long-term effectiveness of current Head Start projects, Republicans as well as Democrats support its expansion and improvement.

One recent suggestion for improving Head Start involves enhancing its educational focus. During the 2000 presidential campaign, candidate George W. Bush recommended transferring it from the Department of Health and Human Services to the Department of Education and emphasizing teaching literacy skills in early childhood education programs. After assuming office and encountering considerable opposition to relocating Head Start, the Bush administration backed away from its plans to transfer the program. But President Bush reiterated his belief that preschool education in general, and Head Start in particular, should prepare young children to learn to read. Indeed, the Head Start reauthorization legislation currently before Congress may require the program to emphasize academic learning and set new educational standards for participating children.[1]

As policy makers and the public debate the wisdom of moving Head Start or increasing its focus on educational components, the program's origins are frequently evoked to justify or explain advocacy for various policy options. For example, many policy makers contend that its founders never intended to design a program that was primarily educational but rather a broader early childhood development intervention for preschoolers. Unfortunately, the scholarly literature about the origin and nature of Head Start and other early childhood education programs in the Kennedy and Johnson administrations is limited and does not provide a balanced, in-depth analysis of the issue.[2]

Helpful introductions to the development of Head Start include Edward Zigler and Susan Muenchow's *Head Start: The Inside Story of America's Most Successful Educational Experiment*.[3] Zigler's insightful personal reflections and scholarly analyses are invaluable because they build on his Washington experiences and his extensive relationships with other key participants. In addition, Zigler and Jeanette Valentine co-edited a useful archival collection of documents and reflections on the early phases titled *Project Head Start: A Legacy of the War on Poverty*.[4]

Other scholars have devoted surprisingly little attention to the origins of Head Start. Although some older studies of the war on poverty may include a few pages or a chapter on the program, their authors lacked access to later archival and oral histories that offer additional insights.[5] More recent scholars usually devote only a few pages to it, as is the case in Barbara Beatty's fine historical study of early childhood education.[6] The comprehensive and otherwise useful new biography *Sarge: The Life and Times of Sargent Shriver* includes a chapter emphasizing Shriver's role in the development of Head Start but fails to acknowledge its diverse and complex origins.[7] Some prominent media columnists are accepting and repeating this biography's interpretation of the project's origins.[8]

A broader and deeper examination of policies toward preschools and Head Start during the Kennedy and Johnson administrations is needed. Although much of the earlier work emphasizes the role of Sargent Shriver, the Robert Cooke Head Start Planning Committee, and early childhood developmentalists, it does not consider other players such as federal education officials and members of Congress as thoroughly. The early contributions of congressional Republicans and the arguments of those who favored making Head Start a more education-oriented program, in particular, are neglected. Related developments in this period, such as Head Start's relation to antipoverty programs and education-improvement initiatives, have not been adequately incorporated. Moreover, scholars have not made full use of the files on these subjects in the National Archives, the Kennedy and Johnson presidential libraries, and regional archives.

This analysis places the origins of Head Start within the broad historical context of the 1950s and early 1960s. It encompasses the "discovery" of poverty, the changing perspectives on early childhood education, and the development of experimental preschool programs funded by the Ford Foundation and other sponsors. This study also explores President John F. Kennedy's attempts to deal with poverty and education and documents his administration's plans for supporting preschools for disadvantaged children. These efforts provided much of the subsequent advisory staff as well as the conceptual framework for many of Johnson's Great Society programs—including Project Head Start.

Drawing extensively on congressional hearings, debates, and reports, this analysis chronicles White House and congressional efforts to create the Office of Economic Opportunity (OEO) and Head Start. At first, the Johnson administration and OEO director Sargent Shriver focused on providing job training for disadvantaged youths and empowering local community action programs—with little attention to early childhood education. But House Republicans, drawing on the testimony of Urie Bronfenbrenner and other experts, championed preschools during the OEO's deliberations in 1964 and the passage of the Elementary and Secondary Education Act (ESEA) of 1965.

As the educational and political value of early childhood programs became increasingly evident in late 1964 and early 1965, the Johnson administration and OEO embraced preschools and created Project Head Start, funding summer preschool programs for more than half a million children. This study therefore focuses on the program's development within the context of the passage and implementation of ESEA and of OEO's Follow Through Program.[9]

The book also considers the challenges faced by Head Start in the second half of the 1960s, including debates about the nature and control of the politically controversial Mississippi Head Start programs, Head Start as an integral part of community action programs, the degree to which it would be an education program, and congressional attempts late in the 1960s to transfer it to the Department of Health, Education, and Welfare. Moreover, local and national evaluations of early childhood education programs as well as growing criticisms and continued defense of Head Start are considered.

This study uses information from the federal government, private foundations, educational organizations, academics, and the mass media. Of particular help were unpublished OEO, congressional, and other government documents located at the National Archives in College Park, Maryland, and the Kennedy and Johnson libraries. Previously conducted oral histories by some of the leading participants in Head Start provided additional information and insightful after-the-fact assessments of events. Specialized collections such as the Wilbur Cohen papers at the Wisconsin Historical Society in Madison, the Citizen's Crusade against Poverty collection at the Walter Reuter Library in Detroit, the Peter Dominick papers at the University of Denver archives, the Albert Quie papers at the Minnesota Historical Society in St. Paul, the records at the Ford Foundation in New York City, and archives at the Joseph P. Kennedy Jr. Foundation in Washington, DC, provided a broader policy perspective on the origins and development of preschools and Head Start.[10]

The book ends by summarizing developments in preschool policy in the late 1950s and 1960s and discussing the valuable contributions of the Kennedy and Johnson administrations to the creation and implementation of Head Start and other early childhood education programs. The chapter also analyzes the relation between politics and policymaking and the way in which that interaction may lead to adverse effects on those whom decision makers are trying to help. The conclusion notes the unanticipated long-term implications of some of the key decisions made during the formative years of Project Head Start—including OEO's decision to immediately provide large numbers of disadvantaged children with underfunded services despite objections from experts as well as leading Democratic and Republican policymakers.

Substantial progress has been made in helping many disadvantaged Americans during the past four decades. Many of those improvements have focused on the elderly. Despite periodic initiatives aimed at providing equal educational opportunities for all children, limited progress has been made in closing the achievement gap between children from disadvantaged households and those living in more fortunate circumstances. Our inability to provide high-quality, comprehensive preschool and K-3 services for disadvantaged children has been particularly disappointing. As we continue to review and revise Head Start, perhaps a broader and more complex analysis of its origins will be helpful. By analyzing the deliberations of policy makers in the Kennedy and Johnson administrations as well as assessing the strengths and weaknesses of their initial preschool policies, we may be able to clarify and improve the policy alternatives facing us today.

ONE

Changing Views of Poverty and Early Child Development

Educational needs in post–World War II America were influenced by societal shifts. For example, educators scrambled to keep pace with demands created by the postwar baby boom.[1] And the tensions that developed following the 1957 launch of *Sputnik* by the Soviets spawned a heightened emphasis on science and math education for more advanced and gifted students.[2] The special needs of economically disadvantaged students went largely unnoticed, however.[3] This trend changed with the belated discovery of poverty in America in the early 1960s. The new focus on domestic policy redirected educational reform efforts toward improving the education of children from poor families. Researchers and policy makers drew from changing views of child development as they began to provide early education for disadvantaged children.

The Discovery of Poverty in America

The economy grew substantially after World War II, following a slight decline between 1945 and 1950 (measured in constant 1958 dollars, personal per capita income fell from $1,870 to $1,810 in that period). In fact, most Americans saw a substantial increase in personal per capita income from 1950 to 1970. In 1955 it was measured at $2,027 and in 1960 it was $2,157, an overall increase of 19.2 percent for the decade. Real per capita personal income climbed to $2,549 in 1965, reaching $3,050 in 1970—an impressive 41.4 percent rate of growth during the 1960s.[4]

America's growing affluence was hailed by observers from varied camps. This new prosperity stimulated a baby boom, increasing the population from 152 million to 181 million between 1950 and 1960. During this period the federal interstate highway system was launched, and more Americans purchased automobiles. Home ownership reached an all-time high as many Americans moved from cities to newly built suburbs. Further, consumers had unprecedented access to leisure products such as televisions and fast food services such as McDonald's. Medical advances such as the development of a polio vaccine, together with improved nutrition, contributed to longer life expectancies.[5]

Not everyone shared equally in this prosperity, however. African Americans, Hispanics, and native Americans were still more likely to be poor and to face discrimination than were most whites, and large pockets of poverty remained in the South and in Appalachia. For example, according to the official 1964 measure of poverty, about one in five Americans lived below the poverty level. Whereas only about 15 percent of whites were designated as poor, almost one-half of African Americans lived below the poverty level.[6]

Yet most Americans remained unaware of—or chose to ignore—the plight of those who remained in poverty; some analysts, policy makers, and politicians, however, made occasional mention of the pockets of poverty and economic backwardness.[7] During the 1960 presidential primary campaign in West Virginia, for example, Appalachian poverty, a major issue, made a lasting impression on the Democratic challenger, John F. Kennedy.[8] In 1962 Harry Caudill published *Night Comes to the Cumberlands,* a vivid description of the region's plight, emphasizing the suffering of poor whites as well as minorities.[9] Michael Harrington's 1962 book *The Other America: Poverty in the United States* also played a key role in publicizing the economic disparities in the United States.[10] Noting the common belief that America now was prosperous, Harrington highlighted the simultaneous presence of widespread poverty. Indeed, much of it was invisible to middle-class America.[11] He documented its various forms, ranging from that affecting the elderly to that affecting alcoholics and the mentally ill, stressing the pervasive culture of poverty that affected all poor individuals. He also pointed out that inferior education and absence of job skills handicapped the working poor.[12]

Harrington's proposed solutions centered on the federal government's providing financial resources to and central coordination of the fight against poverty. He called for a comprehensive approach—including expansion of Social Security, an increase in the minimum wage and the types of jobs to which it would apply, better housing, improved medical care, and elimination of racial prejudice. Interestingly, Harrington did not highlight disadvantaged children's need for improved education.[13]

As awareness of persistent domestic poverty rose in the 1960s, other analysts explored its various forms and chronicled the plight of the poor. The findings were usually optimistic, indicating that poverty could be eliminated in the near future. Such optimism reflected growing faith among academics that recent advances in social science provided the knowledge and tools necessary to improve American society.[14] Thus, heightened awareness of domestic poverty in this period, together with the belief that the nation could eliminate it, inspired many policy makers and academics to search for more effective ways to help disadvantaged Americans.

Changing Roles of Day Care Centers, Nursery Schools, and Kindergartens

Children in the first half of the twentieth century had little opportunity for preschool training, in part because of the strong bias in favor of mothers caring for their children at home.[15] Indeed, the first White House Conference on Children, held in 1909, declared that home life was "the finest product of civilization. Children should not be deprived of it except for urgent and compelling reasons. Except in unusual circumstances, the home should not be broken for reasons of poverty."[16]

Despite this bias, the number of day care centers and day nurseries grew in the late nineteenth and early twentieth centuries. Custodial in nature, these charitable institutions were intended to provide the young children of working mothers both a safe haven and instruction in proper hygiene and self-control. Although poor mothers welcomed another child care option, they resented the accompanying stigma of being charity recipients and inadequate parents.[17] The small number of licensed day nurseries peaked at about seven hundred in 1916 but declined in the 1920s as new state-run mothers' pension programs emphasized home care and social work professionals criticized day nurseries for their lax oversight of participating families.[18]

In the 1920s the nursery school emerged as an attractive alternative to the day nursery. Nursery schools were geared toward middle-class rather than poor families, however, and child development experts saw these institutions as providing an opportunity for middle-class children to obtain better training and education than they received at home. Many nursery schools were affiliated with a university, yet they served only a small number of eligible children. Although the increasingly discredited day nurseries hoped to incorporate the education component as well, they could not afford to provide the same set of services to their poorer clientele.[19]

The Great Depression of the 1930s created hardships for many families, and thus the few remaining day nurseries endeavored to become more flexible in serving children and their families.[20] In September 1933 the federal government set an important precedent for federal involvement in early childhood for the economically disadvantaged by funding emergency public nursery schools through the Federal Emergency Relief Administration (FERA). In 1934 this effort was transferred from FERA to the Works Progress Administration (WPA).[21]

At the height of operations in 1937, the WPA sponsored approximately nineteen hundred nursery schools serving forty thousand children.[22] Federal involvement in early childhood education was justified on the basis that it provided temporary jobs for unemployed teachers, nurses, nutritionists, and cooks. The dynamics of this program proved interesting; although the WPA emphasized the education component of day nurseries, in practice the teachers had no training in early childhood development or education. The quality of federal services could not match that of the better private nursery schools. Federal day nurseries were short-lived, however. As the nation mobilized for World War II and the Great Depression tapered off, the number of WPA nursery schools declined. The program was abandoned in 1943.[23]

The mobilization caused labor shortages in many sectors of the workforce, and women—often mothers—were recruited to staff the defense industry. The temporary labor shortage helped many Americans accept the idea that working mothers were patriotic, although others (such as staff of the U.S. Children's Bureau) opposed the entry of women into the labor force—especially those with children under the age of two. Divisions remained regarding the advisability of this practice, but the war emergency mitigated the most intense public hostility toward it.[24]

In response to the large-scale entry of mothers into the workforce, the Community Facilities Act of 1941 (the Lanham Act) permitted the federal government to fund child care centers; approximately six hundred thousand children participated in such programs between 1942 and 1946.[25] Many of the Lanham Act centers replaced WPA institutions, and a few defense industries even provided their own day care facilities. Although most mothers relied on relatives or neighbors for child care, some took advantage of these additional day nurseries.[26]

Following the postwar demobilization, the Lanham Act was repealed and the federal government ceased to fund day care centers. Although many facilities closed, some survived because the cities and states where they operated continued to fund them. The postwar day care situation resembled that of the 1920s: most working mothers relied on friends and relatives for assistance and a small minority utilized day nurseries or nursery schools. Postwar society, however, nurtured a gradual acceptance of the idea that married women could work outside the home and that their young children might benefit from enrollment in good child care centers.[27]

Although the first half of the twentieth century saw much debate about the benefits and detriments of day nurseries and nursery schools, kindergarten was becoming an acceptable component of education and was being incorporated into public school systems. In fact, the number of kindergarten students rose from 481,000 in 1920 to 723,000 in 1930 and, following a slight decline during the depression, reached one million in 1950 and two million by 1960.[28] The nature of these institutions varied considerably, and few resembled the more rigid model initially prescribed by Friedrich Froebel and his American followers. Most kindergartens operated for only half a day and focused on play and social activities rather than improving cognitive skills.[29] This was not unusual. On the whole, most early twentieth-century day nurseries, nursery schools, and kindergartens did not emphasize cognitive improvement. Instead, these institutions usually offered custodial care for the children of working mothers.

Changing Views of Child Development

Until the mid-twentieth century, leading child development and testing experts assumed that IQ was hereditary and fixed at birth. Moreover, most experts held that children's learning depended on their physical and mental maturation and that there was little point in trying to increase IQ by means of early childhood education. Thus, their analyses focused on groups rather than individuals, and reports detailed intergroup differences in IQ.[30]

A few child developmentalists demurred from this consensus. The scientists at the University of Iowa's Child Welfare Research Station, for example, challenged the idea that a child's IQ was innate, constant, and incapable of enhancement. Bird T. Baldwin, director of the Iowa Station, felt that early childhood training was valuable and established a laboratory to measure preschool children's mental and physical development. In 1927, as a result of his research, Baldwin called for a nationwide system of preschools to help children develop to their full potential. During the 1930s and early 1940s, University of Iowa scientists such as Kurt Lewin, George Stoddard, and Beth Wellman continued to challenge the idea of a hereditary, constant IQ, but they were unable to persuade colleagues at other institutions.[31]

In fact, prominent scholars such as Florence Goodenough and Lewis M. Terman attacked the work of the Iowa scientists. Not only did they reject the idea that IQ was not predetermined at birth, but they criticized the statistical methods employed in the Iowa studies.[32] Thus, dissenting research was suppressed and the prevailing view that IQ remains constant over time and that children's learning depends on maturation dominated the field of child development during the first half of the century.

Donald O. Hebb issued a major challenge to the fixed-IQ orthodoxy in 1949 when he published the ground-breaking book *The Organization of Behavior*. Hebb stressed that differences in IQ stemmed in large part from differences in early learning and environment rather than from variations among brains—a theory that accounted for most of the disparity between whites and African Americans on standardized intelligence tests.[33]

In the 1950s and early 1960s academics' and policy makers' view of early childhood development and education shifted dramatically. Scholars such as J. McVicker Hunt and Benjamin S. Bloom argued that children's intelligence was not fixed at birth and could be significantly altered by improving their environment. In 1961 Hunt published his seminal book *Intelligence and Experiences*. He accepted the biological inheritance theory but argued that children's experiences also influenced their intellectual development.[34] As Hunt later summarized his approach: "Man's nature has not changed since World War II, but some of our conceptions of his nature have been changing rapidly. These changes make sensible the hope that, with improved understanding of early experience, we might counteract some of the worst effects of cultural deprivation and raise substantially the average level of intellectual capacity."[35]

This new approach, according to Hunt, was essential for overcoming the cultural deprivation of economically disadvantaged children—in part by developing effective preschool programs:

> The intellectual inferiority apparent among so many children of parents of low educational and socioeconomic status, regardless of race, is already evident by the time they begin kindergarten or first grade at age 5 or 6. . . . These deficiencies give such children the poor start which so commonly handicaps them ever after in scholastic competition. . . .
>
> At this stage of history and knowledge, no one can blueprint a program of preschool enrichment that will with certainty be an effective antidote

for the cultural deprivation of children. On the other hand, the revolution-ary changes taking place in the traditional beliefs about the development of human capacity and motivation make it sensible to hope that a program of preschool enrichment may ultimately be made effective. The task calls for creative innovations and careful evaluative studies of their effectiveness.[36]

Using eight longitudinal studies of children's physical, mental, and psy-chological development, Bloom supported Hunt's assertion that both envi-ronment and heredity played a key role in establishing IQ. He emphasized the first four years of life in particular as the "critical period" for a child's intellec-tual development: "Thus height growth for boys is almost as great during the 9 months from conception to birth as it is during the 9 years from age 3 to age 12. General intelligence appears to develop as much from conception to age 4 as it does during the 14 years from age 4 to age 18."[37] Yet, reinforcing Hunt's earlier warnings, Bloom pointed out that experts could not pinpoint the strategies or specific programs that helped disadvantaged children learn more effectively—in large part because they did not understand the nature of early learning among humans.[38]

Hunt and Bloom produced some of the earliest and most effective argu-ments for early childhood education in the late 1950s and early 1960s. Their work provided much of the scientific justification for the Head Start pro-gram. But other scholars, drawing on their own work as well as the "discov-ery" of poverty in America, also contributed to the growing interest in early education and compensatory schooling programs.[39] Meetings such as the Arden House Conference on the Preschool Environment of Socially Disad-vantaged Children in 1962 and the University of Chicago's Research Confer-ence on the Education of the Culturally Deprived in 1964 grappled with the issue of poverty and the difficulties faced by poor children in school.[40]

During this period, researchers piloted experimental programs designed to enrich the intellectual experiences of disadvantaged children in cities such as Nashville, New York, and Syracuse.[41] And the Ford Foundation, among other nonprofit organizations, played a key role in funding education projects designed to address the broader concerns of poverty and community devel-opment by means of its Great Cities Schools Program. Two Ford Foundation projects, one in Baltimore and one in North Carolina, even developed preschool programs to meet the needs of disadvantaged children.[42] These efforts contributed to a new awareness that it might be possible to enhance IQ by focusing on improving the learning environment. And these activities set the stage for the launch of Head Start in the mid-1960s.

Education, Poverty, and Early Schooling
in the Kennedy Administration

Most studies of Head Start begin by examining the role of the Johnson administration in early childhood development and education. That approach, however, overlooks the Kennedy administration's substantial contributions to K-12 schooling, poverty elimination, and early childhood education. Moreover, several key Johnson poverty and education policy analysts served in the Kennedy White House, and many of the proposals initiated during the Kennedy administration to address these issues were revised and incorporated into Johnson's war on poverty.

Early Federal Involvement in Education

Although the U.S. Constitution does not directly mention a federal role in education, the government has periodically encouraged schools or helped finance them. The federal government participated in local education even before the 1787 drafting of the Constitution, when the Congress of the Confederation adopted the Survey Ordinance of 1785, reserving one section of every township in the Western Territory for establishment of schools. In 1787 the authors of the Northwest Ordinance declared that "religion, morality, and knowledge being necessary to good government and the happiness of mankind, schools and the means of education shall forever be encouraged."[1] During the Civil War, Congress enacted the Morrill Act, allocating federal land to each state so that states could establish colleges to provide training in agricultural and mechanical arts (the "land-grant colleges"). Congress expanded this legislation in 1890 to help fund the operation of those colleges and amended the Morrill Act again in 1907 and 1935 to increase those subsidies.[2]

Although a federal noncabinet-level Department of Education was created in 1867, it was reduced to the Bureau of Education in 1868 (later reorganized as the Office of Education) owing to controversy about its operation and responsibilities. The agency remained quite small, and it focused on collecting, analyzing, and disseminating statistical information. It was also responsible for such miscellaneous tasks as overseeing education in the Alaska Territory. Oversight of the Office of Education was transferred to the Department of Health, Education and Welfare (HEW) when this agency was created in 1954.[3]

During the late nineteenth and early twentieth centuries, Congress resisted most requests for federal aid for public education. There were, however, a few notable exceptions to this trend. Congress passed the Smith-Hughes Act in 1917 to support courses and teacher training in agriculture, home economics, and trades and industries. During the Great Depression the Public Works Administration provided school construction assistance, and the Federal Emergency Relief Administration funded adult education and nursery school programs. The 1940 Lanham Act authorized federal aid to communities with significant military and defense industry populations. (The Lanham Act preceded the 1950s "impacted" areas aid.) And the 1944 Servicemen's Readjustment Act (GI Bill of Rights) provided educational benefits to veterans.[4]

During both world wars, worries about high illiteracy rates among draftees as well as concern about the uneven quality of state and regional education led to calls for general federal educational aid for schools in states that lacked adequate resources. These attempts, usually led by the Democrats and the National Education Association (NEA), received a major boost in 1946 when the conservative senator Robert A. Taft (R-OH) dropped his opposition and called for general school aid. In 1948 both party platforms endorsed federal aid for education. Although the Senate managed to pass legislation approving general school aid several times in the late 1940s and 1950s, controversies about aiding private schools and funding segregated institutions, together with fear of federal control over local education, doomed most of those proposals. They fared especially poorly in the House of Representatives, where a powerful, conservative Rules Committee scuttled most such initiatives.[5]

Despite these hurdles, federal aid to education after World War II increased during the Truman administration from $292 million in fiscal year 1945 to a peak of $3.3 billion in fiscal year 1949, dropping to $2 billion in fiscal year 1952. During those eight years, the federal government spent a total of $17.7 billion on education. Elementary and secondary schools received only 7 percent of this total, however (and almost two-thirds of this amount was funneled through the 1946 National School Lunch program). In fact, about one-half of total federal education support went to higher education (with veterans' benefits—via the GI Bill of Rights—accounting for 90 percent of such expenditures).[6]

Educational Involvement during the Eisenhower Administration

The administration of Dwight D. Eisenhower expanded federal educational involvement in several areas while reducing the overall federal financial investment. Although Eisenhower had opposed general federal aid to education in 1949, he endorsed classroom construction assistance during his 1952 presidential campaign.[7]

The new areas of federal involvement were varied. The Agricultural Act of 1954 authorized the supply of milk to nonprofit schools, summer camps, and certain childcare programs. Despite Eisenhower's opposition, the impact aid program was not only continued but considerably expanded in scope and funding. In 1950 Congress designated funds with which the National Science Foundation could support research. In addition, Congress passed legislation in 1954 creating the Cooperative Research Program, which allowed the Office of Education to enter into cooperative agreements or contracts with colleges and universities for joint studies of education issues. The largest federal education initiative during the Eisenhower era, however, was the National Defense Education Act (NDEA) of 1958. This legislation was developed in response to the Soviets' successful launch of *Sputnik* a year earlier. The NDEA program endeavored to bolster science, mathematics, and foreign language instruction at all grade levels. It also set an important precedent for federal involvement in education that meets broadly defined national defense needs.[8]

Even when measured in current dollars and considering its expansion in new areas of education, the federal government spent less money on education during the Eisenhower administration than did the Truman administration ($14.7 billion and $17.7 billion, respectively). There were also significant shifts in the ways those funds were spent. Although Eisenhower extended GI educational benefits to Korean War veterans, the share of monies spent on veteran education between 1952 and 1960 declined from more than one-half of all federal education expenditures to less than one-quarter. Federal elementary and secondary spending increased from $1.2 billion to $4.5 billion. As a result of these shifts, the federal government allocated 31 percent of its education funding to elementary and secondary education.[9]

Federal support for higher education fell from $10 billion in the Truman administration to $7.4 billion in the Eisenhower administration, mainly because aid to veterans in colleges and universities dropped from $9 billion to $3.2 billion. Research and development funding, however, rose, and assistance to college and university facilities grew. Aid to college students also increased during this period from $64 to $710 million. Overall, the relative amount of support for higher education dropped from 57 to 50 percent of federal aid.[10]

Lawmakers had numerous hurdles to overcome when implementing these changes. Lukewarm White House support for classroom construction, Republicans' and conservatives' hostility to an expanded federal involvement, northern liberals' insistence on desegregating southern schools, and Protestants' opposition to sharing federal funds with Catholic parochial schools limited federal education initiatives.[11]

Education in the 1960 Presidential Election

Republicans and Democrats brought disparate strengths and weaknesses to the table in the 1960 presidential campaign. The GOP benefited from Eisenhower's eight years of high approval ratings, but they were weakened by decisive losses in other Eisenhower-era political contests. Particularly disheartening was the Democratic sweep of the 1958 midterm elections—the most successful Democratic election since Roosevelt's 1936 landslide victory. Democrats gained 48 seats in the House and 15 seats in the Senate, resulting in impressive majorities of 282 to 154 and 64 to 34, respectively.[12] Following a brief, disappointing exploratory campaign, New York governor Nelson Rockefeller dropped out of the race for the Republican nomination, and the party selected then Vice President Richard M. Nixon as their presidential standardbearer. United States ambassador Henry Lodge was chosen as his running mate.[13]

Democrats sensed an opportunity to recapture the White House, and four

major contenders, all senators, vied for the Democratic nomination: Hubert
H. Humphrey of Minnesota, John F. Kennedy of Massachusetts, Stuart Symington of Missouri, and Lyndon B. Johnson of Texas. Only Humphrey and
Kennedy entered the primaries; Symington and Johnson staked their hopes
on a deadlocked convention that might then offer one of them the nomination. Although Kennedy's Catholicism dominated preconvention debates and
analyses, a series of hard-fought primary victories caused Humphrey to with-
draw after a loss in West Virginia. Kennedy was nominated on the first ballot
at the Los Angeles convention, where he surprised many politicians and liberals by naming Senate Majority Leader Johnson as his running mate—part
of his fall strategy to win the South.[14]

Nominations secure, Kennedy and Nixon turned their attention toward
the November elections. Although much of the contest between them focused on religion and the importance of prior experience in the White
House, differences regarding education surfaced as well. A September 1959
poll revealed that voters trusted Democrats' handling of education more
than Republicans' by a margin of 31 percent to 12 percent (45 percent saw no
difference).[15] During deliberations on an education bill in February 1960,
Democrats maneuvered Vice President Nixon into casting the tie-breaking
vote against an amendment offered by Senator Joseph S. Clark Jr. (D-PA) to
provide $1.1 billion in federal funds for school construction and teachers'
salaries.[16] Although the public favored the former, most opposed the latter.[17]

After his nomination, Nixon countered the Democratic attacks on his education policies, shaping the GOP platform to endorse federal aid for elementary and secondary school construction but opposing assistance for
teachers' salaries.[18] The Democratic platform, however, argued that American education faced a financial crisis necessitating federal intervention including both types of aid.[19]

During the campaign, Kennedy and Nixon raised the issue of education
several times. The *New York Herald Tribune* surveyed both candidates on seven
key education issues that highlighted their differences. The survey focused especially on federal aid for teachers' salaries.[20] Kennedy frequently pointed
out that Republicans had voted against school construction bills and reminded voters that Nixon cast the "tie-breaking vote killing a Democratic bill
giving states money to raise teachers' salaries."[21] During the first debate,
Nixon rebutted Democratic calls for salary assistance, warning viewers that
"we want higher teachers' salaries; we need higher teachers' salaries; but we
also want our education to be free of federal control. When the federal government gets the power to pay teachers, inevitably, in my opinion, it will ac-
quire the power to set standards and to tell the teachers what to teach."[22]

Although education was discussed frequently, neither candidate raised the issue of preschools during the campaign. For example, when Nixon referred to early schooling, he mentioned kindergartens but not preschools.[23] Instead, the candidates focused more on providing aid to public elementary and secondary schools via federal subsidies for construction and salaries—issues that had been debated throughout the 1950s.[24]

The 1960 election was one of the closest in American history. Kennedy managed a narrow popular vote victory of 34,221,349 to 34,108,546. But he carried the electoral college by a decisive vote of 303 to 219.[25] Religion played a significant role in determining whom voters supported: some normally Democratic Protestants, especially in the South and the Midwest, voted for Nixon, and some GOP Catholics in the industrial Northeast crossed party lines and voted for Kennedy. One scholar concluded that, overall, Kennedy's religion cost him popular votes but aided him in the electoral college.[26] Democrats recaptured the White House, but Republicans gained 20 seats in the House and 2 seats in the Senate. These modest gains, however, did not threaten the solid Democratic majority of 263 to 174 in the House and 64 to 36 in the Senate.[27]

The Kennedy Administration and K-12 Education

Although he had a high IQ, John Kennedy's student years were not marked by academic excellence. Kennedy was more interested in social and extracurricular activities than in his studies. Following a mediocre academic performance in his first two years at Harvard University, however, he became interested in international affairs—partly because he spent time abroad with his father, who had been appointed the U.S. ambassador to Great Britain. This interest provided the motivation for his honors thesis about the English appeasement of Hitler; hastily and poorly written, it nonetheless reflected considerable research and contained some interesting insights. With helpful advice from the *New York Times'* Arthur Krock and others, Kennedy revised and published his timely study as *Why England Slept.*[28]

When Kennedy was sent to Congress in 1946, he was assigned to the House Education and Labor Committee; after election to the Senate in 1952, he served on the Labor and Public Welfare Committee, which had jurisdiction over education. Despite these assignments, his involvement in education was modest during most of his tenure in Congress. He often focused more on the interests of his constituents than on those of the nation as a whole. But as he prepared for a possible presidential campaign after 1956, Kennedy began to address education issues more broadly and supported increased federal involvement in public schools.[29]

Following the 1960 victory, the incoming Kennedy administration announced its cabinet members and top White House staff by mid-December. The cabinet was ideologically mixed and included several prominent Republicans. Connecticut governor Abraham Ribicoff was named Secretary of HEW but was regarded as an ineffective administrator.[30] Ribicoff headed this department for less than two years, leaving to run—successfully—for a Senate seat. Thus, much of Kennedy's congressional education agenda was handled by White House Special Counsel Ted Sorensen, Deputy Special Counsel for Budget and Programming Myer (Mike) Feldman, and HEW's assistant secretary for legislation, Wilbur Cohen.[31] The Bureau of the Budget (BOB), under the leadership of David E. Bell, also played a large role in the drafting and vetting of Kennedy administration education initiatives.[32] Unlike Eisenhower, Kennedy did not appoint a chief of staff or delegate much authority outside the White House. The cabinet usually met only once a month as a group and did not play a significant role in decision making.[33]

Many of the new administration's policies had been formulated and announced during the campaign. Kennedy created seven task forces (eventually expanded to twenty-nine) to assist in transition-stage policy planning. Most task force reports appeared in newspapers; eleven of them were also reprinted in a 1961 book, *New Frontiers of the Kennedy Administration*.[34] The Education Task Force recommended that "first priority . . . be given to a vigorous program to lift the [public] schools to a new level of excellence." On the basis of the average daily attendance in public schools, the task force suggested that the federal government provide $30 per annum per child to all states, an additional $20 per child to states with personal income below 70 percent of the national average, and $20 more per child to cities with populations exceeding 300,000 "which are facing unique and grave educational problems." It recommended that these monies be used for school construction, salaries, and educational improvements.[35]

The Education Task Force also called for expanding the federal college housing loan program, providing grants and loans for academic facilities for institutions of higher education, extending for another five years the National Defense Education Act (with some modifications), creating a President's Advisory Committee, taking steps to facilitate fundraising, and covering the indirect costs of research in higher education.[36]

The task force released its influential policy recommendations on January 6, 1961, but the report did not attract immediate widespread public attention.[37] Less than two weeks later, however—and only three days before Kennedy's inauguration—Catholic leaders such as Cardinal Francis Spellman denounced the report as "unfair to most parents of the nation's 6,800,000 parochial and private school children."[38] Kennedy, who had campaigned on a platform federal aid for public elementary and secondary schools only, now faced a difficult dilemma: drafting a politically acceptable legislative package for education aid.[39]

Kennedy met the challenge head-on, making education one of his top five legislative priorities.[40] He set forth his education agenda in a special February 20, 1961, message to Congress.[41] His proposals were based largely on the aid-to-education bill (S. 8) of Senator Patrick McNamara (D-MI), which the Senate had passed in 1960.[42] The administration's initiative slated $2.3 billion for education over three years. Funds were earmarked primarily for public school teachers' salaries and classroom construction, with special emphasis given to assistance for financially impoverished states and depressed urban areas. Kennedy's education package would also authorize loans of $2.8 billion over five years for college and university construction and $892 million for four-year federal need and merit scholarships for college students.[43]

In his education message, Kennedy made it clear that federal funding for elementary and secondary schools would be limited to public schools.[44] Privately he indicated that he would be willing to allocate federal monies to private schools as well, but he shrank from acknowledging this publicly because it contradicted his campaign pledge.[45]

The Senate Committee on Labor and Public Welfare opened hearings on the administration's school-aid bill (S. 1021) on March 8. Committee chairman Wayne Morse (D-OR) skillfully guided the debates, minimizing disagreements about the controversial decision to withhold federal assistance from private schools. The hearings in the House, however, were more acrimonious. Adam Clayton Powell (D-NY), the new chair of the House Committee on Education and Labor, antagonized GOP members with his plans to reorganize the committee and split the oversight of the legislation (H.R. 4970) among three subcommittees. The House school-aid hearings were more contentious than the Senate hearings, and it was clear that the legislation was in serious trouble.[46]

In the face of continued Catholic opposition to the public-school-only provision, the White House and Congress sought to find an acceptable compromise. On April 26, 1961, Kennedy recommended extension and expansion of NDEA because it provided aid for nonpublic schools. He hinted that other proposals addressing the concerns of Catholic and private schools might be added to the act as well. The White House hoped that the proposed expansion would be acceptable to proponents of aid to private schools and facilitate passage of the bill.

On May 11 the Senate Labor Committee reported S. 1021 out of committee by a 12–2 vote. When it reached the Senate floor considerable debate ensued about funding for segregated schools, modifying the state equalization formula, offering states tax rebates rather than direct aid, and expanding the scope of federal aid to education. Barry Goldwater (R-AZ), who opposed general federal aid to education, proposed an amendment that would provide loans for private elementary and secondary school construction. The amendment was rejected by more than a 2–1 margin. However, the final bill passed the Senate by a 49–34 vote.[47]

Following Senate passage, attention shifted to the House version of the bill. The House General Education Subcommittee approved the administration's bill (H.R. 4970) by a 5–3 vote, and the full House Education and Labor Committee reported out a clean bill (H.R. 7300) on an 18–13 vote, sending it to the House floor for consideration. The partisan divisions within the House with regard to the legislation were evident; GOP members unanimously opposed the bill.[48]

Before the House could act on the bill, however, the Rules Committee had to issue a rule allowing the bill to proceed. This committee, which had defeated similar measures in previous years, had been expanded and reorganized in the Eighty-Seventh Congress in order to overcome such historic obstacles.[49] But divisive fights regarding federal aid to church-sponsored schools inspired a coalition of Republicans and southern Democrats to withhold the ruling necessary to allow the administration's bills to proceed. The Rules Committee rejected the school-aid bill as well as the NDEA legislation (H.R. 7904) on an 8–7 vote.[50] Catholic representative James J. Delaney (D-NY) cast the deciding vote after complaining about the lack of assistance for private schools.[51]

In reviewing this period of education history, some writers emphasize the Catholic hierarchy's opposition to public school aid as a key factor in the defeat of the School Assistance Act of 1961 (S. 1021). The most thorough education policy analyst, Lawrence J. McAndrews, disagrees, however, pointing instead to the inability of Catholic lobbies to strongly impact most legislators. All of the Catholic Democrats on the House Education and Labor Committee, for example, supported the legislation, and the Republican members downplayed the church-state controversy. Many opponents of aid were more upset when liberal Democrats expanded the legislation to make permanent the federal government's role in education rather than restricting it to a temporary response to a specific educational emergency. In addition to these provisions, the bill called for support for teachers' salaries, which many members of Congress and the public continued to oppose.[52]

After the Rules Committee blocked movement of H.R. 7904, school-aid proponents employed a little-used mechanism, the "Calendar Wednesday" procedure, to move the revised school-aid bill (H.R. 8890), which now excluded the controversial teachers' salary provision, to the House floor. The Calendar Wednesday procedure required the legislation to win only a majority vote but necessitated that action on the bill be completed within one day. In practice, it would have been easy to delay action. School-aid opponents felt that they could defeat the proposal easily, however, and so they allowed it to proceed expeditiously. The revised bill disappointed even former federal school-aid supporters, and it was defeated by a 242–170 vote.[53]

The administration expressed considerable frustration about the defeat of its education legislation. At a press conference held after the House actions, Kennedy complained that "everyone is for education, but they are all for a different education bill. . . . So it is going to require a good deal of good will on all sides, because the only one who loses today is not the Administration, but the school children who need this assistance."[54]

A *New York Times* editorial blamed both Republicans and Democrats for the failure of the initiatives. But in particular it castigated the Kennedy administration's handling of the legislation.[55] After analyzing the defeat of the administration's K-12 school bill in 1961, McAndrews concluded: "Kennedy entered the White House faced with a smorgasbord of choices in education and, in his first year, too frequently selected the least palatable. He deftly orchestrated a necessary compromise on race, but clumsily maneuvered an unnecessary compromise on religion. His most important concessions, on the salary and permanent support questions, came belatedly and heavy-handedly."[56]

In an effort to salvage the impact aid and NDEA reauthorizations, Representative Powell called for a simple two-year extension for both programs using the "suspension of rules" procedure, which required a two-thirds majority. The administration wanted only a one-year extension so that Congress would be pressured to pass education legislation in 1962, but this plan was thwarted by GOP opposition.[57] The House enacted the two-year extension (H.R. 9000) on a 378–32 vote, and the Senate passed a similar version (S. 2393) the following week.[58]

In the wake of major defeats for Kennedy education bills and in anticipation of upcoming midterm elections, policy makers such as HEW secretary Ribicoff recommended that the White House postpone further action on education legislation until 1963.[59] But in his State of the Union Address on January 1, 1962, Kennedy proposed an education program that was more ambitious than the previous programs—including federal assistance for public school construction and teachers' salaries.[60]

Kennedy provided additional details of his education initiatives the follow-ing month in a special message to Congress. He reiterated his call for federal funds for construction as well as salaries. He also outlined a new proposal to improve teacher quality and discussed assistance for college construction and student scholarships, funds for medical and dental assistance, and support for scientists and engineers. His proposal recommended programs to reduce adult illiteracy, educate migrant workers, and aid handicapped students. Fur-ther, he called for monies to construct nonprofit educational television sta-tions and create a federal advisory council to aid the arts.[61]

Kennedy's 1962 education agenda did not fare well. Initially, it appeared that Congress might be willing to act on a college-aid bill. The House and the Senate passed different versions of the legislation, however; the conference committee could not agree about whether grants or loans should be pro-vided for academic facility construction and student scholarships. As midterm elections neared, partisan and religious divisions intruded and pre-vented any compromise.[62]

Despite calls by the White House for the passage of a general aid bill for elementary and secondary schools, Congress did not want to revisit the con-tentious issues of 1961. The administration was hampered by its own disorga-nization—Ribicoff left in July 1962 to run for the Senate, in part because his political advice about education legislation had been ignored. Although the House Education and Labor General Subcommittee held hearings on the proposed legislation (H.R. 10180), it did not act on the bill, and the Senate did not address the issue.[63] Only one minor education bill, the authorization of federal aid for educational television facilities, passed. The administration's other new proposals all failed.[64]

Seeking a New Approach, Including Preschool Support

The 1961 and 1962 defeats of Kennedy's education proposals encouraged the administration to explore new approaches to packaging improvements to American schools. Of particular importance was the suggestion by the BOB to develop more targeted federal education initiatives. The bureau recom-mended consolidating all education projects within an omnibus bill in hopes of uniting the diverse but often competing advocates of federal aid to educa-tion.

In October 1962 the BOB staff recommended a bill that encompassed a broad "social welfare" approach to education. It proposed that the federal government assist individuals—from childhood to old age—rather than institutions or state and local governments. Moreover, rather than attempting to satisfy different groups of education proponents, the BOB proposed bundling the various proposals into a single bill.[65]

The BOB updated and expanded its recommendations in a November memo stating that "education would now be conceived of as something that goes beyond the confines of school." Thus, because education takes place throughout life, "the conceptual matrix for the education package would be aid and programs for preschool, elementary school, high school, college, graduate, postgraduate, work, work sabbatical, and old age."[66] The only extant details about the preschool proposal are found in an attached summary describing various components of the proposed initiative. Under the category "Educational Programs and Services," the memo recommended an annual $25 million appropriation for "special services for pre-school, in-school, and out-of-school handicapped." Support for preschool education also might have been implicitly assumed under the provisions for "assistance for projects to deal with problems of slum or other depressed areas and special groups," but the document made no mention of specific types of education programs envisioned.[67]

As the BOB issued its memo, the distinguished Bipartisan Citizen's Committee for Federal Aid for Public Elementary and Secondary Education—not surprisingly—recommended more federal assistance. But the panel believed that the federal government should transfer those funds to existing state education aid systems, allowing them the freedom to allocate the monies as necessary. They hoped thereby to promote more local and state control of federal monies. Key individuals within the BOB and the White House opposed this idea, however, and pressed for more federal influence over how the proposed funds would be spent.[68]

As Sorensen drafted the 1963 omnibus education bill, he incorporated many recommendations from the BOB memo of November 8, 1962. Yet he retained the proposal by the Citizen's Committee for Federal Aid that once states received federal money, they would be free to allocate it among various education initiatives. The BOB opposed this provision, advocating instead project grants with specific goals that would give the federal government more control over education reforms.[69]

The BOB memorandums concerning the 1963 omnibus bill targeted preschool as the starting point for schooling—without specifying the role that the federal government might play in this area. Yet this mention served to introduce the need for preschool education, albeit as one of many phases in the life course.[70] The Sorensen draft also emphasized the interrelatedness of a wide variety of projects. The overall package, however, focused on federal funding for construction of facilities for higher education.[71]

In the 1962 midterm elections, Democrats lost two seats in the House but gained four in the Senate.[72] As a result, the balance in Congress remained much the same, though Kennedy had to defeat an effort to strengthen conservatives' hold on the House Rules Committee.[73] As the administration faced the Eighty-Eighth Congress in 1963, tax cuts were the top priority. But federal aid to education continued to be an important issue.[74]

The president signaled his continued commitment to education in his January 14, 1963, State of the Union Address. He departed from the BOB's emphasis on education from "pre-school to old age," instead speaking more narrowly of the period "from grade school through graduate school."[75] Three days later the White House released Kennedy's budget message, which used the BOB approach of addressing specific problems rather than simply providing general aid to institutions and states. Kennedy called for "a program carefully designed to provide a major impetus to the solution of a selected number of critical education problems."[76] Despite the expanded scope of many of the proposed initiatives, the level of funding requested was slightly lower than existing levels.[77]

The administration unveiled its educations plans in more detail in the education message that Kennedy delivered to Congress on January 29, 1963. As one of three fundamental guidelines for the legislation, he mentioned the important role of preschool education in the learning process in offering "an appraisal of the entire range of education problems, viewing educational opportunity as a continuous life-long process, starting with pre-school training and extending through elementary and secondary schools, college, graduate education, vocational education, job training and retraining, adult education, and such general community educational resources as the public library."[78]

In his discussion of the reforms necessary to improve elementary and secondary education, Kennedy reiterated more traditional messages such as the need for higher teacher salaries, more classroom construction, extension of the National Defense Education Act, and reauthorization of impact aid. Yet he also highlighted the need to more effectively help disadvantaged students by "initiating pilot, experimental, or demonstration projects to meet special education problems, particularly in slums and depressed rural and urban areas."[79]

Most media reaction to the proposed legislation was as expected. A *New York Times* editorial, for example, praised the initiative: "Educationally, the new approach chosen by the President for this bill as a whole has much to be said for it. It puts a premium on quality improvement, thus trying to prevent the Federal funds from being used ineffectively by being spread too thin."[80]

Congress greeted the administration's 1963 omnibus education bill (H.R.

3000, S. 580) with considerable skepticism, preferring to deal with legislation in a more traditional, piecemeal manner. Representative Edith Green (D-OR) warned that she did not "think [that] the Administration has any chance of getting an omnibus bill through this year."[81] The Kennedy bill included about twenty-five education projects that carried an estimated price tag of $5 billion. The House and the Senate held hearings on the bill, and many witnesses expressed concern about the attempt to consolidate all programs into a single package.[82]

On May 22, 1963, Powell reported that the administration was willing to abandon its omnibus approach. Thus his House Committee on Education and Labor separated the legislation into four separate bills: (1) a college aid bill, (2) an elementary and secondary assistance program, (3) reauthorization of impact aid, and (4) a collection of other administration requests including the NDEA, adult education, and teacher quality improvement. Powell indicated that he had little hope that the elementary and secondary legislation would be enacted in that session of the Eighty-Eighth Congress.[83]

Despite the skepticism, Congress managed to pass five major education bills in 1963: (1) a college construction bill, (2) a vocational education initiative, (3) a program for teachers of handicapped students, (4) a one-year extension of the NEDA, and (5) a two-year renewal of impact aid. The administration's decision to split its omnibus education bill and start with the least controversial components proved a useful strategy to pass many of its initiatives.[84]

The aid to elementary and secondary schools was, however, doomed from the outset. Almost all stakeholders and observers recognized the difficulty of resolving the impasse regarding assistance to private schools. Wayne Morse, leader of the Senate's Democratic education caucus, saw little hope for enacting any K-12 bill and quietly began to explore other ways of framing the issue in the next session of Congress. Neither the House nor the Senate reported out any bill in 1963. Indeed, not wishing to reopen divisive past battles, both the White House and Congress focused on passing the less controversial education bills.[85]

The Kennedy administration's record with respect to education legislation is mixed. Although the White House managed to expand federal funding in areas such as higher education, impact aid, vocational education, and educational television, it failed to enact any large-scale federal aid program for elementary and secondary schools.

The debates and setbacks in that area, however, persuaded NEA and National Catholic Welfare Conference lobbyists that they needed to cooperate among themselves if they expected to pass any future legislation. (This move set the stage for the Johnson administration's 1964 and 1965 initiatives.) The focus on addressing specific problems and permitting more federal influence over education paved the way for a series of federal education projects during the next five years. And early childhood education was discussed, although the results were minimal. Moreover, BOB staff, who had developed and recommended many of these educational approaches and programs, were poised to assist in drafting the ambitious Great Society and War on Poverty projects.

The Ford Foundation and Early Childhood Education

Much of the federal government's expanded role in education during this era involved constructing facilities for higher education, increasing university research funding, and more impact aid for communities with large numbers of military personnel. Little was done to provide direct aid for K-12 education, and—though awareness of the issue within the BOB did grow—early childhood education received scant attention.

In the private sector, however, interest in early childhood education programs rose during the late 1950s and early 1960s. Exploration of the issue was centered at several experimental sites, including those in Nashville, New York, and Syracuse. Researchers developed programs to help disadvantaged youths increase their chances of success by enrolling them in such programs. The Ford Foundation was one of the most influential organizations in this emerging movement. Although it did not particularly emphasize preschool programs among its grantees, its early childhood initiatives formed a significant part of its Great Cities School Improvement Program in the early 1960s. These initiatives became part of federal policy makers' thinking because foundation and government employees interacted significantly in dealing with juvenile delinquency programs. The Ford Foundation was also able to communicate to key individuals its vision for a comprehensive approach for helping inner cities. As such, the influence of the foundation's Gray Areas Program on government policy was large.

In the late 1940s and early 1950s the Ford Foundation shifted its focus from state-level to national projects. It quickly developed strong international programs, too, but in the early 1950s its domestic initiatives were neither particularly coherent nor very effective.[86] In the mid-1950s, however, Paul N. Ylvisaker became director of the public affairs unit, and he focused his group on urban redevelopment and metropolitan governance problems. He directed special attention to initiatives designed to alleviate human suffering stemming from the deteriorating areas (so-called gray areas) between a city's central business district and its affluent and growing suburbs.[87]

Most of the education projects that the foundation supported during the 1950s focused on improving adult education, K-12 teacher training, undergraduate education, and educational television.[88] But in January 1959 the education division was approached by the school superintendents of fourteen major cities requesting funds to help them reconceptualize and reorganize operations in their districts.[89] To meet this request, the education division partnered with the public affairs unit and developed the Great Cities School Improvement Program, a ten-city program that supported school systems in providing aid to their disadvantaged students.[90]

Henry Saltzman of the public affairs department prepared a paper explaining that the Great Cities program would focus on the ways in which schools could help disadvantaged students in neighborhoods undergoing urban renewal. He mentioned the need for preschool programs and for a curricular emphasis on reading, among other suggestions. The scholars Peter Marris and Martin Rein, later commissioned by the Ford Foundation to examine the initial Great Cities projects, concluded that the grantees were neither as coordinated nor as effective as the public affairs division had envisioned.[91]

Ylvisaker viewed educational improvement grants as only a beginning, however. "From the start," he wrote, "the school grants have been regarded as a stepping-stone to larger grants that would stimulate broader and more coherent community approaches to the physical and human problems of the gray areas."[92]

While working toward this end, the public affairs unit was influenced by Richard A. Cloward and Lloyd E. Ohlin, who were studying juvenile delinquency at Columbia University's School of Social Work. They advocated a comprehensive approach to improving urban communities rather than funding for targeted projects.[93] Thus, the public affairs unit funded additional programs in several Great Cities communities in an effort to foster comprehensive community planning and programs that would improve job opportunities, access to education, affordable housing, and health care.[94]

This new approach is seen in the discussion in the foundation's 1962 annual report of plans to help recent migrants to the gray areas: "The programs are concentrated on adjustment of newcomers—especially members of racial minorities—to urban life. They concern the lack of school programs adapted to the special school needs of children in transitional and slum neighborhoods; critical school dropout rates; housing needs; unemployment; family instability; and above-average rates of crime, juvenile delinquency, and serious health problems." The report also mentions the role of preschool education, though this discussion is limited to the City of Oakland: "In the schools, reception centers have been established for new pupils, and remedial-reading experts are working with children at all grade levels and with preschool children." As part of a related youth development initiative, the public affairs unit provided similar assistance for preschool children in Baltimore and New York.[95]

As part of its 1963 funding agenda, the public affairs unit expanded its Gray Areas initiative to include Philadelphia and Washington, DC, and it supported a statewide fund in North Carolina designed to help local schools and community agencies improve education and employment opportunities. It also provided nearly a half million dollars for preschool programs in eight Pennsylvania districts.[96]

As the 1960s progressed, the foundation continued to build on these early investments in preschool education. In 1964 it provided a second grant to the Institute for Developmental Studies to develop preschool materials and techniques. Even after the federal government began funding Head Start programs, the foundation maintained its support for this work. For example, the it granted $1 million to the Bank Street College of Education, a pioneer in early childhood education.[97]

The Ford Foundation and the Kennedy Administration

As the federal government became more involved in Head Start, however, the Ford Foundation moved away from such projects and concentrated on funding other domestic initiatives. When its new president, McGeorge Bundy, arrived, Ylvisaker was forced out. Indeed, his departure may have contributed to the foundation's diminished interest in funding early childhood education programs because Bundy favored increased funding for civil rights activists seeking racial justice in America and supporting controversial education initiatives such as the decentralization of New York City schools.[98] Despite this new focus, the foundation still financed occasional early education initiatives. For example, it joined with several other organizations to fund *Sesame Street*, an experimental television program.[99]

Although the foundation's focus had shifted from early childhood education, information about foundation-supported programs in this area indirectly found its way into the Kennedy administration because foundation staff and federal government employees often worked together on juvenile delinquency and urban antipoverty programs. These unusually close working relationships provided ample opportunities to share information about both preschool programs and other foundation initiatives to help disadvantaged Americans.

These initiatives were of tremendous interest to the federal government, because the 1950s saw widespread fear—often greatly exaggerated—about juvenile delinquency and crime.[100] In fact, the Eisenhower administration held a national conference on juvenile delinquency, calling for $5 million in annual grants to states to help them combat youth crime. Despite the modest funding request and the continued public concerns about juvenile delinquency, Congress passed no legislation to this effect.[101]

The Kennedy administration inherited these concerns, and in May 1961 it created the President's Committee on Juvenile Delinquency and Youth Crime, headed by Attorney General Robert F. Kennedy. David Hackett, Robert Kennedy's close friend and Milton Academy classmate, was appointed the executive director. As the committee explored ways to address this issue, David Hunter and Dyke Brown of the Ford Foundation introduced Hackett to the Mobilization for Youth philosophy and put him in touch with one of their key consultants and grantees, Lloyd Ohlin, who had done significant research on the topic. Mobilization for Youth was a program that adopted Ohlin's and Cloward's ideas about dealing with juvenile delinquency by fostering opportunities for young people and increasing community participation and power. This foundation-facilitated relationship was to prove valuable for the administration's domestic agenda.[102]

In addition to his affiliation with Columbia University's School of Social Work, Ohlin co-directed research for the New York Mobilization for Youth program and with Richard Cloward wrote an influential monograph calling for a more comprehensive approach to addressing juvenile delinquency.[103] They also acknowledged the relatively low educational aspirations of and inadequate opportunities available to disadvantaged inner-city youth. They did not propose any special programs—such as early childhood education—to address these inadequacies, however.[104] Cloward and Ohlin drew on their experiences with Mobilization for Youth to stress the need for client participation. Moreover, they viewed the world in terms of power, believing that protest and conflict were necessary to stimulate community action and change existing institutions.[105]

On the basis of this collaboration, Ohlin was persuaded to join the attorney general's staff and later served on the President's Committee on Juvenile Delinquency and Youth Crime as special assistant from HEW. He also worked closely with Hackett to draft the an administration bill designed to address delinquency prevention. Congress approved this legislation, the Juvenile Delinquency and Youth Offenses Control Act of 1961, authorizing $10 million annually for three years to fund research and demonstration projects. This marked the first time Congress was able to enact legislation in this area. There was remarkably little controversy as both chambers passed the bill on a voice vote.[106]

The legislation did not, as the Eisenhower administration had proposed, include direct grants for fighting delinquency but instead emphasized the need for new approaches to reducing the problem and providing training and technical assistance.[107] Following passage of the act, Ohlin was appointed executive director of the newly created HEW Office of Juvenile Delinquency. From this vantage point he continued to work with Hackett and others concerned about broader issues of poverty.[108]

Implementation of the Juvenile Delinquency and Youth Offenses Control Act was more complex than its passage had been. Indeed, the application process for demonstration grants was so complicated that cities could not hope to win awards without substantial federal assistance. Thus projects funded by the Ford Foundation benefited from the new guidelines because several former foundation staff members helped draft the act's funding criteria, worked for this federal program, or served as grant reviewers. Moreover, foundation projects had already incorporated Cloward and Ohlin's comprehensive approach and were touted as models for the Control Act initiative, and so officials and reviewers in Washington were inclined to view these projects in a positive light. Not surprisingly, Mobilization for Youth was the first major demonstration project to receive federal funds, and it served as the prototype for other grantees. In addition, four of six Gray Area projects supported by the Ford Foundation were among the seventeen pilot communities to receive federal money for preventing juvenile delinquency.[109]

The prominent role of Ford Foundation projects in the new federal juvenile delinquency program meant that early childhood education—a key component in most existing foundation programs—was widely publicized and often imitated by other applicants. Although neither the foundation nor the federal government made preschool programs a project centerpiece, early childhood education was seen as a normal and desirable component of comprehensive efforts to improve deteriorating inner cities.[110] In addition, Robert Kennedy emphasized the need for preschool education programs to help disadvantaged students who entered regular schools unprepared for the work they would face.[111]

As a result, the Ford Foundation and federal Control Act programs made improving education—including preschool education—a top priority in practice: "Despite the diversity of their communities, the projects' analysis of needs led them to adopt many of the same remedies. . . . Nearly all initiated pre-school classes, where children of poorly educated and not very articulate parents could be trained in the conceptual skills they needed to hold their own in school."[112] Given the high costs of schooling children and the limited monies available to the programs, however, much of the demonstration project's education effort went into improving educators' perceptions about the intellectual capabilities of disadvantaged inner-city children. Few major or radical changes were introduced into regular schools; this reflected the conservatism of teachers as well as school administrators. Most innovations were introduced in programs intended to supplement existing classroom practices such as extending education into "holidays, evenings, or early childhood by summer school, after school and pre-school programmes, without challenging the everyday classroom routine."[113]

Although evaluations of education programs' effectiveness were slow in coming, interim results from the Oakland project presented a picture of mixed results: "The pre-school programme seemed to improve linguistic skills, judging by the performance of experimental and control groups of children on a reading-readiness test. But a rather similar language enrichment programme for pre-kindergarten, kindergarten and first grade children at a child care centre did not show any demonstrable improvement."[114]

Efforts to develop preschool programs in the late 1950s and early 1960s provided valuable information for policy makers who developed federal programs in early childhood education. The Ford Foundation's key role in funding many urban preschool programs, together with its indirect but influential contributions to Project Head Start, have not been adequately appreciated or documented.[115]

The Kennedy Administration Begins the War on Poverty

Although the candidates mentioned poverty during the 1960 presidential campaign, most of these references were to international, not domestic, concerns.[116] Nor did Kennedy at first make eradication of poverty a priority; it became a focal point following the tax cuts of 1962. During its first two years, the Kennedy White House was more concerned with finding ways to stimulate economic growth. In August 1962 the president, acting on the recommendations of the Council of Economic Advisers (CEA) and other economists, endorsed across-the-board tax cuts. Because tax cuts often contribute to higher budget deficits and in this case faced strong public disapproval, however, opponents were able to delay the progress of the proposed tax reduction legislation through Congress until 1963. The bill passed the House in September 1963 but was enacted by the Senate only in early 1964.[117]

Responding to criticisms that the proposed tax cuts favored the middle and upper classes and ignored the poor, the president at a December 1962 economic review session asked CEA chair Walter Heller for information about the extent and nature of poverty in the United States.[118] Heller assigned Robert J. Lampman, an expert on wealth and income distribution and a recently hired CEA staff member on leave from the University of Wisconsin, to research the topic. Swamped with pressing work on the proposed tax cuts, Lampman did not complete his memorandum to Kennedy until May 1963. He found that considerable progress had been made in reducing poverty in the late 1940s and early 1950s but that the rate of improvement had slowed. As a result, Lampman and other administration analysts sought new ways to combat poverty. Their suggestions focused on programs that would improve education, retrain unskilled youths, and provide other rehabilitation initiatives for the economically disadvantaged.[119]

Other factors influenced Kennedy's perspective on domestic poverty. For example, although he probably did not read Michael Harrington's *The Other America,* in March 1963 he saw a lengthy review of the book by Dwight Macdonald in the *New Yorker.* This reinforced his growing concerns about the continued presence of pockets of domestic poverty.[120]

As the White House began to anticipate Kennedy's reelection campaign, advisers sought new campaign themes. Helping the poor seemed a promising area in which to expand federal initiatives. An article in the *New York Herald Tribune* in June 1963 suggested that the GOP planned to introduce its own antipoverty program, and potential Republican competition drew additional White House attention to the issue.

When preparing for the 1964 legislative session, Heller asked Lampman to assemble an informal group of government officials to discuss poverty. Lampman did so, and when he returned to the University of Wisconsin in late 1963, William Capron, another CEA staff member, convened the weekly meetings.[121] Dubbed the "Saturday Club," the group considered alternative definitions of poverty and possible solutions to the problem. Much concern focused on the need for better education and job training opportunities for disadvantaged Americans. As one participant noted in late October, the "group's consensus leans toward relying on a wide range of programs. Preventive and remedial programs, such as improved education, training and health services deserve the first priority."[122]

On the basis of these informal staff discussions and signals from the White House that the issue of poverty should be pursued further, the secretaries of HEW, Agriculture, Labor, and Commerce, together with the Housing and Home Finance agency and BOB directors, formed an interagency task force on poverty. Heller chaired the task force; on November 5 he informed the group that the Kennedy administration had decided to highlight the issue in its 1964 legislative proposals.[123] Heller outlined some of the general characteristics of this effort: "We need programs to (1) *prevent entry* into poverty, (2) *promote exits* from poverty by enlarging employment potential and opportunities, and (3) *alleviate* the difficulties of those (such as the aged) for whom prevention of poverty and promotion of exits from poverty are not feasible."[124]

The memo included illustrative possibilities in the area of education such as "enrichment programs for deprived youth (demonstration), day care, counselling, special classes, keep schools open after hours in slum areas."[125] Heller asked each of the assembled departments and agencies for assistance in "(1) examining in broad terms existing programs; (2) suggesting imaginative *new* programs; (3) suggesting redirections for existing programs (including programs already recommended by the Administration but not yet enacted); and (4) suggesting increased funding or reorganization of existing programs if you believe it appropriate."[126]

More than 150 proposals were submitted, most of which were unimaginative reiterations of standard practices. The CEA hoped to report to the White House by Thanksgiving, but the proposals were so numerous and complex that it asked the BOB to assist in evaluating them.[127]

One particularly interesting response to Heller's memo came from HEW secretary Anthony Celebrezze.[128] After discussing Social Security benefits, hospital insurance, and credit union services for low-income groups, Celebrezze turned to educational matters—including increasing teacher salaries and supporting public elementary and secondary school construction. The secretary then emphasized special projects in educationally disadvantaged communities, reminding Heller that these programs had been part of the administration's unsuccessful 1963 public elementary and secondary school proposal. Celebrezze wanted the new antipoverty initiative to highlight the special education projects and recommended a separate bill to achieve those objectives.[129] Although preschools could be readily accommodated under the special education rubric, notably, when Celebrezze provided specific examples, he focused on youth programs and other projects rather than early childhood education.[130]

Research had progressed to the point that when in October Kennedy directed his closest advisors to start work on 1964 campaign issues, as Ted Sorensen recollected, "foremost among the new items was a comprehensive, coordinated attack on poverty."[131] In November the president also remarked to adviser Arthur Schlesinger that "the time has come to organize a national assault on the causes of poverty, a comprehensive program across the board."[132]

At the first planning meeting for his reelection campaign on November 13, 1963, Kennedy shared a *New York Times* article about poverty in eastern Kentucky and announced that he wanted a "crash program" to assist the poor of that state.[133] Peace and prosperity were to be the themes of the 1964 campaign—but he wanted to emphasize prosperity by attacking the problems caused by domestic pockets of poverty.[134]

Heller met with Kennedy on November 19, just prior to a trip to Japan, in order to see if the White House was still interested in assigning a large number of staff members to developing an ambitious antipoverty program. The president acknowledged that members of the middle class might be threatened by a war on poverty, but he wanted the CEA staff to develop legislative plans for combating poverty in 1964. "Yes, Walter, I am definitely going to have something in the line of an attack on poverty in my program. I don't know what yet. But yes, keep your boys at work, and come back to me in a couple of weeks."[135]

Three days later Kennedy was assassinated in Dallas.

THREE

Educational Policy, the War on Poverty, and the 1964 Election

Following Kennedy's assassination in Dallas on November 22, 1963, Vice President Lyndon Baines Johnson became the thirty-sixth president of the United States. The transition was difficult for both the nation and its new president. As America mourned Kennedy's death and contemplated its future, Johnson faced the challenge of simultaneously uniting the nation, consoling Kennedy's family and close friends, reassuring world leaders about American foreign policy, installing his aides in the White House while retaining Kennedy appointees, and preparing for both the 1964 legislative session and the presidential election. Some wondered whether Johnson could win the confidence of liberal Democrats and fulfill Kennedy's domestic agenda. Despite these uncertainties, he not only passed the historic War on Poverty legislation but won reelection by a landslide during his first year in office.

Johnson Endorses the War on Poverty

On his return from Dallas, Johnson met these challenges head-on. In addition to reassuring national and international leaders, he consulted with key government officials concerning necessary tasks. On his first day in the White House he saw a dozen outside visitors, answered many incoming calls, and made almost three dozen telephone calls. He also met with several advisors and aides.[1]

Among the individuals consulted that first day was Walter Heller, chairman of the Council of Economic Advisors (CEA), who briefed the president on the nation's economic condition and Kennedy's proposed tax cut. Heller also discussed the Kennedy administration's tentative plans to combat poverty. For several months, he explained, the interagency poverty task force had been assembling and coordinating department and agency proposals, but no overall theme or agenda had emerged.[2] Johnson's reaction to Heller's description of the initiative was enthusiastic and unequivocal: "That's my kind of program. I'll find money for it one way or another. If I have to, I'll take away money from things to get money for people."[3]

Johnson had not been involved in these efforts, nor was he familiar with the academic or the popular literature concerning American poverty. But having grown up in the Texas hill country among struggling farmers and ranchers, Johnson was genuinely interested in the plight of the poor. Although he had amassed a sizable family estate and frequently sided with wealthy, powerful interests, he remembered his upbringing and sympathized with friends and neighbors living in poverty.[4]

Following Johnson's quick endorsement of Kennedy's poverty initiative, the White House staff resumed efforts to develop an antipoverty strategy. By mid-December the White House reached a decision to include a section about poverty in the *Economic Report of the President*. The White House also added a $500 million line item designed to aid disadvantaged Americans to its draft of the fiscal year 1965 budget. Moreover, the interagency poverty task force continued efforts to draft legislation to address the problem.[5]

Planning the War on Poverty

Responding to the Johnson administration's decision to proceed with an antipoverty initiative, William M. Capron and Burton Weisbrod, CEA staffers who coordinated the Kennedy administration's interagency poverty task force, drafted a preliminary memo on December 2 that outlined a possible strategy. They pointed out that many Americans experienced difficulty earning a living owing to scanty education and training opportunities, poor health and physical disabilities, and limited employment options. Inadequate community and regional sociocultural environments, which handicapped children especially, were also factors.[6]

Capron and Weisbrod argued that the Johnson administration's anti-poverty initiatives should focus on providing disadvantaged youth with better education and training opportunities. Because children and youth are affected by their overall environment, they recommended that the initiative "include measures designed to provide exits from poverty for those of working age. For in a sense poverty is often an inherited disease." They called for coordination of federal, state, and local endeavors. They did not, however, emphasize a community-action approach to the War on Poverty, although this strategy soon emerged as a key organizing principle. Indeed, they offered few specific recommendations. They did, however, indicate that a permanent Cabinet Committee on Poverty should be seriously considered. The Capron and Weisbrod memo also pointed to an inadequate understanding of the problem, stating that "in connection with the announced major attack on poverty, we recommend that 5 or 6 major demonstration projects be undertaken." Moreover, they emphasized that the entire program required a long-term effort: "We suggest a 10-year program for which *specific* targets should be set not only for the end period but also for some interim dates."[7]

One major element of the preliminary strategy included upgrading extant child education and youth training programs. The draft also called for "specific vocational training, improved job counseling and a youth-oriented employment service activity. . . . The Administration's proposed Youth Employment Act is a central feature of such a program." Though early childhood education was not singled out, they did call for community facilities and services "as a partial offset to the inadequate homes in which many children and youth are forced to live because of the poverty of their parents."[8] These centers were to provide social, cultural, and athletic activities for the disadvantaged children, but this provision did not mention educational assistance.

Internal responses to the memo were positive. Most respondents endorsed an attack on poverty, but they offered few corrections and additions. Most also supported the focus on disadvantaged youth; however, the importance of early childhood education was not yet discussed.

Heller, who was responsible for assembling Johnson's antipoverty initiative, convened a meeting of representatives from HEW, the BOB, and the CEA. The group reviewed the CEA staffers' preliminary strategy. This draft was slated for discussion at a White House meeting with Theodore Sorensen two days later. The meeting was generally helpful in clarifying Heller's approach and resulted in a draft memo from Heller to Sorensen. William Cannon, assistant chief of the Office of Legislative Reference at the BOB, contributed key language for the memo, calling for "well-organized local action and self-help under Federal guidance." Such a community approach dated from earlier initiatives by the Ford Foundation and the President's Committee on Juvenile Delinquency and Youth Crime.[9] Thus, Cannon's crucial addition channeled much of the War on Poverty into the Community Action Program (CAP).

Heller's December 20 memo to Sorensen suggested that the "attack on poverty" serve as a major component of the 1964 legislative program; it also recommended that Johnson deliver a special message emphasizing that "the major focus of the attack on poverty is youth: to *prevent* entry into poverty, and indicat[ing] that additional purposes will be to encourage *exit* from poverty and to *alleviate* the hardships of those living in poverty."[10] In a three-page attachment to his memo, Heller highlighted the CAP as "the key new element in any realistic attack on poverty" that "relies on well-organized local initiative, action, and self-help under Federally-approved plans and with Federal support."[11] The CAP would begin with about ten demonstration projects—an urban and a rural site in each of the five major regions of theUnited States funded at up to $10 million annually. The projects would emphasize human development rather than economic growth; they would coordinate existing antipoverty projects, provide flexible assistance to the disadvantaged, and take into account the different types of poverty in each locality.[12]

In addition to the proposed Community Action Program, Heller recommended other possible initiatives such as allocating $200 million to "special projects for elementary and secondary education (already included in HEW budget; shift to 'poverty'?)."[13]

Many opinions emerged at the December 20 meeting in Sorensen's office. Most of the cabinet and agency officials present opposed a separate antipoverty initiative, preferring to place proposed programs within their respective jurisdictions. Secretary of Labor Willard Wirtz, for example, argued strongly against any new agencies; the proposed initiatives could easily be operated by the Departments of Labor and HEW. Attorney General Robert F. Kennedy also held this view. Key BOB members—William Cannon, Kermit Gordon, and Charles L. Schultze—and CEA staff economist William Capron, however, believed that the poverty initiative should be housed in a new agency. Otherwise, they feared, "it would be gobbled up in the usual bureaucratic crap."[14]

For his part, Assistant Secretary of HEW Wilbur Cohen advocated general aid to education as the centerpiece of any attack on poverty. He argued that "elementary and secondary education should have the highest priority as part of an antipoverty and illiteracy campaign." Thus, he believed, the strategy should "make the community action program the second string to the bow rather than the first string."[15] By the end of the meeting, community action proponents prevailed; this approach would be the framework for the antipoverty initiative, although the comparatively modest proposal for demonstration projects gave way to an ambitious, large-scale initiative.

Over Christmas, Johnson invited Gordon and Heller to his ranch in Texas. They discussed the antipoverty strategy at considerable length, and Gordon and Heller continued to advocate a modest pilot venture involving demonstration projects in only a few cities. Johnson, however, wanted a broader, bolder undertaking that would reallocate $500 million from existing programs and add another $500 million in new monies that would become available following anticipated cuts in the defense budget. The participants agreed to call the initiative the "War on Poverty." Johnson supported the title, recalling that "the military image carried with it connotations of victories and defeats that could prove misleading. But I wanted to rally the nation, to sound a call to arms which would stir people in the government, in private industry, and on campuses to lend their talents to a massive effort to eliminate the evil."[16]

An earlier memo from BOB staff members William Cannon and Sam Hughes to Heller had enthusiastically advocated placing the antipoverty programs under the control of community action organizations. Heller and Gordon endorsed this approach, proposing it to Johnson at the meeting in Texas. On the basis of his experiences as a former teacher and his tenure as Texas director of the National Youth Administration in the 1930s, Johnson agreed to this approach as well. Later he wrote that "Gordon and Heller jointly recommended that we give the local organization idea a try, although they warned me of the risks—particularly the political risks—that might make the outcome uncertain." But Johnson welcomed the risk: "Community participation would give focus to our efforts. I realized that a program as massive as the one we were contemplating might shake up many existing institutions, but I decided that some shaking up might be needed to get a bold new program moving. I thought that local governments had to be challenged to be awakened."[17]

On January 8, 1964, Johnson used his first State of the Union speech to unveil an ambitious legislative program including an "all-out war on human poverty and unemployment."[18] He announced that "this Administration today here and now declares unconditional war on poverty in America. . . . It will not be a short or easy struggle—no single weapon or strategy will suffice—but we shall not rest until that war is won."[19] The president also urged better opportunities for all Americans and stressed the need to prevent future instances of poverty. Amazingly, this historic crusade to dramatically increase domestic assistance to the disadvantaged was to be achieved without raising overall federal spending.[20]

Labeling the initiative the "War on Poverty" was an important symbolic and political decision. The metaphor associated with declaring a war and winning it played a key role in generating public and congressional support for the rapid passage of the legislation in 1964, and it portrayed Johnson as a dynamic leader who was fulfilling Kennedy's unfinished agenda. At the same time, however, that rhetorical strategy also contributed to unrealistic expectations, encouraged ambitious and sometimes ill-prepared programs, and later helped stimulate a conservative backlash that limited the ability of Washington policy makers to help disadvantaged Americans.[21]

Two weeks after the speech, the White House published a detailed analysis of the problem in its *Economic Report of the President*. The lengthy section concerning poverty, written primarily by CEA staff member Robert Lampman during the Kennedy administration, warned of a "vicious circle" of poverty, "passed from parents to children."[22] The CEA outlined a broad strategy for combating the problem in the report. Suggestions included maintaining high employment rates, accelerating domestic economic growth, fighting discrimination, increasing job opportunities for youth, improving the nation's physical health, and promoting adult job training. The council also recommended expanding educational opportunities for poor children. It specifically mentioned preschool education among other essential services: "The school must play a larger role in the development of poor youngsters if they are to have, in fact, 'equal opportunity.' This often means that schooling must start on a pre-school basis and include a broad range of more intensive services. The President's program against poverty will propose project grants to strengthen educational services to children of the poor."[23]

Debating Education's Role in the War on Poverty

Following Johnson's announcement, wrangling about where the initiative would be housed and what recommendations would be included in the legislation began. Wilbur Cohen's recommendation that the War on Poverty be led by a new assistant secretary of HEW chairing an Interdepartmental Committee on Poverty was discarded.[24] Instead, the newly created Office of Economic Opportunity (OEO) would be an independent agency within the White House headed by an independent director. In light of this decision, the secretary of HEW, Anthony Celebrezze, continued to push for a 1964 general education aid bill separate from the War on Poverty package but including some of the educational provisions proposed for the poverty initiative.

The Bureau of the Budget disagreed with Celebrezze and Cohen, stating that "it must be recognized that the elementary-secondary bill may go down the drain, and the Administration would not only lose this significant education measure but also a key element in its attack on poverty."[25] The BOB staff also feared that public schools might be too cautious to initiate new programs for dealing with poor children. In addition, the troublesome politics of providing services to private school students might be minimized if the services were structured as special education programs external to public school systems.[26]

Disappointed by the BOB's opposition to a separate education bill, Celebrezze, Cohen, and HEW next tried to remove the administration's education proposals from the antipoverty initiative. But CEA staff members such as Capron held another view. They wanted to keep the special antipoverty projects—including education projects—within the War on Poverty package, because they were more likely to pass there than if they were attached to the education legislation. Moreover, the CEA argued that, if included in the antipoverty package, education would be less subject to rigid administrative regulations. Finally, CEA staff believed that including education initiatives within the poverty bill would make the entire package more politically attractive. Indeed, Bill Moyers, a special assistant to Johnson, placed them there because the president felt that they would effectively "beef up" the proposal.[27]

Following Johnson's announcement of the War on Poverty, the CEA asked HEW to draft a bill, and stakeholders met at the White House on January 23, 1964, to discuss the HEW proposal. Labor Secretary Wirtz attacked the draft as too narrowly focused on education and welfare. Wirtz wanted stronger emphasis on job training opportunities, higher minimum wages, and better employment opportunities. The meeting ended in a stalemate and reinforced the need for someone to oversee and guide the administration's antipoverty initiative—both within the federal government and on Capitol Hill.[28]

Although HEW lost the battle to lead the antipoverty issue or shepherd a separate education bill in 1964, the participants reached a compromise at the end of January 1964 that created a second title, "Educational Improvement in Low Income Areas," within the proposed legislation. Local groups were to provide advice to these educational improvement projects, and community action agencies would be required to approve them. Public schools, however, would plan and administer the programs. The draft bill set aside $140 million to meet the special educational needs of low-income families. Among the eight programs was a recommendation for "establishing and strengthening community and other efforts designed to improve the educational climate of a community through (1) improving the readiness of pre-school children to

benefit from formal educational opportunities, (2) paying the cost of trans-
porting students to cultural programs and to centers providing special guidance or health diagnostic services or remedial education, and (3) providing
mobile reading centers with skilled librarian services and reading specialists."[29] A later study of education and the War on Poverty concluded that the
proposed compromise on education was not well thought-out from a research or policy perspective: "The compensatory solution the title proposed
was weak, the view of educational change vague. Nor did the title represent
an effort to gain knowledge about the educational process of deprived children. The title established a committee to review and evaluate projects
funded by the title. But since there were no provisions for reports from local
areas, and since educational goals were imprecise, this provision would probably yield little useful information for later policy-makers."[30]

Shriver Joins the War on Poverty

Johnson, anxious for someone to shepherd his antipoverty initiative through
the political maze of federal agencies, special interests, and congressional
skepticism, decided that Sargent Shriver would be an excellent director of
and salesman for the program. Shriver, John F. Kennedy's brother-in-law, was
the popular head of the Peace Corps and worked well with both Democrats
and Republicans.[31] When Shriver returned from an official overseas trip, he
met with Johnson to report on Peace Corps activities. During the meeting
Johnson shifted the conversation to the War on Poverty; almost immediately
afterwards he pressed Shriver to become its director. After considerable cajol-
ing from Johnson, Shriver reluctantly accepted, but he insisted on continuing
as Peace Corps director as well. Johnson acquiesced, and he announced
Shriver's appointment on February 1.[32]

Shriver was unfamiliar with domestic poverty issues in general and with
early interagency task force research in particular. He became concerned
when he discovered that the entire $500 million program budget was to be
spent under the rubric of community action. He feared that, as allocated, the
money thus spent during the following year would be an inefficient investment. Shriver and some of his associates worried that primary reliance on
community action might not produce tangible results in time for the next
congressional appropriations hearings.[33] Moreover, as William Cannon later
recalled, Shriver initially was not interested in hearing about community action proposals. Instead, he "was much more interested in what eventually became the Job Corps because that fitted [his goals]. He could take these tough
ghetto kids off the street and make citizens out of them."[34]

Thus, following his appointment, Shriver moved quickly to reconsider the proposed antipoverty initiative. On February 4, 1964, he convened a large, all-day meeting of key antipoverty officials to explore various alternatives. Heller delivered an hourlong update on the progress so far and called for selected large-scale community action demonstration programs. As expected, Wirtz attacked Heller's proposal and argued that the War on Poverty should not be waged solely by a few pilot projects scattered across the nation. He reemphasized the need for increased focus on jobs and job training programs for the poor. Representatives from other departments and agencies who also felt slighted by Heller's suggestions echoed Wirtz's criticisms. As a result, it was decided that the administration's antipoverty program should include other proposals in addition to the community action programs.[35]

Although Shriver was open to suggestions for innovative alternatives, he was also eager to consolidate as many existing poverty projects as possible under his new agency's jurisdiction. James Adler, a staff member at the Department of Labor and later the acting director of the men's Urban Job Corps centers, described Shriver's rationale for bringing together existing and proposed programs: "I think he wanted to have a billion-dollar price tag on it . . . and yet he didn't have $1 billion of new budgetary money to spend. . . . So part of his strategy was to utilize existing programs that had already been submitted but would have been assigned to other departments, and to pull them into a coordinated effort to utilize their money that way."[36]

A new Poverty Task Force was hastily established as Shriver and his co-workers spent the next five weeks frantically exploring various proposals. Shriver spoke with many different experts and considered a wide variety of options. No minutes were kept, but the meetings did generate numerous memos and eventually led to detailed papers recommending language and content for the president's anticipated speech about poverty and the accompanying draft legislation. Ann Hamilton, a former Peace Corps staff member and recent addition to Shriver's Poverty Task Force, described the atmosphere of those meetings as "very open, very free-flowing, very unstructured in the early days, the kind of place where ideas were freely and hotly exchanged."[37] Some observers of the task force were less impressed by the director's openness. One characterized Shriver as a "dilettante with a propensity for schoolgirl enthusiasm."[38]

The task force was hampered in its progress by very difficult working conditions. It lacked both budget and staff and depended on other agencies or volunteers for assistance. William Kelly Jr., who would become assistant director for management for the Office of Economic Opportunity, remembered his initial attempts to normalize operations: "The first thing I tried to do," he explained, "was to bring some semblance of logistic logic out of what we had. It wasn't quite clear as to how many people we had on the task force, because they were scattered all over town. The task force had a very debilitating problem in that it didn't have any money, and we couldn't pay for such simple things as printing."[39]

Anticipating the onset of the 1964 legislative season, Cannon began in mid-February to urge the Poverty Task Force to draft legislation. In response, Adam Yarmolinsky, special assistant secretary to the Secretary of Defense, whom many expected to be appointed Shriver's deputy, recruited Norbert Schlei and others to work on crafting the bill over a February weekend. Under rather chaotic conditions, a more final version of the legislation was drafted with input from a diverse set of government officials such as Patrick Moynihan, Schultze, and Wirtz as well as outside advisers such as Michael Harrington. Throughout the process, Shriver admonished the group to "make the language as general as possible, because we want to be able to do anything that we think will lead to an improvement in the economic condition of people."[40]

When the task force finished drafting the antipoverty bill, it had changed shape considerably. No longer did the bill consist of a community action section and a separate education section. Instead, the legislation contained six sections, including the Job Corps and the Volunteers in Service to America (VISTA). Education reform had shifted from a centerpiece to a smaller, less visible component. Moreover, funds previously designated as distinct education projects had been allocated to job training programs.

During the drafting process, questions about maintaining church-state boundaries with respect to educational assistance—similar to those faced by the Eisenhower and Kennedy administrations—surfaced. To minimize potential political problems, the Poverty Task Force altered its February 24 draft to omit mention of specific educational grants; as an alternative it listed fourteen programs as possible activities, including "establishing programs for the benefit of pre-school children" under the community action section.[41] This element was retained in the community action section of the March 2 draft.[42] Later, concern that Congress might try to mandate additional specific activities prompted the task force to omit even the list of suggested activities in its final draft.[43] On March 17, however, Shriver delivered a special presentation on the War on Poverty to Congress, and in it he listed some examples of possible community activities—including "establishing programs for the benefit of preschool children."[44]

Some later analysts were disappointed by the work of the task force and by the resulting legislative proposal. For example, the historian Julie Roy Jeffrey argued that "despite the different models of educational reform that task force participants held, Heller's group never seems to have explored them. Nor does the group seem to have systematically evaluated research on the general relationship between education and poverty, or more mundane matters such as whether compensatory education programs were success-ful." Jeffrey noted that "when the task force changed as Shriver became head of planning in 1964, the new group primarily concerned itself with political appeal, not careful evaluation. The new legislative proposal, the Economic Opportunity bill, did not rest on any firmer analytical grounds than the orig-inal measure."[45]

The Economic Opportunity Act of 1964

On March 16, 1964, Johnson delivered to Congress both a special message about poverty and a package of proposals designed to effect its eradication. He again called for "a national war on poverty."[46] He outlined the five major components of his Economic Opportunity Act, including providing oppor-tunities for five hundred thousand underprivileged Americans "to develop skills, continue education, and find useful work."[47] He also designated Shriver as the director of the new Office of Economic Opportunity.

The following day, the House Education and Labor Committee's Ad Hoc Subcommittee on the Poverty War Program began hearings on the proposed legislation (H.R. 10440) that ran from March 17 to April 28. During the twenty days' worth of House hearings, fifty-six supporters and nine opponents were invited to testify. Four additional witnesses provided advice but offered no opinion of the merits of the legislation. The bill was backed by most Demo-crats and opposed by most Republicans. In fact, Republicans complained that Chairman Adam Clayton Powell (D-NY) refused to invite many opponents to testify and that he scheduled hearings at irregular hours without informing GOP members.[48]

The role of education was the subject of much heated discussion during House and Senate hearings. Members of both parties complained about the lack of attention given to schools in particular and education in general in the War on Poverty. Moreover, administration officials offered contradictory tes-timony about the role of education in the OEO. On one hand, Robert F. Kennedy, a witness in the House hearings, acknowledged the poor condition of American public schooling and outlined the ways in which the Economic Opportunity Act (often called the OEO bill) might help remedy the system's deficiencies. On the other, Shriver testified before the Senate that the OEO legislation was not intended to offer advice regarding public education; at the federal level, he argued, this task was better left to the Commissioner of Education.[49]

One GOP invitee, Cornell University professor Urie Bronfenbrenner, a social psychologist and expert in early childhood development, offered key testimony before the House.[50] He complained that the bill was written too vaguely and did not address the need for more early childhood education. "The bill before you gives primary attention to the age group between 16 and 22. Well and good, but it does not hit at the heart of the matter. . . . To me, this means striking at poverty where it hits first and [is] most damaging—in early childhood."[51] Bronfenbrenner pointed to recent scholarship that indicated the importance of early childhood. "We now have research evidence indicating that the environment of poverty has its most debilitating effect on the very young children in the first few years of life. As Martin Deutsch and other investigators have shown, growing up in poverty often means growing up in a situation in which stimulation is at a minimum. . . . The result is a child so retarded in his development that when he gets to school he is unable to profit from the experience. What is more, the effect is cumulative; the longer he remains in school, the further behind he gets."[52]

What was needed, according to Bronfenbrenner, was a package of early childhood education programs delivered by means of "the establishment of day-care centers in the deprived areas." He rejected existing day-care programs in favor of new ones. "The new centers should not be mere babysitting establishments, but should include scheduled programs of stimulation and training for infants and preschoolers in order to provide the conditions necessary for normal physical and mental development."[53] Bronfenbrenner acknowledged that under Title II of the bill local communities were permitted to set up early education programs. But he feared that many localities would fail to do so because the legislation specifically emphasized education for older youths.

Although only four members of Congress participated in the late-afternoon session (one Democrat and three Republicans), it proved to be very important for emphasizing the need for more attention to early childhood education. Republican representatives Charles E. Goodell (R-NY) and Albert H. Quie (R-MN) were particularly interested in Bronfenbrenner's testimony, which they frequently cited when Republicans proposed their own programs to address this need. Indeed, Quie initially drew heavily on Bronfenbrenner's suggestions in his decision to develop GOP plans for supporting preschools.[54]

Five day later, when Jack Conway, a member of the Poverty Task Force, testified on the last day of hearings before the House Education and Labor Committee, he stated that "improving the education of these children is essential in helping them to break out of the insidious cycle of poverty." He pointed out that "pre-school education can help prepare the youngest children for school and to keep them from falling behind as soon as they enter. Education can help the father, too. Literacy instruction can help him reach the level where he can benefit from job training."[55]

Committee Republicans raised significant objections to the pending poverty legislation, claiming that current agency heads opposed OEO's duplication of services and warning that the federal government would bypass states by dealing directly with public and private entities in local communities. On the last day of that set of House hearings, the ranking minority member, Peter Frelinghuysen Jr. (R-NJ), introduced the GOP's antipoverty initiative (H.R. 11050), a counterproposal to H.R. 10440, which authorized a three-year, $1.5 billion poverty program administered by the states and requiring them to provide a larger share of the funding. Preschools were not explicitly mentioned, but they could have been funded under the section related to special teachers and special services "for schools serving socially or economically depressed communities or neighborhoods.[56]

The White House geared up for a close fight in the House by astutely recruiting Phil Landrum (D-GA), a conservative southerner, to sponsor H.R. 10440.[57] On May 26 the House Committee on Education and Labor approved the revised bill (H.R. 11377) on a straight party-line vote, adding in the process an adult literacy program and a migrant worker assistance provision. General aid to education was forbidden under the community action section of the bill, but special remedial education was permitted. The committee authorized the program for three years, but it only authorized a one-year appropriation of $962.5 million. This move would force the White House to return to Congress in 1965 to obtain continued appropriations.

The House committee's report on the Economic Opportunity Act of 1964 praised the legislation because it "would authorize programs to attack the causes of poverty—lack of education, poor health, absence of a marketable skill, and unstable family life."[58] In analyzing Title II of the community action section, the committee only briefly mentioned preschool children. It said that community centers might be used to "provide day care for preschool-age children, study centers, volunteer or professional tutoring programs, health and social work services, and special library services, and classrooms might be used for remedial instruction for groups of parents or children with language difficulties. Such programs would be separate from the regular required curriculum of any school or school systems."[59]

Committee Republicans issued a minority report attacking the War on Poverty as wasteful, ineffective, and intrusive.[60] The GOP also cited Bronfenbrenner's statement that the Democratic legislation was too focused on providing services for youths and should address the roots of poverty in preschool children.[61] The minority report concluded that "vital priorities, such as the acute needs of the very young children among the poor, are completely ignored. Priorities are indispensable if limited funds are to accomplish meaningful results."[62]

The bill was reported to the House on June 3, but it was blocked in the House Rules Committee for two months. This occurred in part because Howard W. Smith (D-VA), its chair, thought the bill was too vague and that the Job Corps provision would allow coeducational and interracial job camps.[63]

While the bill languished in the House Rules Committee, the Senate Labor and Public Welfare Committee Select Subcommittee on Poverty held four days' worth of hearings on its antipoverty bill (S. 2642) between June 17 and June 25. The Senate devoted much less time and attention to the issue of poverty in the public hearings than had the House. Most of the attention was focused on issues relating to job training for youth or the role of the federal government; the issue of preschools was mentioned only in passing.[64]

The full Senate committee marked up the bill on July 7, reporting it out on a 13–2 vote. Only Senators Barry Goldwater (R-AZ) and John Tower (R-TX) voted in opposition to the legislation. The Senate version was basically similar to the House bill. The full Senate passed S. 2642 by a 61–34 vote on July 23 and authorized $947.5 million for fiscal year 1965.

The Senate Committee on Labor and Public Welfare issued its Report on the Economic Opportunity Act of 1964 about six weeks after the House Committee on Education and Labor filed its document. It noted that "the central core of the poverty program is the community action program, which relies upon the traditional and time-tested American methods of organized local community action to help individuals, families and whole communities to help themselves. Each of the other programs authorized by this bill will contribute to and reinforce the efforts of the community to strike at poverty at its source."[65]

The Senate committee emphasized the importance of education, stating that "although it recognizes that effective community action will involve activities in a wide variety of fields, the committee wishes to direct attention to the programs of educational assistance authorized by this part. It is expected that virtually every community action plan will include a broad-scale attack on the special education problems of the poor."[66] Whereas the House report referred to young children only in passing, the Senate report explicitly mentioned the need for preschools to give poor children a head start. "Creation of and assistance to preschool, day care, or nursery centers for 3- to 5-year-olds.

This will provide an opportunity for a head start by canceling out deficiencies associated with poverty that are instrumental in school failure."[67]

Only Goldwater and Tower issued a minority report strongly criticizing the Economic Opportunity Act of 1964. "We consider it an attempt to reap political rewards from the American people's natural and human desire to improve the lot of our less fortunate citizens," they wrote. "This bill, with its generous use of programs tried during the depression-ridden thirties, is illusory in leaving untouched the difficulties which prevent some Americans from sharing in our general prosperity." While they attacked the unlimited powers delegated to the "poverty czar" and the lack of attention to state and local officials, they did not discuss early childhood education. They did, however, urge readers to consult the "excellent" and "comprehensive" House minority views of the administration's bill.[68]

Senators Jacob K. Javits (R-NY) and Winston L. Prouty (R-VT) added more supportive individual views of the legislation. But they expressed disappointment in the scant attention given to education and the needs of the elderly. Neither addressed the issue of preschool education in his brief statement.[69]

On July 28 the House Rules Committee, on an 8–7 vote, finally granted a rule for debate. Both sides now courted conservative southern Democrats. To garner their support, the Democratic leadership agreed to give governors veto power both community action projects and Job Corps programs. And over Shriver's strenuous objections, the White House promised that Yarmolinsky, whom conservatives considered a radical, would not be appointed deputy administrator. The bill passed the House on August 8 by a surprisingly large 266–185 margin. Republicans opposed the bill 22–145. All 144 northern Democrats endorsed the legislation, whereas southern Democrats were split 60–40.[70]

The House version was almost identical to the Senate version, but the House extended gubernatorial veto power over OEO's administration of the CAP. In addition, the House added an amendment to the provision for the Job Corps requiring all recipients to swear that they did not support subversive organizations. On August 11 the Senate accepted the House amendments on a voice vote, and Johnson signed the legislation on August 20.[71]

Mounting Interest in Early Childhood Education

During the 1964 deliberations about the OEO, the White House focused mainly on ensuring the availability of job-related services for youth and developing community action programs. Shriver and other War on Poverty officials paid little, if any, attention, to early childhood education. During House deliberations, Cohen and HEW also showed little interest in preschool education. But HEW memos did sometimes discuss the need to provide special education services for culturally deprived children, and the agency's lists of permissible education expenditures made frequent, if brief, mention of early education programs.

In May, this idea received another boost when Charles E. Silberman published an article in *Harper's Magazine* advocating early education programs for poor children. Silberman noted that "the slum child does not learn to read properly in the first two grades. . . . Poor reading skill at the start is the major cause of school dropouts and subsequent unemployment." Citing the work of Martin Deutsch, director of the Institute of Developmental Studies of New York Medical College, Silberman explained, "the reason we have failed is that we start much too late, after the damage is already done . . . the environment in which lower-class Negro and white children grow up does not provide the intellectual and sensory stimulus they so desperately need."[72]

In view of the severity and intransigence of the educational and cultural deprivations experienced by disadvantaged children, Silberman called for "a radical reorganization of American elementary education." He urged enrolling students in school at younger ages and providing them with a new type of nursery school education. "To reverse the effects of a starved environment," he explained, "the schools must begin admitting children at the age of three or four, instead of at five or six. The nursery school holds the key to the future—but a very different kind of nursery school from the one most Americans are familiar with."[73]

He described the research and demonstration nursery school projects Deutsch had established in ten New York City public schools and five daycare centers. "The curriculum is designed to teach the youngsters the verbal and perceptual skills they need in order to learn to read, and also to bolster their sense of self." Silberman detailed other types of stimulation provided in Deutsch's nursery schools, including an emphasis on teaching labeling of common items and using puppets and other objects "to drive home the relation between people and things."[74]

Silberman was optimistic about the benefits of extending public education down to the nursery level. "The youngsters in Deutsch's experimental classes show significant improvements in IQ test scores. . . . Kindergarten teachers who receive youngsters exposed to even as little as six months of Deutsch's experimental program are almost speechless with enthusiasm. In all their years of teaching, they say, they have never had slum youngsters enter as well-equipped intellectually, as alert, as interested, or as well-behaved."[75]

Silberman's article was favorably noticed by Washington policy makers. For example, Representative William S. Moorhead (D-PA), in a statement on the War on Poverty, recommended that the members of the House Subcommittee on the War on Poverty Program "give careful consideration to Mr. Silberman's proposals. In fact, I believe that a highly profitable study could be made of the pilot programs upon which Mr. Silberman bases his proposals."[76]

Commissioner of Education Francis Keppel had not emphasized preschool education in earlier discussions of education and poverty. In a February 15 speech before the American Association of School Administrators, for example, Keppel called for improving instruction and overall school quality in inner-city slums. "We must bring the school into the community's life and the community into the school. We must reach out to these parents, as they are now reaching out to us," he urged.[77] But he failed to discuss—or even to mention—the importance of early childhood education.

Yet he began to speak out on early childhood education in mid-1964. In a speech to the National Education Association (NEA) on June 29, 1964, Keppel stated: "If we in education begin our work with 3 and 4 year olds, with nursery school classes, we have a powerful chance to be influential in cancelling out deprivations that will otherwise affect every aspect of their lives. If we wait to act until they reach the 3rd grade, or the 6th grade, or 8th grade, our prognosis for change is dramatically diminished."[78]

As interest in preschool education increased among child development experts, House GOP members, and the public, Keppel asked consultant Harry Levin to provide a brief assessment of preschool programs geared toward disadvantaged children. Levin completed his report on August 24 (only four days after the president signed the Economic Opportunity Act of 1964). Levin acknowledged the growing interest in compensatory preschool programs. "This combination of circumstances—knowledge about the urban disadvantaged child, the experiences of various pilot programs, the imminence of large scale support and the explicit injunction that such programs are one of the intentions of the 'war on poverty'—makes a large scale establishment of preschools inevitable."[79]

Following an eight-page summary of the research on early childhood education and development, Levin discussed existing preschool programs, beginning with those developed by Deutsch (citing Silberman's article extensively). Levin then summarized a dozen similar preschool programs across the nation, discussing issues they faced and the trends he observed. His twenty-seven-page report concluded by acknowledging that the Office of Education (OE) had not been very interested in preschool education. But he felt that the OE would be "the appropriate locus for leadership in curriculum development, teacher training and research instigation for compensatory pre-schools."[80] Levin urged that the OE work closely with the new Office of Economic Opportunity—perhaps by having OEO delegate its early childhood education responsibilities to OE.

Using information and analyses from Levin's report and additional sources, Keppel began to speak more often about the importance of early childhood education. For example, in his October 23 speech before the Council for Basic Education, he discussed how to educate disadvantaged children. Citing the work of Deutsch and other early childhood experts, he stressed that "children learn more and much earlier than we have heretofore believed possible [and] . . . we had best start with them earlier than we have in the past."[81] He referred to Silberman's call for a nationwide program of preschool education and listed some cities that were already implementing the recommendations, highlighting progress in preschool education and citing preliminary evidence from teachers and parents.[82]

Johnson Postpones Major Education Initiatives in 1964

Although the EOA downplayed the role of education, the White House continued to view schooling as an important vehicle for helping the poor. Indeed, Johnson knew firsthand that education was one of the few ways disadvantaged children could escape poverty, and he had advocated strongly for public education throughout his political career—a trend that continued in his presidency.[83] As a youngster he had not distinguished himself academically. Often refusing to complete homework, he had relied instead on an ability to impress teachers with his wit and agility. Earlier antics notwithstanding, the twenty-one-year-old Johnson had found himself in Cotulla, Texas, as teacher and principal of a small, neglected Mexican American school. He had proved to be a tireless, dedicated instructor.[84]

As Senate Majority Leader he had supported efforts to provide more federal assistance to education. Kennedy, however, made only limited use of Johnson's skill in southern politics and Capitol Hill connections when trying to pass his ill-fated K-12 education policies. (The 1963 Higher Education bill was quickly resolved in early November, but the vocational education bill remained deadlocked in House-Senate conference.) Johnson, however, moved decisively on education after assuming the presidency; less than a week after Kennedy's assassination, he addressed a joint session of Congress and urged passage of the vocational education bill.[85] Later, he personally intervened with the conferees, persuading them to reach an agreement. In mid-December 1963 he signed both the higher education and vocational education bills, touting them as the first two major accomplishments of "the Education Congress of 1963."[86]

As Johnson prepared for the 1964 legislative session, his top three priorities were to pass Kennedy's tax cut, enact a civil rights bill, and pass his antipoverty legislation. He did not plan to push K-12 education reform in this session because the issue remained divisive and might hinder both his other legislative initiatives and his chances for election in the fall.[87]

This decision concerned many within the administration and outside it. In addition to discussions about the role of education in the war on poverty, the debates about the introduction of separate education initiatives in the 1964 session also intensified. In a December 17, 1963, memo to the secretary of HEW, Anthony Celebrezze, Cohen argued that "elementary and secondary education should have the highest priority as part of an antipoverty and illiteracy campaign."[88] And, as mentioned above, when Wilbur Cohen realized that the administration would not formulate a separate elementary and secondary education bill, he suggested that the administration add elements of the 1963 K-12 education bill to the antipoverty legislation.

Responding to an outline of a proposed poverty program dated January 6, 1964, Cohen also questioned the antipoverty initiative's seemingly exclusive emphasis on community action programs and urged that the War on Poverty be administered by HEW and overseen by an Interdepartmental Committee on Poverty headed by an additional assistant secretary of HEW. Cohen spelled out in considerable detail the possible funding sources and proposed projects for the initiative, including education programs, but he did not emphasize the need for preschool programs. He wanted $365 million of the proposed $500 million in new funds to be distributed by HEW, and he was willing to earmark $450 million for community action programs. Under the auspices of community action, he advocated a broad range of services, "the provision of which would contribute to lifting people out of conditions of poverty and raise their educational, health, and skill levels to those enjoyed by other Americans." But of the seven new areas of activity (such as summer jobs for high school youth), none explicitly targeted preschool activities. Although preschool programs could be encompassed under Cohen's broad definition of community action services, he gave no indication that early childhood education should be a priority.[89]

Cohen's recommendations for the centrality of education and its placement within HEW were rejected. He therefore suggested minimizing formal schooling provisions in the EOA antipoverty bill and waiting for the administration to introduce a comprehensive K-12 education bill—in which education initiatives would be overseen by HEW and reflect recent, albeit unsuccessful, Kennedy administration efforts to provide federal assistance to elementary and secondary schools.

In the meantime, education was mentioned briefly in the administration's budget message of January 21, 1964. After praising passage of the higher education and vocational education bills, Johnson called for additional legislation, reiterating earlier calls for general aid to boost teacher salaries, build classrooms, and support special education initiatives in the proposed community action programs.[90]

Although the administration aggressively lobbied for passage of the poverty legislation, it did not attempt to pass elementary and secondary school legislation in 1964. The Eighty-eighth Congress did renew the 1958 National Defense Education Act, pass a one-year extension of the federal impact aid legislation, and expand assistance for library programs.[91] Johnson frequently applauded the achievements of this Congress, calling it "the greatest education Congress in the history of the Republic."[92]

The Gardner Task Force and Early Childhood Education

Anticipating both a landslide victory in the 1964 presidential election and a more Democratic Eighty-ninth Congress, Johnson created task forces to make legislative recommendations to the White House. The rationale for these stemmed from his May 22 "Great Society" speech at the University of Michigan, in which he stated that "we are going to assemble the best thought and the broadest knowledge from all over the world. . . . I intend to establish working groups to prepare a series of White House conferences and meetings—on the cities, on natural beauty, on the quality of education and on other emerging challenges. And from these meetings and from this inspiration and from these studies we will begin to set our course toward the Great Society."[93]

Among the first thirteen task forces was the Education Task Force. It was headed by John W. Gardner, president of the Carnegie Corporation. William B. Cannon of the BOB was appointed executive secretary and Emerson J. Elliot his alternate. Gardner's fourteen-member blue ribbon task force, like the others, included many academics and figures in higher education, specifically Clark Kerr, David Riesman, Paul C. Reinert, Ralph W. Tyler, Stephen J. Wright, and Jerrold R. Zacharias. A few state and school officials—among them James E. Allen Jr. and Sidney P. Marland—were also included. Commissioner of Education Francis Keppel and White House liaison Richard Goodwin rounded out the panel.[94]

The task force's reports and recommendations were due at the White House in early November and were to be kept secret until then.[95] The task force first convened on July 20 and 21 in a meeting that also included a brief session with Johnson. Although the group met only three more times, it assembled thirty-one papers, including two specific to early childhood education. Barbara Biber, professor at the Bank Street College of Education, contributed a paper reviewing extant studies of nursery schools and noting that these institutions were not similar to standard primary schools.[96]

Biber acknowledged that most in-depth studies of nursery schools analyzed middle-class children, and their data therefore were not necessarily applicable when determining the needs of disadvantaged children. Moreover, she was concerned that given the limited knowledge of effective early education methods, policy makers might prematurely insist on a particular, fixed set of practices for all children despite variations in their circumstances. Therefore, she called for the "establishment, through federal support, of demonstration centers for the pre-school child in locations selected for diversity of population characteristics and need."[97]

John Goodlad contributed an essay about improving childhood education in elementary and secondary schools. He included a sympathetic discussion of early childhood schooling, observing that "we care more about the attitudes and abilities of those who provide for our pets than about the qualifications of those who educate our very young in schools."[98] He recommended that

> the United States Office of Health, Education, and Welfare attack the problems identified above on a four-fold front: (1) Documentation of current provisions for nursery school and kindergarten (public and private) education, including an appraisal of and recommendations for the improvement of programs and staffs. (2) Documentation of environmental deficiencies surrounding children not enrolled in early childhood schooling and the formulation of recommendations for the supplementary environments to be provided in nursery schools and kindergartens. (3) Financial support for the creation of model nursery schools and kindergartens in those most disadvantaged environments of the United States, these schools to serve as part of continuous N-K to grade 12 demonstration centers. (4) Financial support to research efforts designed to determine the effects of environmental manipulations in schools based on careful diagnosis of and educational prescriptions for the individual.[99]

The Gardner Task Force was not the only entity interested in early childhood education. Abandoning its earlier relative neglect of preschools, HEW indicated that this issue was a priority. A preliminary HEW memo dated October 23, 1964, regarding possible 1965 education legislation suggested $100 million in "aid for preschool and kindergarten education. A grant program to stimulate establishment of preschool classes throughout the Nation; would serve *all* children on precedent of Economic Opportunity Act."[100] Four days later, HEW issued a list of major legislative proposals that it was considering. Included was a $100 million line item to "establish a major new grant program to stimulate preschool construction for children."[101]

Thus in late October HEW seemed eager to spend $100 million on preschool education, but the agency had not decided how to invest these funds. Because the OEO's mission was to help disadvantaged youngsters, HEW explored ways to provide preschool services to all children, not only the impoverished. Alternatively, HEW proposed to use its funds to construct preschool facilities—perhaps in hopes of circumventing the problems associated with supporting religious institutions.

The Gardner Task Force sent its report to the White House on November 14, 1964. The group emphasized that all children should have an opportunity to learn, lamenting that "yet even today, children of disadvantaged background are deprived of normal access to educational opportunity."[102] After recounting the difficulties facing poor children, the report praised the OEO and expressed confidence that "that program will be the vehicle for much that needs doing."[103] Along those lines, the report described how preschool programs can help disadvantaged children but warned policy makers to proceed cautiously because little was known about the most effective ways of implementing those interventions.[104]

The report also discussed the job-training programs planned by OEO and how they could help disadvantaged students. Similarly, the report addressed educational needs of the physically and mentally handicapped as well as those who were neither poor nor handicapped but were unsuccessful in school. It concluded that "much can be done in educating the disadvantaged under the Economic Opportunity Act of 1964. Given the generally conceded importance of education in an attack on poverty, and given also the perspectives on the nature of educational disadvantage outlined in this report, we recommend a substantial increase in funds under that Act."[105]

Thus the task force, like HEW, acknowledged the importance of preschool education and called for its expansion. Unlike HEW, however, the task force viewed preschool education primarily as a resource for the disadvantaged rather than an opportunity for all children. Moreover, it seemed to expect that the newly created OEO, not HEW, should provide special help for disadvantaged students by means of early childhood education programs, job-training assistance, and services for physically and mentally handicapped children.

Education and Poverty in the 1964 Elections

As Republicans and Democrats prepared for the 1964 elections, sharp differences emerged between the parties with regard to most issues—including education and poverty. The Republican Party experienced significant upheaval as support for Governor Nelson Rockefeller (R-NY) collapsed (in large part owing to the controversy surrounding his divorce and remarriage). Rockefeller's misfortunes left the eastern establishment scrambling to find a replacement. Since the 1960 election, however, conservative Republicans had quietly mobilized and had persuaded Arizona senator Barry M. Goldwater to run in the 1964 presidential race.[106]

The GOP signaled a sharp move to the right when it nominated Goldwater instead of Pennsylvania governor William W. Scranton by an 883–214 vote at its convention in San Francisco. The convention rejected the more moderate, internationalist wing of the Republican Party, and Goldwater left no doubt about his position, telling the convention, "Extremism in the defense of liberty is no vice. Moderation in the pursuit of justice is no virtue."[107] A hitherto unknown New York congressman, William E. Miller, was selected as Goldwater's running mate.

The conservatives who wrote the 1964 GOP platform rejected some of the more moderate positions the party had adopted four years earlier. Whereas the 1960 platform had endorsed federal aid for school construction and accepted a federal role in assisting higher education, the 1964 platform promised "maximum restraint of Federal intrusions into matters more productively left to the individual."[108] The GOP platform also attacked the Democrats for "failing the poor."[109]

At the 1964 Democratic national convention in Atlantic City, delegates nominated Johnson by acclamation. Johnson ended speculation about his choice of running mate by selecting Senator Hubert Humphrey (D-MN), whom delegates nominated on the first ballot. The Democrats revealed a platform that, unlike its GOP counterpart, was designed to appeal to the broadest possible number of voters. It was twice as long as the Republican document. The platform first listed the 1960 Democratic pledges regarding education and then detailed the achievements of Kennedy and Johnson: passing the Higher Education Facilities Act of 1963, the Vocational Education Act of 1963, and the Library Services and Construction Act of 1964.[110]

The Democrats continued by promising to "carry the War on Poverty forward as a total war against the causes of human want." In describing aid to depressed areas in the United States, the platform praised the five titles within the Economic Opportunity Act of 1964, making brief mention of the community action programs.[111] Interestingly, although other EOA titles offered specific illustrations of their services and programs, the community action programs did not indicate possible local programs such as preschools. Sargent Shriver, however, in his testimony before the Democratic Platform Committee, discussed the War on Poverty and noted that the EOA "means that, for the first time, kids can start first grade with an equal chance because they are able to attend pre-school classes."[112]

The 1960 presidential campaign had featured Kennedy and Nixon competing for undecided voters in the political center and had resulted in an extremely close contest; the 1964 contest provided voters a "choice, not an echo." The difference between Goldwater and Johnson was significant with respect to a series of key issues. But it was clear from the beginning of the fall campaign that Johnson was the stronger candidate and that Goldwater was unlikely to prevail. Not only did he frighten many independent voters, but large numbers of moderate and liberal Republicans were also wary of him. Theodore White explained this phenomenon in his best-selling analysis of the 1964 campaign. "Of Barry Goldwater's campaign," he wrote, "it may be fairly said that no man ever began a Presidential effort more deeply wounded by his own nomination, suffering more insurmountable handicaps. And then it must be added that he made the worst of them."[113]

Johnson refused to debate Goldwater, so voters could not make direct comparisons between the two candidates' positions. Instead, each campaign focused on its own messages. And the media, more Democratically oriented than usual during that election, contributed to the widespread perception of Goldwater as an extremist who threatened world peace and endangered domestic prosperity.[114] Unlike the situation four years earlier, voters in 1964 perceived major differences between the Democrats and the Republicans.[115]

Their decisive lead notwithstanding, Johnson and his staff campaigned vigorously and effectively, making the War on Poverty and the need to improve education key components of the Democratic message. The value of early childhood education or preschool programs, however, went unmentioned by Johnson throughout the fall campaign—although he highlighted other education initiatives and programs.[116] Moreover, Johnson did not acknowledge early schooling in his 1964 campaign book, which did discuss education and poverty at length.[117]

Humphrey's 1964 book *War on Poverty,* however, published before his nomination as Johnson's running mate, notes the importance of early childhood education—including working closely with the mother—in breaking the cycle of poverty. "We must begin much earlier with the preschoolers. We should establish voluntary nursery schools in our slum areas. Children from these deprived neighborhoods are out of step from the first day of school; their home environment does not permit them to compete on an equal basis from the very beginning. Such nursery schools should involve the mother as well as the child so that she may assist in the educational process."[118]

Johnson was reelected by the largest margin in American history. He received sixteen million more votes than Goldwater, winning the popular vote 61.1 to 38.5 percent and sweeping 486 of 538 electoral votes. Perhaps even more important than this decisive win was the net gain of two Democratic seats in the Senate and thirty-eight seats in the House. These victories solidified Democratic power in the Eighty-ninth Congress, yielding a majority of 62–38 and 295–140 in the Senate and the House, respectively. Further, the 1964 elections paved the way for the 1965 passage of both the historic Elementary and Secondary Education Act and additional support for the War on Poverty.[119]

FOUR

Organizing OEO and Passing ESEA

After the passage of the Economic Opportunity Act (EOA) of 1964, the Johnson administration organized the Office of Economic Opportunity (OEO). A key OEO initiative, the Community Action Program (CAP), eventually considered early childhood education and developed Project Head Start in 1965. At the same time, Congress enacted the Elementary and Secondary Education Act (ESEA) of 1965, which provided compensatory education for disadvantaged students in K-12 schools and specifically addressed the issue of preschool education. During the deliberations about ESEA, Republicans led the way in supporting early childhood education. Democrats criticized that stance, accusing the GOP of focusing too narrowly on young children. In the end, Congress passed the administration's bill with few changes.

The Founding of OEO

Johnson signed the Economic Opportunity Act (Public Law 88–452) on August 20, 1964, in the White House Rose Garden. At that ceremony, he pledged, "We will work with them through our communities all over the country to develop comprehensive community action programs—with remedial education, with job training, with retraining, with health and employment counseling, with neighborhood improvement. We will strike at poverty's roots."[1]

The organizational plan for the newly created OEO was a curious mixture of elements reflecting the personal dispositions of some key policy makers as well as internal and external political compromises necessary to enact the legislation. As Sar Levitan, one of the best contemporary analysts of OEO, put it, "It is apparent from the legislative history of the Economic Opportunity Act that no over-all rational plan dictated either the selection of programs to be included in the Act or their distribution between the new OEO and federal agencies already in the poverty business. The distribution was essentially pragmatic, involving two sets of factors: existing agencies' expectations that they would 'get their share' of the new program, and the preferences of Shriver and his associates backed by the President."[2]

To reflect the preferences of the Bureau of the Budget (BOB) and Sargent Shriver, Johnson placed OEO within the Executive Office of the President rather than within a department. Several cabinet members and other officials strongly objected to the placement of a major agency (especially one including operating duties) within White House operations, which were usually reserved for staff or advisory agencies.[3]

As anticipated, Shriver was appointed director of OEO on October 16, 1964. At the swearing-in ceremony, Johnson spoke of the need for leadership and declared, "I have selected the best equipped by personality, by training, by head and heart and heels." He again reminded the audience that poverty would be eliminated soon: "So it's a very high privilege for me to be here on this occasion to observe the swearing in of the man who will start this year not to abolish slavery in this country, but a most noble calling to abolish poverty in this country."[4]

Shriver's responsibilities for the first year and a half were split between administering OEO and overseeing the Peace Corps.[5] The office was a difficult agency to manage because its staff tended to see themselves as fairly autonomous. Jule M. Sugarman, associate director of Head Start and deputy associate director of CAP, observed that "OEO has, I think, attracted more bright and more individualistically thinking people than almost any federal program that I've ever seen. But the result of that was nobody was willing to accept the authority of anybody else to make a decision. Every issue had to be fought out time and time again."[6]

Although Shriver excelled in working with the president and with Congress, he was not considered an effective administrator. As director of the Peace Corps, he was praised for his enthusiasm and energy, but questions were raised about his management style and ability to retain staff.[7] Similarly, assistant attorney general Norbert A. Schlei, head of the Office of Legal Counsel and a member of the 1964 task force headed by Shriver that drafted the EOA, remembered Shriver's creative enthusiasm but also his difficulty in deciding which course to pursue. "Sarge has tremendous enthusiasm and charm and he can persuade people. He's tremendously creative, has lots of ideas. But he has more ideas, by far, than he has good ideas, and he needs somebody who is close to him who can shoot down the bad ideas and preserve the ones that are brilliant and good. Sarge is not able, like many people, to do that himself." He also acknowledged that "Sarge is not a good, methodical administrator. He works in bursts of tremendous creativity and energy, and then he has to regroup and do his thinking and so on."[8]

Initially, Shriver's strengths and weaknesses were nicely complemented by Adam Yarmolinsky.[9] But Yarmolinsky was not nominated as the deputy administrator because of strong opposition from southern members of Congress. They and conservatives feared that Yarmolinsky was too radical and might insist on desegregating all OEO activities.[10] As Schlei noted, "When [Shriver] had Adam, the whole operation kept right on going because Adam administered it and made it all happen and went around picking up the pieces. When he left I felt the whole operation began slowly to unravel, and I think that he was a very, very significant loss to the whole operation."[11]

The crucial post of deputy director was filled by a series of short-term administrators. Jack T. Conway was on loan to the federal government from the United Auto Workers Union. A former member of the Kennedy administration, he had just been appointed assistant director of the CAP. Conway became OEO's deputy director in February 1965 but took a leave of absence until May in order to care for his ailing father. He then left the federal government in October to return to Detroit. Though an experienced administrator, Conway was absent during much of the crucial time when OEO was organized and staffed.[12]

Bernie Boutin replaced Conway but was unhappy at OEO and did not want to stay. Boutin found that many OEO employees were particularly hard to manage because they viewed themselves as independent operators. Nor did he accommodate Shriver's administrative style. Boutin recalled, "Sarge was very inaccessible. He was on the road an awful lot. Sarge is probably the greatest salesman that I've ever met. He could sell things to anybody. But his short suit, truthfully, was management. . . . Sarge, once he got something going, would lose interest in it and wanted to jump on to something else. Yet as deputy, I was limited as to what I could do without his final stamp of approval, and we had some very violent disagreements on that."[13] Shriver agreed that Boutin and he could not get along. Shriver felt that Boutin was "much more accustomed to working in what ordinary people would say [was] an orderly way, or a systematic way, and he was accustomed to having certain things delegated for him to do. . . . He found it impossible, unbearable, with me."[14]

Bertrand M. Harding, a career government employee, was designated as Boutin's replacement in June 1966 and finally provided much-needed leadership in that position.[15] During 1967, for example, while Shriver devoted his energies to the political problems facing OEO in Congress, Harding handled most of the agency's internal operations.[16] When Shriver left in March 1968 to become ambassador to France, Harding replaced him as the acting director.[17] Johnson tried but failed to persuade his White House special assistant, Joseph A. Califano Jr., to replace Shriver as director.[18]

The lack of continuity in the office of the deputy director plagued OEO. According to Harding, Shriver acknowledged that although he had a reputation for "gobbling up deputies," he considered himself a fairly reasonable person and cited his ability to work well with Bill Moyers, his former deputy at the Peace Corps.[19]

Overall, OEO faced serious management problems such as lack of adequate internal coordination. Critics charged that OEO hired too many high-priced personnel and that their rapid turnover contributed to the lack of continuity and consistency in the administration of the programs. In addition, OEO had difficulty in identifying and hiring employees skilled in dealing with poverty issues. Yet the number of staff almost tripled in its first four years— from 1,259 employees in fiscal year 1965 to 3,216 staff in fiscal year 1968. The great majority of top OEO officials were recruited from the federal government, with the rest gathered from businesses, state or local government, the education community, and other sources.[20]

The OEO's advisory board did not strengthen the agency to any great extent. Although the various advisory groups, such as the Economic Opportunity Council and the National Advisory Council on Economic Opportunity, reviewed some OEO activities and provided suggestions, none played a key role in the agency's operation. The National Economic Opportunity Council, responsible for coordinating federal poverty programs, proved inadequate as an advisory group; other federal agencies viewed the group as ineffective and too beholden to OEO's particular interests.[21]

The agency maintained almost a dozen staff offices to assist it in the War on Poverty. The Office of Research, Plans, Programs, and Evaluation assessed various programs and supported research efforts relating to poverty. The Information Center provided statistics and current information about the operation of the agency's programs. The Office of Inspection investigated accusations of wrongdoing in OEO programs. In addition, the Office of Civil Rights, the Office of General Counsel, the Office of Public Affairs, and the Office of Congressional Relations provided assistance.[22]

Reflecting Shriver's interests, as well as the political challenges facing the agency, OEO appointed assistant directors to operate several of its key programs—VISTA (the domestic Peace Corps), the Job Corps, and the CAP. As other federal service providers such the Labor Department and HEW became increasingly disillusioned with OEO—and later as the GOP gained influence in Congress after the 1966 midterm elections—OEO was pressured to transfer some of its programs to other federal agencies. The agency agreed to delegate to others responsibility for running some programs by means of interagency agreements. For example, the Department of Labor operated the Neighborhood Youth Corps, the Agriculture Department administered rural loans, and HEW oversaw the Follow Through Program.

Concerns about the inability of OEO to administer its own programs or coordinate other antipoverty projects led to suggestions for reorganizing the agency and transferring its direct operating functions to other federal entities. Questions were raised within the Bureau of the Budget in 1965 about whether certain programs should be transferred elsewhere. These plans were fueled by Johnson's fear that Shriver might help Robert Kennedy seek the presidency in 1968. In late 1965 Johnson asked his special assistant, Califano, to secretly "look at dismantling OEO and moving its programs to other existing government departments and agencies."[23] Califano personally did not doubt Shriver's loyalty to Johnson, but he felt that the president's faith in his OEO director waxed and waned. Califano reported that "Johnson couldn't look at Shriver without trying to see whether Robert Kennedy was in the shadows behind his brother-in-law."[24]

Califano discovered that all of OEO's functions and funds could be delegated to existing departments and agencies. Although this would cause considerable political turmoil, it could be combined with the organization of the Department of Housing and Urban Development (HUD) and the appointment of Shriver as its director. Califano concluded that "the reorganization of the War Against Poverty, the designation of Shriver as HUD Secretary (with a Negro Under Secretary), the placing of the Community Action Program and Poverty coordination functions in the HUD, would be a typically dramatic Johnsonian move that would be received with applause across the board."[25]

On December 21, 1965, the White House Task Force on Urban Problems recommended that the community action programs be moved from OEO to the newly created HUD. And the Heineman Task Force on Government Organization suggested a year later that major antipoverty programs, such as the Jobs Corps and Head Start, be delegated to the Departments of Labor and HEW, respectively.[26] Ultimately, however, Johnson, fearing a major bureaucratic debate within the administration as well as strong political opposition on Capitol Hill, decided not to reorganize OEO. As Califano later wrote, Johnson "did not wish to give Shriver's brother-in-law Robert Kennedy and congressional liberals any ammunition to accuse him of shorting the needs of the poor because of the Vietnam War."[27]

In mid-1965 OEO set up seven regional offices, paralleling the regional organization of the Labor Department's Neighborhood Youth Corps. The agency's Washington-based units varied greatly in their willingness to decentralize operations. The Job Corps, for example, continued mainly as a national program and was not decentralized significantly. After September 1965, however, regional offices increasingly handled CAP projects by means of local grants. Because CAP emphasized local control of its grantees from its creation, it was more willing to accept regional decentralization than OEO programs that maintained their national orientation.[28]

Although Johnson and Shriver pledged to eliminate poverty in the near future, neither the White House nor Congress provided sufficient funds to attain that ambitious goal. The first-year appropriation of $800 million came late and was intended to fund only about three-fourths of fiscal year 1965. Much of that money reflected the transfer of existing federal antipoverty programs to OEO rather than the allotment of new money. The appropriations rose to $1.5 billion in fiscal year 1966 and reached $1.77 billion in fiscal year 1968.[29]

Federal aid to the poor increased substantially during the Johnson administration, but only a small proportion of it was given to OEO. Total federal aid to the poor almost doubled from $13.4 billion in fiscal year 1964 to $23.9 billion in fiscal year Y1968. Yet OEO accounted for only an estimated one-fifth or one-sixth of those expenditures. The costs of the Vietnam War later restricted federal contributions. But even when overseas involvement was less demanding on the treasury, the White House chose to minimize political opposition by requesting only a limited poverty budget for fiscal year 1965.[30]

Responsibility for coordinating all federal poverty-related programs rested nominally with OEO. But in practice, the agency paid little attention to this assignment and was not very successful in the few areas targeted for coordination. Attempts to coordinate OEO's manpower training programs with the Labor Department were disappointing. And coordination of OEO's Head Start with early childhood education programs under ESEA were ineffective. Even Follow Through, delegated to HEW from the beginning, was not closely aligned to Head Start, as intended.

The Community Action Program, Title II of the Economic Opportunity Act, was the centerpiece of the Office of Economic Opportunity. Although there was little agreement about the exact intent of the legislation establishing CAP, throughout the deliberations regarding the War on Poverty that office was viewed as a key element. Indeed, as discussed in some of the earlier antipoverty proposals considered during the Kennedy and the Johnson administrations, CAP was seen as a broad umbrella under which various local activities could be supported.

In a special message to Congress concerning the War on Poverty given on March 16, 1964, Johnson emphasized the role of local citizens in planning and implementing CAP's antipoverty initiatives.[31] Rather than a specific set of program recommendations with detailed guidelines for implementation, CAP was to be a general strategy for combating poverty at the local level. The final legislation, drawing heavily on the original language drafted by the Johnson administration, called on local community action programs to be "developed, conducted, and administered with the maximum feasible participation of residents of the areas and members of the groups served."[32]

Neither the White House nor the Eighty-eighth Congress devoted much attention to clarifying the meaning of the phrase "maximum feasible participation of residents." At the time, few expected the issue to become as controversial as it proved to be later. Neighborhood activists in some communities challenged their political leaders by using the resources provided through their local community action agencies (CAAs). Moreover, local control sometimes led to inadequate oversight of federal funds.

The controversy about control of the CAPs grew and eventually led to congressional requirements that local CAAs be initiated, or at least endorsed, by state and local officials. White House staffer James C. Gaither recalled that "Community Action . . . was probably the most troublesome, because it was a broad umbrella under which communities could try almost anything they wanted to try as long as it was directed at the problems of the poor. Almost by definition they had problems of accounting and charges of rip-offs. Some of them were bad and some were very good. But they created enormous political problems in the cities."[33] Moreover, in 1966 Congress mandated that at least one-third of CAA boards be composed of representatives of the poor.

The first acting assistant director for CAP was Jack Conway, who left in February 1965 to head the Industrial Union Department of the AFL-CIO; later that same month, he returned to become the OEO's deputy director. He was replaced by Theodore M. Berry the following month. Berry had been elected to the Cincinnati City Council and held prominent positions in civil rights organizations—including stints as president of the NAACP's Cincinnati branch and as a member of the NAACP's national board of directors.[34] Shriver had recommended the appointment because of Berry's leadership experience with the Cincinnati community action program as well as OEO's efforts to recruit more African American administrators.

Yet Berry and Shriver did not get along. Berry opposed Shriver's efforts to interfere with the operation of CAP. By August 1965 Shriver was trying to replace Berry, asking him for his resignation for health reasons following Berry's serious gallbladder operation. After his convalescence, Berry returned to his office but found one of Shriver's assistants sitting there and refusing to leave because Shriver had instructed him to stay. When Berry threatened to confront Shriver, who was scheduled to meet a group of black social workers, he was allowed to reclaim his office. The hostility between the two persisted—with periodic (but incorrect) information being planted in the news media about Berry's anticipated resignation. Yet Berry persevered and remained as the assistant director of CAP during the rest of the Johnson administration.[35]

The Community Action Program was the largest component of OEO. Of the $5.7 billion allocated to OEO from fiscal year 1965 to fiscal year 1968, $2.56 billion (44.9 percent) went to CAP. The next largest allocation, $2.33 billion (40.9 percent), went to the Title I programs (Job Corps, Neighborhood Youth Corps, and comprehensive employment and special impact). Together, both titles accounted for nearly seven-eighths of OEO allocations during those years.[36]

The Community Action Program funded more than a thousand community action agencies; those in large cities such as New York, Chicago, and Los Angeles received millions of dollars in the same period. Not only did smaller communities receive less overall funding, but rural areas in general secured disproportionately less money than urban communities. And there was considerable variation among communities in the amount of funding per person served.[37]

Although in principle CAP allowed the local CAAs to make their own decisions about what types of services to provide to local residents, in practice CAP also funded several national emphasis programs (such as Head Start, Upward Bound, and Legal Services) without necessarily going through the CAAs. From fiscal year 1965 to fiscal year 1968, almost one-half of CAP funds (49.7 percent) went to these national emphasis programs, 39.0 percent went to local initiative programs, and another 11.3 percent was spent on support initiatives such as training, technical assistance, program administration, and research or program evaluation. By far the most popular and best funded CAP activity was a national emphasis program, Head Start, which received 38.0 percent of all CAP monies.[38]

Although Shriver was not officially designated as OEO director until October 6, 1964, the appropriations for the agency passed three days earlier. The need to spend those monies quickly meant that OEO had little opportunity to explore the various alternatives for initial funding. Because the White House did not want poverty funds distributed prior to the election, the first grants were not announced until November 25. Most of the November grants went to existing entities that were already combating poverty.

The administration's announcements of the initial grants did not emphasize early childhood education. Instead they focused more on training programs for disadvantaged youths. The program descriptions indicate, however, that at least some grantees planned to use part of that money for early childhood education.

OEO Begins Its Focus on Early Childhood Education

During legislative deliberation regarding OEO, the White House had decided not to specify the particular services to be offered by CAAs. The administration feared that listing services in the bill might encourage members of Congress to add their own favorite programs and limit CAP's flexibility at the local level.[39]

Neither OEO nor CAP officials paid much attention to early childhood education. Norbert Schlei, a key participant in drafting the administration's EOA legislation, for example, remembered discussions regarding early childhood education but could not recall whether it was mentioned in the final bill.[40] Similarly, Christopher Weeks, a member of the Poverty Task Force and later director of Job Corps, acknowledged that preschool education initially was assumed to be part of CAP programs but not considered a particularly important component.[41] Once OEO was established, however, a series of events encouraged Shriver to start exploring preschool education in October. First, Republicans indicated interest in early childhood education during Urie Bronfenbrenner's testimony at the April 23 House hearing regarding antipoverty initiatives.[42] An alternative bill (H.R. 11050) offered by Representative Peter Frelinghuysen (R-NJ) called for providing remedial education, including the possibility of preschool training, for disadvantaged students in poor districts.[43] And Representative Albert Quie (R-MN) called for legislation to improve the training of preschool teachers.[44]

Competition within the administration also may have spurred OEO into action. Commissioner of Education Francis Keppel requested an analysis of preschool programs. Harry Levin, the consultant who completed that report in August 1964, praised the programs and outlined several possible courses of action for the Office of Education in the area of early childhood education.[45]

In June 1964, as HEW began to plan for the next legislative session, the department omitted "aid for extension of kindergarten or preschool education" from the priority list for the Eighty-ninth Congress.[46] But it soon reversed its position. In September 1964 HEW proposed an education program for 1965 that included funds for supporting early education either by constructing nursery school facilities or by funding early childhood education programs for the disadvantaged. Its November 1964 draft of the budget for the proposed Elementary and Secondary Education Act of 1965, for example, included $400 million for "preschool and kindergarten education."[47] Some HEW officials favored keeping the proposed program within the department, but it was acknowledged by December that additional monies for preschools and kindergartens could be administered by OEO. Unless OEO moved quickly, however, it was possible that HEW might preempt the antipoverty program in this area and claim preschools and kindergartens for themselves in the forthcoming K-12 legislation for 1965.

Finally, Gardner's task force explored the issue of early childhood education and solicited a few papers that supported federal involvement. The draft report of the task force, which Shriver or his aides most likely read, recommended federal involvement in early childhood education and went so far as to say that the antipoverty program should be responsible for developing this initiative.[48] Perhaps Sugarman was referring to the Biber and Goodlad papers, which had been prepared earlier for the task force. The influence on Shriver, however, may have come later from the specific recommendations about OEO and preschools contained in the secret final report of the task force, released internally to the White House in the fall of 1964.

Although Sargent Shriver had not emphasized preschool education in planning the War on Poverty, he was sympathetic to the idea because of his earlier experiences.[49] His wife, Eunice Kennedy Shriver, was active in advocating early intervention programs for helping the intellectually disabled. The Kennedy family's long-standing concern about this issue arose as a result of the mental retardation of Rosemary Kennedy, Eunice's older sister. Although Rosemary's condition was not widely known for many years, the family created the Joseph P. Kennedy Jr. Foundation in 1946 in part to address this issue.[50] As executive director of the Kennedy Foundation, Sargent Shriver was familiar with its activities in the late 1950s and early 1960s. As part of the effort to educate the public about intellectual disability, Eunice Shriver publicized her sister's condition in a widely circulated 1962 *Saturday Evening Post* article.[51]

Eunice Shriver, who was appointed a consultant to the President's Panel on Mental Retardation in October 1961, served as an informal liaison to her brother, President John F. Kennedy, for that issue. Indeed, a historian who has analyzed the panel argued that "far from being a peripheral 'consultant,' Eunice was really the head of the panel."[52] It released a report the following year discussing both the biological and the environment aspects of mental retardation.[53] The panel noted a relatively high incidence of mental retardation among the "culturally deprived" and described the inadequate home environments of young, disadvantaged children in rural and urban slums.[54]

The panel believed that cultural deprivation is reversible but that "methods of offsetting such impoverishment must be used long before the typical school entrance age of six years."[55] The panel rejected using traditional, middle-class day-care centers and nursery schools for helping disadvantaged young children. Instead of focusing on fostering good health habits and providing nutritious lunches, the panel wanted the new centers to focus on "the development of the modes of learning to understand, on more abstract levels, the world of things and people, of communities with others, and of developing attitudes conducive to school learning."[56]

Sargent Shriver's involvement with the Kennedy Foundation and the issue of mental retardation also put him in touch with Susan Gray's pioneering preschool projects at George Peabody's Teachers' College. The Kennedy Foundation had funded her ten-week summer early training project for mildly retarded children at Murfreesboro, Tennessee; when Shriver visited Gray's program, he was impressed to learn that "if you intervene effectively and intelligently at, let's say, three, four, or five years of age, you can actually change the IQ of mentally retarded children."[57] In addition, while serving as president of the Chicago School Board for five years, Shriver had argued for summer school programs to offer extra help for disadvantaged students, as well as to provide employment for public school teachers.[58]

Interestingly, although early childhood education had been widely discussed by various officials in the Kennedy and the Johnson administrations, Shriver was apparently uninformed about the discussions.[59] He initially relied on the mental retardation studies funded by the Kennedy Foundation—such as the works of Gray and Philip Dodge on child nutrition—not the early childhood education programs associated with the War on Poverty. Shriver admitted that he did not pay much attention to the theoretical work on child development that had influenced other educators and policy makers: "We didn't know anything about theoretical models; none of us was a scientist, least of all me."[60]

Shriver may not have been familiar with much of this evidence, but his involvement with the Kennedy Foundation demonstrated his ability to work quickly and closely with academic experts in the field to assess the best scientific evidence and leading scholarship.[61] Shriver did consult with prominent early childhood education experts such as Harvard professor Jerome Bruner, but when they questioned his decision to move ahead quickly with low-cost summer Head Start programs, he ignored their advice.[62] Instead, Shriver chose to rely on his long-time scientific advisers and friends; although they may not have been the top research specialists in this area, Shriver was comfortable working with them and could count on their cooperation.

In October Shriver was preparing for the 1965 legislative session. At a senior OEO staff meeting, he indicated that among the issues he was considering was a multiservice summer program involving health, nutrition, and immunizations for children about to enter kindergarten or the first grade. Wade Robinson asked his special assistant, Polly Greenberg, to prepare a staff paper on preschools and parent involvement. She completed the paper on October 31.[63]

In late November, Bill Moyers and Myer Feldman held discussions at the White House about development of the legislative program for 1965. One of the three documents discussed was Sargent Shriver's proposal for the War on Poverty, which was organized along "four key life cycle stages . . . early childhood, late adolescence, middle life, and the older years."[64] Shriver's memo listed several broad areas of early childhood problems such as lack of prenatal care, handicaps, lack of health care for the poor, and children who "enter school already badly retarded by the environment of their first five years of life." To address these problems, Shriver recommended focusing "special attention through community action on pre-natal health care for the poor, medical care and preventive health services for children, and pre-school programs aimed at overcoming the educational handicaps of the disadvantaged child."[65]

Previous studies focus almost exclusively on OEO's leadership in initiating and developing Head Start. But they ignore the contributions of the Office of Education (OE) in the Department of Health, Education, and Welfare—especially the work of OE's new Office of Programs for Education of the Disadvantaged (OPED). That entity, which started working with OEO in mid-November 1964, assisted the antipoverty agency in reviewing the educational components of proposed CAAs as well as helping with other related activities. On December 10, for example, a staff member from OPED participated in a workshop held in conjunction with the Urban League National Leadership Conference. The title of the workshop was "Pre-School and Elementary Programs."[66]

A week later, OPED proposed a mid-December meeting at the Office of

Education to discuss plans for a large-scale summer preschool initiative by OEO:

> The preschool programs will be part of a special eight (8) week OEO effort for the summer of 1965. They will reach some 100,000 children in some 300–400 communities. Representatives from six universities in various parts of the country will take part in this first large meeting on the subject; those invited to participate are the outstanding experts on preschool education. The focal point of this meeting is to discuss the possibility of establishing regional centers in early childhood education in strategic sections of the country to be funded jointly by the Office of Education and Office of Economic Opportunity. The centers would be concerned with research, demonstration, training, and evaluation in the field of preschool education and would work closely with those involved in administering the Teacher Training Institute Program under Title XI of the NDEA.[67]

The Office of Economic Opportunity and the Office of Education were already working together in early December to plan for a large-scale summer preschool initiative well before Robert Cooke's Head Start Planning Committee had been created. Moreover, many of the OEO-funded projects discussed in December already had preschools as key components. Sixty percent of the first twenty Community Action Agencies funded by the end of 1964 included preschools. As the OPED analyst wrote: "The use of pre-school programs by the vast majority of the 15 communities [that had an education component] should be noted. This is by far the most popular program and reflects the recognition of the handicaps with which low-income children begin school."[68]

In late November or early December Shriver had asked Richard Boone to explore possible endeavors in the area of early childhood education and suggested that he contact Robert Cooke, chair of pediatrics at the Johns Hopkins Medical School, member of President Kennedy's Panel on Mental Retardation, and the Shriver family's pediatrician.[69] Cooke was a distinguished scientific adviser to the Kennedy Foundation and had worked closely with Eunice and Sargent Shriver on mental retardation issues.[70]

Boone drafted a memo in December suggesting that children in the early childhood education projects receive medical screening and nutrition assistance and that one-quarter of the hired staff be paraprofessionals (recruited mainly from among the parents of the enrolled children).[71] The decision was made to call the new initiative "Project Head Start."[72]

Because Boone did not have time to follow up on his assignment, Sugarman took over the task. In December Sugarman met with Cooke and Ed-

ward Devans, the deputy director of health in Maryland and also a member
of the Panel on Mental Retardation. They discussed the composition of a
possible planning committee for Head Start. Sugarman recalled that "the
common thread that united most of these people was their shared experiences in working on various programs related to the President's Panel on
Mental Retardation. Curiously, the Committee included only one professional educator (George Bain, former superintendent of schools for the city
of Baltimore) and two early-childhood educators (John Niemeyer, president
of Bank Street College of Education, and James Hymes, one of America's
best-known early-childhood experts)."[73]

The medical and psychological backgrounds of most of the panel members, according to Sugarman, predisposed the group against education programs. "They were deeply skeptical about the public schools and already
committed by their experience to a belief that learning could not take place
without major changes in the child's environment. These attitudes were per-
fectly compatible with the prevailing view of OEO staff that existing educational institutions had failed and that the War on Poverty had to be a total
war. In my judgment these attitudes were correct."[74]

The White House Preschool Initiative

Before the Cooke Planning Committee had a chance to meet, the White
House had already decided to launch a preschool initiative. In his annual message to Congress concerning the state of the union on January 4, 1965, Johnson called for a major new federal education initiative—including preschool
education.[75] A week later he elaborated his education plans in his special
message to Congress. He announced additional details regarding his proposed preschool program—including its location within OEO's Community
Action Program rather than in HEW (although preschool education could
also be included in other institutions such as schools serving low-income
families). It was also the first time that Johnson called the initiative "Head
Start."[76]

In contrast to Shriver's focus on preschools associated with mental retardation, Johnson's message mentioned urban programs in Baltimore and New
York City that emphasized education and poverty. Johnson concluded the section on preschools by announcing a special Head Start summer program and
indicating that the other proposed federal education programs might also
support early childhood education.[77]

Johnson's announcement of Project Head Start was enthusiastically endorsed by the mass media. An editorial in the *Washington Post*, for example, praised the proposed programs. "The preschool projects outlined by the President in his education message on Tuesday are perhaps the most imaginative and hopeful aspects of the whole education program. They afford a possibility of getting at the root cause of school dropouts; and they may serve to make education meaningful in later years to innumerable young students who otherwise would be wholly unprepared to receive it or benefit from it."[78]

Head Start received further White House support when on January 14 Sargent Shriver met with Lady Bird Johnson and her press secretary, Liz Carpenter. Lady Bird Johnson, in her daily diary, reported that discussion about Operation Head Start. "This program will attempt to give one hundred thousand underprivileged children in the five- and six-year-old age bracket a 'head start,' before they enter the first grade in September. It will include a medical examination, one good free meal a day, and the simplest rudimentary teaching in manners and vocabulary improvement. The course will last eight weeks."[79]

Shriver earlier had asked the psychologist Jerome Bruner how many children should be enrolled in the summer program. Bruner had replied that no more than twenty-five hundred children could be accommodated because there were not enough qualified teachers to handle any more than this number.[80] The administration's decision to accommodate the larger number of children mentioned by Lady Bird Johnson was made before the newly appointed Head Start Planning Committee made any recommendations. As late as early February 1965, however, the Johnson administration had not confirmed that OEO would administer the new program.[81]

Cooke's Head Start Planning Committee

The Head Start Planning Committee met eight times in Washington and New York during January and February. Cooke chaired the committee, and OEO's Sugarman served as executive director. Shriver briefly attended some of the sessions, but he usually did not participate actively in the discussions. Shriver emphasized the educational aspects of early childhood education, but the committee stressed the need for a medical component and a comprehensive child development approach. Throughout its deliberations the panel highlighted parental involvement, based in part on some panelists' experience with mental retardation work.[82]

Some members of the Head Start Planning Committee were either personal friends of Shriver or had worked closely with him and the Kennedy Foundation in the area of mental retardation. Although this relationship facilitated the committee's relationship with Shriver, it also may have inhibited its members from publicly challenging the administration's decision to rapidly implement a large-scale Head Start program for the summer of 1965. Urie Bronfenbrenner, one of the committee members, recounts the disagreements about the initial scope of the initiative:

> Another vivid memory is a controversial meeting with Sargent Shriver at which we presented the first draft of our plan for the Head Start program. In substance, it was very close to what became the final document (which was entitled "Improving the Opportunities and Achievements of the Children of the Poor"), but it differed in proposed scope. Several members of the Committee, including myself, were arguing for the importance of trying out our ideas on a small scale before implementing them with large numbers of children in all sections of the country. We argued that some of the things we were proposing had never been done before and might prove to be ineffective, or even worse, have some negative impact. But Sarge saw things differently. From his perspective as director of the Office of Economic Opportunity, he viewed the needs of poor families in America as desperate and immediate. We had to effect a major change in our society now. The people couldn't wait.
>
> He said he respected us as experts in our fields, but that we were not political realists. If we were to go ahead with the kind of small-scale program we were talking about, it would no doubt be excellent and serve a small number of families very well. But few would know about it, and it would have no lasting effect. "We're going to write Head Start across the face of this nation so that no Congress and no president can ever destroy it," he said.[83]

Edward Zigler, another member of the committee, offered a somewhat different perspective on why these experts failed to challenge the administration's decision to execute a large-scale Head Start summer program:

> No doubt aware of how we would respond, Shriver never asked the Planning Committee to address the fundamental issue of program size. Most of the committee members thought that Head Start ought to begin as a small pilot program and be tested. After all, most of us were academics, more familiar with conducting experiments than launching government programs. How could a group of scientists say Head Start was going to be a good thing when it hadn't first been tested?

Despite that unofficial consensus, the committee, without ever voting on the issue, agreed to support—or at least not oppose—the Johnson administration's decision to proceed immediately with a nationwide Head Start program that would serve 100,000 children. The only reference to the issue is a modest plea not to sacrifice quality for quantity: "During the early stages it would be preferable to encourage comprehensive programs for fewer children than to attempt to reach vast numbers of children with limited programs." Why did we all agree to stay silent on the basic issue of program size? The simplest answer is that we weren't really given a choice. As Bob Cooke put it, "Shriver didn't tell us as a committee that it had to be other than a pilot program, but he certainly let me as the committee chair know and convinced me that it was the way to go." Cooke remembers Shriver's telling him, "Look, you academicians are purists here. If the nation is ever going to have any program, it has to be done right away. If we study it, it will be studied to death and it never will come to fruition."

Cooke went along with Shriver because he respected his political judgment. After all, Cooke remembered the Peace Corps when it consisted of Shriver and a secretary. With Cooke on Shriver's side, the committee had little choice but to agree, even if only tacitly, that the program should begin on a large scale.[84]

The Head Start Planning Committee unanimously endorsed its February 1965 report, "Improving the Opportunities and Achievements of the Children of the Poor," and forwarded it to Shriver. As expected, the group agreed that early childhood is a critical period for development and that enough already was known to provide help for disadvantaged students.[85] The committee advocated comprehensive, high-quality programs and believed that many of them could be implemented immediately.

> It is clear that successful programs of this type must be comprehensive, involving activities generally associated with the fields of health, social services, and education. Similarly it is clear that the program must focus on the problems of child and parent and that these activities need to be carefully integrated with programs for the school years. During the early stages of any programs assisted by the Office of Economic Opportunity it would be preferable to encourage comprehensive programs for fewer children than to attempt to reach vast numbers of children with limited programs. The Office of Economic Opportunity should generally avoid financing programs which do not have at least a minimum level and quality of activities from each of the three fields of effort.

The need for and urgency of these programs is such that they should be initiated immediately. Many programs could begin in the summer of 1965. These would help provide a more complete picture of national needs for use in future planning.[86]

The committee acknowledged the severe shortage of qualified teachers and recommended additional training programs for childhood educators.[87] Their report also emphasized the role of parents in providing various types of assistance. Although most of the proposed tasks were nonteaching activities, teaching opportunities were not precluded, particularly in providing assistance in specialized areas such as singing and painting.[88]

The committee did not pay sufficient attention to staffing the projects with high-quality teachers. James L. Hymes Jr., a member of the committee, later recalled that "we never did face up to the disadvantaged young child's need for skilled and trained teachers; we never did face up to the need for top-flight educational leadership in what was to be a massive educational program." Instead, Hymes felt that "in 1965 I detected that 'anyone can teach young kids,' and that feeling persists today. . . . Throughout, at all levels, Head Start was never staffed to produce consistently good educational programs, and Head Start children were shortchanged because of this."[89]

At the same time, other committee members were concerned that elementary public school teachers might not be appropriate as Head Start instructors. One early childhood education specialist, D. Keith Osborn, noted that "the major fear was that we would end up with one large reading program and no concern for the whole child. We feared that well-meaning elementary school teachers would be concerned with teaching kids curriculum and lose sight of the larger goals of Head Start. And we were also concerned that teachers would not work with parents, particularly since public schools seldom included parents in program planning."[90]

Despite the committee's willingness to cooperate with the administration's plans for Head Start for the summer of 1965, many of its members did not believe that the proposed services would significantly help the one hundred thousand disadvantaged children who would be participating. Zigler recalled, "Few of us on the Planning Committee really believed that an eight-week summer program could produce many lasting benefits in children's lives; we certainly didn't think that a couple of meals a day and some vaccinations could 'cure' poverty. But the estimated $18 million price tag for the entire summer Head Start program was about the same as the cost of two fighter bombers at the time. If the nation could spend so much money on a war that was benefitting no one, why couldn't it spend a fraction of that amount on poor children in Head Start? The program certainly wouldn't do any harm; it might even do some good."[91]

Organization of Project Head Start

After the Head Start Planning Committee had completed most of its work, Shriver selected Julius Richmond as director of the program.[92] Richmond, a Syracuse pediatrician, had started a program in the 1950s for disadvantaged infants. Shriver recruited him in February 1965 but only on the condition that Richmond could continue his job as dean of the Upstate Medical Center at the State University of New York at Syracuse. Although Richmond was an experienced and knowledgeable researcher, his late arrival in Washington and multiple responsibilities limited his influence on the implementation of Head Start. Moreover, he contracted pulmonary tuberculosis within a year and was confined to bed, further hampering his work with the program.[93]

Jule Sugarman served as deputy director of Head Start and helped compensate for Richmond's inability to work full-time in Washington. Although not an expert in early child development, Sugarman excelled as an administrator who understood the bureaucracy and could get things done under difficult circumstances. Like Shriver, Sugarman sometimes appeared to be more concerned with the public image and political viability of Head Start than with the ability of the program to provide high-quality services for disadvantaged children.

Several crucial but hasty decisions were made in early 1965 that influenced the nature of Head Start. Concerning the question of the recommended child-teacher ratio for Head Start programs, Sugarman suggested a ratio of twenty or thirty children to one adult—comparable to the staffing pattern of many kindergartens. Richmond, who had considerable experience with early childhood education programs, disagreed and decided that the ratio should be fifteen students per teacher (with two additional adults as assistants).[94]

Regarding cost, Martin Deutsch, director of the Institute of Developmental Studies of New York Medical College, believed that approximately $1,000 per student would cover the salary of a competent teacher and adequate classroom facilities for a summer program—an amount well above what OEO policy makers had envisioned. At one point Shriver needed a quick estimate of the summer program's cost per student and gave Sugarman an hour to provide the answer. Rather than consulting experts and carefully assessing the various estimates, Sugarman offered his own guess, reflecting the idea that the Head Start projects could do with inexpensive and poorly trained teachers: "So another fellow and I sat down over a ham sandwich at the Madison hotel and arrived at $180 per child for an eight-week program. We rushed that figure to Shriver. Sure enough, when the press releases came out, that figure was the figure used for the average cost per child."[95]

Once OEO publicized its estimated average cost per student, applicants tried to stay within those informal guidelines.[96] As a result, many applicants may have hesitated to ask for much more money, and those that did probably faced strong questioning from the reviewers. In addition, once Shriver and other officials publicly announced that the 1965 summer initiative had significantly helped disadvantaged students, it would have been awkward for the program directors to request more money per student. Finally, because the administration and OEO emphasized the large number of disadvantaged students assisted, program directors found it difficult to obtain higher teacher salaries: any effort to significantly improve the quality and cost of teaching staff would prevent programs from serving as many children. Not surprisingly, subsequent congressional allocations of monies for Head Start usually were explained in terms of expanding the length of the program or increasing the number of children served rather than enhancing the quality of the teachers by raising their salaries.

Passage of the Elementary and Secondary Education Act and Early Childhood Education in 1965

Following Johnson's special message on education on January 12, 1965, the White House's Elementary and Secondary Education Act (ESEA) was introduced in the House (H.R. 2362) by Carl D. Perkins (D-KY) and in the Senate (S. 370) by Wayne L. Morse (D-OR). Thanks to Johnson's landslide reelection in 1964, the Eighty-ninth Congress was much more Democratic and liberal, making the enactment of the administration's initiative much easier. Also, Congress already had passed the Civil Rights Act of 1964, stipulating that organizations practicing segregation were ineligible for federal funds. This act lessened the opposition of some southern legislators who earlier had felt that they had to vote against federal education legislation in an effort to fend off school integration. Moreover, staunch opponents of assistance to church-supported private schools such as the National Education Association now were ready to compromise in order to obtain federal funds for K-12 public schools.[97]

The Johnson administration did not try to enact federal general aid for K-12 education or obtain school construction funds. Instead, it sought categorical assistance for disadvantaged students in both public and private schools. (The categorical aid under Title I was defined so broadly, however, that in practice this bill almost resembled a general aid-to-education approach.)[98] The underlying rationale behind this strategy, the child-benefit approach, appeared to be a way of circumventing constitutional and political opposition to federal assistance to K-12 education.[99] The proposed legislation consisted of five titles, the first of which provided assistance for disadvantaged students and authorized five-sixths of the total ESEA package. The other sections supported school library resources and provided instructional materials (Title II), created supplementary educational centers and services (Title III), established educational research and development laboratories (Title IV), and provided funds for state departments of education (Title V).[100]

The bill was enacted unusually quickly, largely because of the sizable Democratic majority in Congress, prior negotiated agreements among key participants, and the insistence of the White House and congressional Democratic leadership on opposing any major or controversial amendments to the administration's bill.[101] The House began hearings on January 22 and concluded them on February 2. House Democrats vowed not to add any amendments, jeopardizing the fragile coalition that had reached informal agreements on the bill. Republican members of the General Education Subcommittee boycotted the bill's markup to protest the hasty consideration of legislation.[102] The full House Committee on Education and Labor debated the bill in executive session for almost a week and reported it favorably by a 23–8 vote on March 8; the Democrats unanimously supported the legislation, while all but two of the GOP members dissented.[103]

Most studies of early childhood education overlook debates about federal funding for preschools during the passage of ESEA. They also ignore the GOP's enthusiasm and support for early childhood in 1964 and 1965.[104] Yet it was the Republicans who specifically invited Bronfenbrenner and were the most impressed by his testimony about the need for preschool education during the 1964 hearings on OEO. And it was a Republican, Representative Albert Quie (MN), who in August 1964 requested federal funds for teachers to help disadvantaged children between ages three and six. "A special corps of teachers—'like those who are now trained to teach the mentally or physically handicapped'—should be established to aid the socially and culturally handicapped."[105] In addition, a GOP task force followed up by issuing a "Pre-School Plan for Republicans" that "emphasized the need for pre-school education among the poverty-stricken and disadvantaged children of our country."[106]

In his January 12 education message, Johnson had supported early childhood education and assigned that task to OEO. Although the administration's ESEA bill acknowledged the need for remedial education, it appeared to authorize assistance only for children aged five and older. On March 8, 1965, the Republican members of the House Committee on Education and Labor criticized their Democratic colleagues for this omission and added a minority response to the *Committee Report on the Elementary and Secondary Education Act of 1965* that concluded that "any bill designated to upgrade and modernize American education which does not focus on preschool training is antiquated before it is even enacted. The most imaginative innovations of recent years in teaching techniques and equipment have been made at the preschool level. Let's not attempt a step forward by starting 10 years behind."[107]

On the same day that the House committee's report was released, the GOP announced its own alternative education legislation. Representatives Charles Goodell (R-NY), William Ayers (R-OH), and Thomas Curtis (R-MO) co-sponsored the Education Initiative Act (H.R. 6349), which provided federal tax credits to anyone paying state or local school taxes. They argued that families would be better helped by tax assistance than by categorical aid to public and private schools. Tax assistance was seen as less intrusive and more equitable to parents regardless of whether their children attended public or private schools.[108]

The GOP education package included Quie's proposal for $300 million in annual direct grants to states. The states would allocate the money to schools serving children aged three through seven whose families' incomes were less than $3,000 (compared to the administration's threshold of $2,000). The administration's Title I aid formula provided more money per disadvantaged student in wealthier communities than it did to those residing in poorer areas such as Mississippi and Alabama. Quie's preschool assistance plan would have allocated to all poor children the same amount of federal funds, regardless of location. Whereas the administration's Title I program provided only a small proportion of the total cost of educating a disadvantaged student, the GOP version called for the federal government to finance a larger share of the overall costs of preschools.[109]

Because the larger Republican proposal included tax relief, it had to be vetted by the Ways and Means Committee, as well as by the Education and Labor Committee. The Democratic leadership accused the Republicans of simply trying to delay the administration's bill. In addition, they attacked the GOP's education tax credits, likening them to Goldwater's election promises, which voters overwhelmingly had rejected the previous November. Without approval from the Rules Committee to proceed and facing the unwillingness of the Ways and Means Committee to even hold hearings on the GOP proposal, the Republican alternative could not be offered as a simple amendment to the White House's bill, which now went to the House floor.[110]

The House debated ESEA for three days, addressing the allocation formula for Title I, the types of aid provided to public schools, and the role of the federal government in K-12 education. The issue of early childhood education dominated the debates. One reason for this focus was the full-committee minority report's complaint that the administration's bill precluded the use of Title I monies for preschool education.

Considerable confusion ensued regarding whether Title I monies could be used for preschool programs. The White House's original bill did not emphasize the use of Title I funds for preschools, and the funding allocation's age range of five years to seventeen years suggested that the target population was not young children. The exclusion of Title I funding for preschool children seemed to be reinforced in Johnson's January 12 education speech, in which he designated OEO as the agency to deal with preschool programs.

Although Johnson had not highlighted OEO's inclusion in the administration's legislation, HEW continued to lobby for preschool programs and wanted them placed in the Office of Education. Preparing for a discussion with Perkins regarding possible amendments to the administration's bill, Cohen suggested to Commissioner of Education Keppel that the administration "include [a] new part in title I of the bill for preschool and nursery school education with authorization of $150 million. Assign responsibility to Office of Education. Preclude use of title II EOA funds for this purpose. Allotment [for children aged] 3–5."[111]

In early March, House Democrats—probably responding to growing GOP criticism regarding the absence of early childhood education and the suggestions of Senator Robert F. Kennedy (D-NY)—added to Title I language permitting the funding of preschool programs. The White House asked congressional Democrats to minimize amendments to the bill. It was particularly important that the Senate accept the House version so that the bill would not be delayed by lengthy conference proceedings. This tactic would hamper House Republicans' efforts to thwart the administration's bill. Therefore, during the deliberations by the House Committee on Education and Labor, the administration asked key Democratic senators for changes they deemed essential to ESEA.[112]

Robert F. Kennedy had met with Cohen in February 1965 to discuss possible changes to the House version of ESEA. According to Cohen, Kennedy proposed that "the program . . . encourage local school boards to provide pre-school programs for children ages 3–5."[113] Moreover, Kennedy wanted to transfer OEO's education programs to the Office of Education. "There should be an elimination of the 'overlap' between the antipoverty program (title II—Community Action Program) insofar as educational programs are concerned by transferring responsibility for educational programs in the antipoverty program to educational agencies." The administration incorporated preschool programs into the House's draft bill, but at that time the administration and the House were still debating among themselves the issue of overlap with OEO in education programs.[114]

Early debates on the House floor regarding Title I and preschool education provide interesting insights into how some members of Congress now envisioned the legislation. After continued criticisms from their Republican colleagues, the House Democrats defended themselves. Perkins, floor manager for ESEA, summarized the Education and Labor Committee's March 2 amendments and changes, including the important clarification that "preschool programs [are] one of the means by which public local educational agencies may improve educational opportunities for educationally deprived children."[115] The amendment permitting use of Title I funds for preschool programs was added less than a week before the final committee report on ESEA was released on March 8; because the minority views did not take that change into consideration, Perkins criticized the Republicans for claiming that ESEA did not allow or emphasize early childhood education.[116]

Perkins, attacking the proposed Republican alternative education bill, used its early childhood education provision to refute the idea that the Democrats favored more federal control than the Republicans. "Despite the minority's professed desire to preserve local public school autonomy over local school policy, its so-called substitute would make it mandatory for local school districts to provide preschool programs irrespective of any consideration of local needs."[117]

Although the Democrats now allowed Title I funding for preschools, they did not share Quie's and his GOP colleagues' enthusiasm for targeting help for young disadvantaged children. Indeed, Perkins described the Republicans' interest in early childhood education simply as a clever ruse to avoid providing federal assistance to older students: "However, the real interest by the minority in pre-school seems simply to be a prelude to their so-called substitute legislation which would limit benefits to 3 to 8 year olds, thus cutting out several million educationally deprived children from receiving broadened and increased educational opportunities."[118]

When Quie offered his early childhood substitute for Title I the following day, he disagreed with the way Perkins and the other Democrats characterized the GOP's exceptionally strong interest in preschool education. He reiterated its importance, citing various studies funded by the Ford Foundation and others. Then Quie shared his broader and more philosophical rationale for federal involvement in this issue in particular:

> My reason for offering this [amendment] is [that] I believe the Federal Government has the responsibility to improve the educational level of children before the first grade. In my philosophy I believe that the States and local governments have the responsibilities in grades 1 through 12. The Federal Government has assisted for many years to a substantial degree in the grades above 12, at the higher educational levels. However, here is an area of great unmet need. The educationally deprived child being talked about for these 2 days in the bill . . . are the ones who have been lost before they ever reached school for first grade. The children who are poverty stricken and result in the unemployed; the ones we were trying to reach last year in the antipoverty bill for the most part were lost before they ever attended public schools. We heard a great deal of testimony about these children. They are the easiest to reach and you can motivate them easier at this age than they can be at a subsequent age. The correction you have to make later on can be prevented if you have special programs designed to reach children ages 3 to 6. . . .
>
> There is no sense in having all these expensive programs . . . trying to reach these kids at a later age and permit the breeding ground to continue. We must have the program specifically designed to reach these young people and the later programs will not be necessary.[119]

In urging support for his amendment, Quie complained that the administration's assignment of preschool education to OEO would not lead to a close relation between early childhood education and the public schools.[120]

During floor debate on March 25, Quie did acknowledge that ESEA had been amended to allow the use of Title I funds for preschool programs. But he continued to insist that Democratic interest in and attention to early childhood education was minimal and explained his substitute amendment for Title I. Quie proposed $300 million annually for preschools and special education centers serving children aged three to seven whose families' yearly incomes were less than $3,000. After one year of full federal support, states desiring continued participation would be required to contribute, while federal funding would diminish to two-thirds of the total costs.[121]

Several Republicans praised Quie's amendment, but Democrats, as expected, opposed it as too prescriptive and too narrowly focused on early childhood. Representative John Brademas (D-IN) also pointed out that the GOP proposals provided less overall assistance for children of all ages than did the Democratic alternative.[122] Quie's amendment was defeated on a voice vote.

The House debates also provided interesting insights into the ideas of some members regarding preschool teachers' qualifications. For example, in his amendment to Title I, Quie reiterated his call for a specially trained teaching corps and incentives to teach disadvantaged children.[123] And Democrats as well as Republicans raised the need for higher qualifications for preschool educators. Representative Andrew Jacobs (D-IN), for example, discussed the limitations of "culturally deprived" parents in educating their own children and noted the need for "highly trained" preschool teachers.[124]

After a three-day floor debate, but with almost no changes, the House passed ESEA by a 263–153 roll-call vote on March 26. A majority of the Republicans (96–35) and southern Democrats (54–41) were opposed. But overwhelming support from northern Democrats (187–3) was sufficient to pass the legislation.[125]

The Senate hearings on S. 370, which went on for seven days, began on February 11. More than one hundred persons testified before the Senate Subcommittee on Education, but there was less partisan division than in the House because Republican members did not feel that the bill was rushed. Senator Morse and the administration had decided to postpone further action in order to await House passage of ESEA.[126]

Concerned that delays and changes might ensue if the bill had to be returned to the House following a House-Senate conference, the Senate Committee on Labor and Public Welfare accepted the House version without changes.[127] The accompanying report expounded on several issues that were of concern to the senators but did not address early childhood education in any depth; the senators accepted the House's decision to permit but not require the use of Title I funds for preschool education (as Kennedy had urged).[128] Perhaps responding to Kennedy's previous suggestions, the senators clarified the relation between the Office of Education and OEO regarding the coordination of education activities.[129] Thus, the report gave local school boards primary responsibility for providing services such as preschool education. But CAAs might provide or supplement preschool education programs with health, social, parental, and nutritional services.[130]

The full Senate began discussing H.R. 2362 on April 6. Most of the floor discussion dealt with issues such as the Title I aid formula. But Senator Ralph Yarborough (D-TX) did mention the importance of early childhood education and shared a letter from John Silber outlining plans for preschools.[131] Several attempts to amend the House bill in the Senate were defeated. On April 9 the Senate easily approved the House version by a 73–18 majority.

Democrats overwhelmingly approved the bill (55–4), whereas Republicans supported it by a much narrower margin (18–14).[132]

Johnson signed the legislation two days later in a special ceremony at the one-room schoolhouse he had attended at age four. Katherine Deadrich Loney, his first teacher, was present at that historic occasion in Johnson City, Texas. Johnson praised the passage of the act and proudly noted that the legislation "represents a major new commitment of the Federal Government to quality and equality in the schooling that we offer our young people. I predict that all of those of both parties of Congress who supported the enactment of this legislation will be remembered in history as men and women who began a new day of greatness in American society."[133]

With the passage of ESEA, the federal government committed itself to providing major educational assistance for disadvantaged children. The House Republicans' amendment to replace Title I with a major early preschool initiative failed, but in the process the benefits of early childhood education received widespread publicity and discussion among policy makers. Republicans and Democrats alike praised preschool programs and saw them as a particularly effective means of helping culturally disadvantaged children. And preschool programs now were clearly acknowledged as permissible and desirable Title I expenditures for local school districts.[134]

Implementing, Evaluating, and Improving Head Start Programs

In 1965 the Office of Economic Opportunity's Community Action Program (CAP) launched eight-week summer Head Start programs, designed to prepare disadvantaged children to enter school and succeed in their education, throughout the nation. Unfortunately, early evaluations indicated that the programs did not significantly help poor children make long-term intellectual gains. Thus, analysts and policymakers worked to establish year-round early childhood programs and improve the quality of existing Head Start services. This goal was increasingly elusive, however, as the critics questioned the efficacy of Head Start, OEO faced mounting criticism, and the Johnson administration's resources increasingly were absorbed by the conflict in Vietnam.

The 1965 Launch of Head Start

After Johnson's January 12 education message to Congress, which called for federal support for preschools, the OEO stepped up efforts to create Head Start programs for the summer of 1965. Johnson continued to encourage this effort. On February 17, 1965, he wrote to the House and the Senate and requested that they double funding for the War on Poverty. The letter mentioned the administration's progress in that effort and described planned Head Start activities: "We will, this year, provide a school readiness program for over 100,000 children about to enter kindergarten. This will help them overcome the handicaps of experience and feeling which flow from poverty and permit them to receive the full advantages of school experience."[1]

Many people participated in the Head Start launch. Lady Bird Johnson, who had agreed to serve as its honorary chair, hosted a tea at the White House on February 19 on the project's behalf. About four hundred guests crowded into the East Room to hear the first lady announce the summer program and request volunteers to staff the classes.[2] During her many discussions on behalf of Head Start, she emphasized target children's extreme cultural and intellectual deprivation and isolation. "Some don't know even a hundred words because they have not heard a hundred words. Some don't know how to sit in a chair because they don't have as much as a chair. Some have never seen a book or held a flower."[3]

Further efforts to aid disadvantaged children included plans for expansion of the program. On March 8 Johnson made public the "President's Report to the Nation on Poverty," a document prepared for Congress. In an attachment, the White House revealed plans to spend $50 million for summer Head Start classes in 1965 and budgeted $150 million for year-round early childhood education programs in fiscal year 1966.[4]

Four months remained before the summer programs were to begin, and OEO accelerated its efforts to solicit applicants. Shriver wrote thirty-five thousand letters to public health directors, school superintendents, mayors, and social service commissioners. In addition, OEO contacted America's three hundred poorest counties and informed them about opportunities to qualify for Head Start funding. The application deadline was set at April 15, less than two months after the initial public announcement. The programs were scheduled to begin in late June or early July.[5]

Included in OEO's information packet for Head Start applicants was a forty-eight-page booklet describing the summer program's general objectives.[6] The booklet emphasized that local programs, when planning, should consider it "essential that the following broad goals be uppermost in the planning of Head Start programs."[7] These broad goals focus heavily on medical, cultural, and self-esteem or self-discovery activities. Encouragement to develop academically—by learning the alphabet or developing emergent literacy skills—is largely absent from the lengthy list of "broad goals." This relative neglect of preschools' educational component roughly parallels the Cooke Head Start Planning Committee's mid-February recommendations for the program's emphases.[8]

The booklet stressed the need to recruit and train a professional staff that had "training or experience in working with young children." Community volunteers were needed—including neighborhood residents, "especially parents of children at the Center, who have the potential to work well with children. Parents may either be volunteers or paid employees of the Center."[9] The summer programs also needed well-trained professionals, but OEO acknowledged the difficulty of recruiting them.[10] Thus, it emphasized engaging neighborhood residents and parents to staff Head Start programs.[11]

The response to OEO's invitation to apply for funding was overwhelming. Its Community Action Program staff worked diligently to process the flood of applications. But they often had to rely on short-cuts and irregular grant-processing procedures in order to handle the overflow. The CAP staff worked closely with other federal agencies, such as the Office of Programs for the Education of Disadvantaged in the Department of Health, Education, and Welfare, and they recruited volunteers and government interns to help.[12] This hectic pace led some observers to call the entire operation "Project Rush-Rush."[13]

Because the White House was committed to a massive summer program despite the limited time available to recruit providers, pressure was applied to process applicants quickly and to lower the quality standards for the projects. When OEO employees such as Polly Greenberg objected to funding low-quality proposals, they were removed from the applicant screening process. As Greenberg's immediate supervisor explained to her, "I know it's hard on you. But to lots of the staff, you are the symbol of quality, and we have to hang you publicly so everyone will see that quality is passé and quickness is the rule of the day."[14]

Jule Sugarman, the deputy director of CAP, acknowledged the agency's unorthodox funding approach prior to start of the 1965 summer programs. "We departed rather dramatically from the previous government grant programs, which for the most part are conceived of as quality experimentations, trying to develop new services in a quality fashion. As a result of that decision, we got a wide mix in the variety of programs and we created an enormous range of back-up services."[15]

Despite the low quality of some of the applications, OEO funded approximately 82 percent of them.[16] On May 18 the White House announced that twenty-five hundred summer Head Start projects would operate eleven thousand Child Development Centers and help five hundred and thirty thousand children of the poor. In a Rose Garden ceremony, Johnson announced that "this means that nearly half the preschool children of poverty will get a head start on their future. These children will receive preschool training to prepare them for regular school in September. They will get medical and dental attention that they badly need, and parents will receive counseling on improving the home environment."[17]

The White House Conference on Education

On July 21 and 22, 1965, as OEO was launching this massive initiative, the administration sponsored a widely publicized, well-attended conference on education, the successor to the education conference that the Eisenhower administration had sponsored a decade earlier. Topics discussed at the two-day meeting, chaired by John W. Gardner, president of the Carnegie Corporation and head of Johnson's 1964 Education Task Force, ranged from preschool to postgraduate education. The roughly five hundred attendees included some of America's prominent educators and policy makers.[18]

Each of the eighteen special sessions included a commissioned paper and a panel of experts to discuss the issue highlighted in that unit. A session concerning preschools featured a paper by University of Chicago education professor J. W. Getzels. Getzels, not a preschool educator himself, reviewed the state of knowledge about early childhood education and noted that "numerous studies attest to the view that the development of both general and specific cognitive abilities—the abilities required for success in school—is determined in many critical ways by the availability of relevant experiences in the pre-school environment."[19] He emphasized the great diversity in early childhood education programs, explaining that preschools existed in about seventy cities (new Head Start programs not included).

After discussing three general, albeit diverse, approaches to early childhood education, he acknowledged that there are "no systematic comparisons of the relative effectiveness, say, of what we have called the supplementary and academic-preparatory procedures." Moreover, he explained several longitudinal studies suggesting that although participating children's performance improved initially, those relative gains did not persist.[20]

When Getzels discussed the Head Start programs, he raised several key questions about their implementation and efficacy. "What, for example, are the criteria for selecting activities from the available alternatives? On what basis will the effectiveness of what is being done be evaluated? Granted, it is difficult to see how any educational harm can come to the children, and there may be residual gains in medical care and keeping them off the streets."[21]

During the preschool session many experts also expressed support for preschool programs. For example, Howard Samuels, president of the Kordite Corporation, urged support for "a national commitment for a war on ignorance" focused on the preschool child. He argued that "no city or State can come to grips with problem. The Federal Government must accept the responsibility for educating the culturally deprived child." Marion Folsom, secretary of HEW during the Eisenhower administration, agreed and asked: "With the problem so clear, why is it taking so long to get to the solution?" Project Head Start's director, Julius Richmond, pointed out that the public consensus on the value of early childhood education was evidenced by the "flood of proposals" for summer programs. And Representative Al Quie (R-MN) expressed concern that so little emphasis had been placed on preschool education; he promised to offer an amendment to ESEA that would incorporate programs like Head Start into existing schools. The superintendent of schools for Wichita, Kansas, L. H. Shepoiser, praised Quie's proposal and added: "We need to loosen up the Elementary and Secondary School Act and incorporate all aspects of the Head Start programs." Shepoiser further urged that the medical and health services included in Head Start programs be maintained when the program was incorporated into the schools.[22]

A few educators also raised concerns. The Chicago educator J. Deton Brooks Jr., for example, feared that programs like Head Start would "get buried in the traditional educational system" and that these initiatives should therefore operate within the context of community action programs.[23]

1965 Summer Head Start Programs

Despite the formidable challenges involved in creating and staffing summer Head Start programs on such short notice, OEO succeeded in helping five hundred and sixty thousand disadvantaged children during the summer of 1965. The total cost for the effort was $84 million—$150 per student in the eight-week program. More than three-fourths of the money was spent on daily needs such as personnel, equipment, and child transportation. Six percent was allocated to medical, dental, and psychological health, 8 percent was spent on nutrition, and 1.7 percent was dedicated to recruiting parents and families and providing them with social services. Another 2 percent was allocated for research, evaluation, and training; the remaining 5 percent was used to administer the programs.[24]

Participating children were somewhat older than Head Start participants today. Only 14.7 percent were under age five; 44.2 percent were five years old, and 41 percent were six years old or older. This age pattern occurred in part because summer programs attracted older children than did the year-round programs that were instituted later.[25]

One positive aspect of the summer programs received less publicity than the primary goal of helping disadvantaged children: Head Start generated a large number of jobs for adults. In a memo to the president, Shriver noted that "Head Start will provide paid summer employment to approximately 100,000 people. There will be close to 40,000 paid professionals and 60,000 paid neighborhood workers. In addition, another 100,000 will be involved during the summer on a full-time volunteer basis." Shriver concluded that "it would be difficult to determine which is the greater benefit—the additional income provided to 100,000 or the opportunity to serve for another 100,000."[26] At the end of that summer's frenzied effort, Johnson applauded the success of the programs in helping half a million youngsters. "Before this summer, they were on the road to despair. They were on the road to that wasteland of ignorance in which the children of the poor grow up and become the parents of the poor."[27]

Robert Cooke, chair of the Head Start Planning Committee, also praised the summer program's achievements. He singled out intelligence gains among disadvantaged youngsters in particular. "The evidence is overwhelming that major improvement in intelligence, stability and achievement can result from improved early childhood experience whereas change in later years is most difficult to effect. Carefully controlled studies have now shown that remarkable improvement in intellectual performance can be expected from early childhood enrichment."[28]

Others, however—even those sympathetic to the project—were less convinced of the quality and effectiveness of the programs funded that summer. Edward Zigler, a member of the Cooke committee, commented:

> While Head Start did capture the hearts and minds of Americans in a way no other publicly funded social program has yet managed to do, the frenzied distribution of grants during that first summer contributed to a long-term problem that still plagues Head Start—wide disparities in program quality. While some Head Start programs are excellent, many are mediocre, and some are downright poor.
>
> Haste was certainly an important factor, if not the only factor, in the uneven quality. I remember watching the screening process late one evening in the spring of 1965. Because a large, but temporary, labor pool was needed to process the applications, Sugarman hired substitute teachers to

supplement the volunteers and help screen the grant requests at night. They had a virtual assembly line set up. The only sound was the repetitious thumping of rubber stamps as the reviewers scanned each application, checked five boxes, and sent them on for funding.

Impressed by the organization and the dedication, I nevertheless worried about the end product. I asked Sugarman if he was concerned about the quality of the applications. "Don't worry," he assured me. "Of course, we'll fund some bad programs. But after the program is implemented, we'll close down any programs that are bad and shift funds to better programs."

Caught up in the spirit that night, I was prepared to believe Sugarman. But a few years later I found that it is not so easy for administrators to stop the flow of federal funds to a program once it had started. One of the first questions I asked after assuming the responsibility for overseeing Head Start in 1970 was how many of the original programs had been closed down. Dick Orton, another Head Start pioneer and someone who by that time was directing the Head Start bureau at the new Office of Child Development (OCD), paused and scratched his head. "Well, Ed, there *was* one program we *almost* closed down."[29]

Year-Round Head Start Programs

From the beginning, many early childhood educators and policy makers doubted that an eight-week summer program would be sufficient to effect lasting change among the impoverished. Foreseeing this, the administration announced in March that it intended to fund year-round preschool programs. In August 1965 Johnson reiterated that support and announced funding for year-round Head Start programs beginning that fall. He also planned to continue summer sessions; moreover, he indicated that special "follow-through" programs were necessary for youngsters who attended the summer programs.[30]

Despite growing questions regarding summer programs' efficacy, they were continued. Because its budget was limited, the administration was reluctant to shift its resources to the more effective—but more expensive— year-round programs when it could serve large numbers of youngsters in the much less expensive summer programs.

When in March 1967 OEO proposed shifting $20 million from the summer programs to the full-year programs, Charles L. Schultze, director of the Bureau of the Budget, objected. Schultze conceded that "it is true that summer programs seem to have a *low* educational effectiveness. There is a good case for the OEO proposed shift—on the merits."[31] But he reminded everyone that summer Head Start programs were very popular and therefore should not be cut—lest others insist on restoring them using supplemental funds. The White House agreed with Schultze, and OEO was not allowed to transfer the monies to the year-round programs.[32]

Following the BOB's decision, OEO even refused to allow local transfers of monies from summer to full-year Head Start projects. In theory, CAAs should have had the authority to plan and administer their own programs. But when they tried to shift the funds, Shriver refused, saying, "because of the limited amount of money available, it has been determined that no increase in the number of Head Start children in full-year programs will be permitted at the expense of the summer program."[33] Continued political pressure, however, forced OEO to relax its prohibition on transferring funds at the local level.[34]

The number of children enrolled in summer programs actually grew by 13,000 from 1965 to 1966. In 1967 enrollment decreased substantially from 573,000 to 466,000, but in the summer of 1968 OEO enrolled an additional 8,000 children. Funding for summer Head Start programs increased by one-fifth, from $84 million in 1965 to $101.5 million in 1968.[35]

The year-round Head Start programs were also expanding. The number of children served shot from 20,000 in 1965 to 160,000 in 1966; 215,000 children participated in 1967, but this number leveled off at 218,000 in 1968. Funding for year-round programs also increased—from $8 million in 1965 to $239 million in 1968. The increased funding was useful, because the year-round programs were five to seven times as expensive to run as were summer programs. Moreover, the two types of programs differed in the populations they served. Whereas 30 to 40 percent of summer Head Start children were aged six or older, less than 10 percent of those in the year-round programs were that old.[36]

Children enrolled in the Head Start programs did indeed come from disadvantaged backgrounds. In fact, among 1966–1967 year-round participants, 7 percent had not visited a doctor and 31 percent had not seen a dentist in the previous two years. Thirty percent lived in households from which the father was absent; 27 percent were in homes receiving welfare. Fourteen percent lived in homes without interior running water, and 34 percent lacked telephone service.[37]

In theory, the programs relied on high-quality teachers and small class sizes (one professional teacher for every fifteen children). In practice, of course, it was difficult to find enough well-trained educators. Head Start, like other CAPs, relied heavily on volunteers and paraprofessionals to assist trained teachers.[38] Ideally, this would result in a ratio of one adult for every five children. During fiscal year 1968, approximately thirty thousand paraprofessionals and thirty-nine thousand volunteers staffed year-round projects; an additional fifty thousand paraprofessionals and almost twice as many volunteers participated in the summer programs. Many volunteers were the parents of the Head Start children. Among paraprofessionals in the year-round programs, 31 percent were white, 45 percent African American, 12 percent Hispanic, and 8 percent American Indian. More than eight of ten staffers were paid, and they were also overwhelmingly female. Most lacked postsecondary education, and approximately three of ten had at most a tenth-grade education. Although OEO stressed plans to train teachers and paraprofessionals needing additional education, fewer than one-quarter of the latter had received any university-sponsored training.[39]

Growing Criticism of OEO

While Head Start became one of the most popular Great Society programs, OEO itself faced mounting criticism.[40] For example, Republicans—and many conservative Democrats—questioned the agency's wasteful practices. Moreover, many political leaders and policy makers were particularly upset by the legislative requirement of "maximum feasible participation" in CAPs. This was an ambiguous and initially little-noticed requirement evoked by some local activists to challenge or bypass local governments and elected officials. Finally, continued disagreements regarding which stakeholders should have representation on CAA boards and what powers should be allocated to these participants undermined political support for OEO among many state and local politicians.[41]

White House aide James Gaither, involved in oversight of the War on Poverty from 1966 to 1969, acknowledged the political difficulties encountered by the CAP: "We tended, over time, to de-emphasize the Community Action label. . . . Community Action struck most people as a violent kind of movement. . . . As I recall, in all of the materials which we prepared for the President, we avoided the use of that label."[42]

Shriver was not immune to rising criticisms of OEO, and he used the popularity of Project Head Start to offset increasingly negative attitudes toward OEO. "Faced with local and congressional hostility, I felt that National Emphasis programs, one of them being Head Start, could ameliorate some of this hostility to OEO's CAP efforts by establishing certain national programs that many communities would consider desirable. . . . Otherwise, the Community Action Program would be looked upon exclusively as an effort to empower the poor politically and economically."[43] Not surprisingly, Shriver opposed any efforts to transfer Head Start from OEO.

But not everyone in OEO was pleased with the extraordinary attention and resources Shriver devoted to Head Start. Some Washington bureaucrats resented Shriver's direct involvement in decisions about the program and the manner in which he bypassed regular CAP decision-making channels. The program's director, Julius Richmond, also remembers the resentment of community action participants who felt that Shriver, rather than the local group, was making the key decisions.[44] Some OEO officials felt that other areas of the program suffered because such a high proportion of funds went to Head Start programs and because, as they saw it, Head Start staff members were second-class employees.[45]

In addition, some local community action agencies resented the funding and privileges earmarked for Head Start programs instead of other services. For example, local activists wanted to exercise more control over staff selection; they were particularly eager to hire people from the local community for Head Start positions and distrusted the so-called outside experts sent to advise them on early child development and care.[46] Shriver explained that "some of the philosophers or theorists of community action did not believe in what they called 'services.' They believed that OEO should not give services to poor people. Rather, we should *empower* poor people politically and economically." Shriver pointed out that Saul Alinsky, an influential community organizer, "called our whole effort at OEO 'political pornography.' What he meant was that we were not really giving poor people the power to change their own conditions, economically or otherwise; that OEO was therefore a palliative, and all we were doing was spoon-feeding the poor with programs like Head Start. Consequently, some Community Action agencies did not want the Head Start program."[47]

Other local activists insisted that Head Start and community action must be linked, arguing that the former was meaningless without community reforms. Thomas Levin, the first executive director of the Child Development Group of Mississippi (CDGM), for example, testified before a congressional panel in 1967 that "Head Start must be an instrument for social change. Preschool education for communities of the poor which prepares the child for a better life without mobilizing the community for social change is an educational and sociological 'fraud.'" Levin went on to explain that "the child cannot be redeemed without redeeming the community. The community cannot be redeemed without application of vigorous community organization and social action principles which are needed to achieve an imaginative, creative, and effective Head Start program—or any other that is addressing itself to the education, social, or health needs of the poor."[48]

The Mississippi Head Start Controversy

One of the few major political-social controversies involving the program erupted in Mississippi in 1965. A coalition of northern and Mississippi civil rights supporters, in conjunction with the Mary Holmes Junior College, created the nation's largest Head Start program. The group received a grant in May 1965 to establish eighty-five centers in forty-five counties to serve six thousand children. The CDGM, the corporation subcontracting to operate the programs, began working under difficult logistical and political circumstances. Polly Greenberg, a former OEO official in Washington, DC, and a key CDGM participant, documented the accomplishments and difficulties that the organization faced.[49]

Powerful state political leaders—for example, Senator John Stennis (D-MS), an ardent segregationist and powerful member of the Senate Appropriations Committee, opposed delivery of Head Start services under the auspices of local African American groups; he accused CDGM of wasting funding and siphoning monies to support the Mississippi Freedom Democratic Party (MFDP).[50] Mississippi governor Paul B. Johnson drafted a letter to the president in which he attempted to link CDGM to the antiwar movement. "While Mississippi boys are dying in the defense of the freedom of others in South Vietnam, a federal agency, Office of Economic Opportunity, grants American dollars to an organization that has openly opposed America's policy in South Vietnam and urged Negroes to ignore Selective Service calls."[51]

Even the staff members who were the most closely involved in investigating the allegations of impropriety were divided regarding the seriousness of the charges against CDGM. Julius Richmond downplayed the irregularities and thought that the lack of financial receipts was so infrequent that the investigation "was a kind of a 'Star Chamber' proceeding."[52] On the other hand, OEO general counsel Donald M. Baker recalled that "in the year of its great crisis, CDGM came to be a tool of the black militants. . . . The fact of the matter is, a lot of our money went to pay for the automobiles and to feed the marchers on that Selma march. . . . Perhaps in some respects the worst thing about it was that in many areas it was converted from a child-oriented program to a public employment program for adult Negroes. They were hiring illiterate, untrained Negroes, and not infrequently requiring a certain amount of militancy from them, [to], in essence . . . baby-sit the children."[53]

Several investigations produced a disputed number of examples of fraud or mismanagement, and CDGM's auditing system was deemed inadequate to handle the task at hand.[54] Following strong, persistent pressure from Stennis and other southerners in Congress, OEO stopped CDGM's funding. As Shriver explained, "In America, one of the most effective ways to attack anything the government is doing to show that money is being misused. . . . Therefore, from the beginning, we at OEO tried to enlist people to go down to Mississippi who were extremely responsible from a fiscal viewpoint. . . . For a long time we did a pretty good job. . . . What finally happened, however, was that, despite our efforts the records CDGM had kept were simply not good enough to stand up to intense congressional scrutiny."[55]

Following the Johnson administration's termination of CDGM contracts and funding of a new group, Mississippi Action for Progress (MAP), many liberal leaders—especially in the North—denounced Shriver's actions.[56] Opponents placed a full-page ad in the New York Times that read "Say it isn't so, Sargent Shriver" and criticized Shriver personally.[57]

The Citizens Crusade Against Poverty (CCAP), a group of liberal organizations and individuals organized to fight poverty, denounced Shriver's decision and created a special panel to investigate the decision to terminate CDGM's funding.[58] The CCAP Board of Inquiry cleared CDGM and stated that for the previous two years CDGM "had proven to be a highly successful and significant program providing quality preschool experiences for a large number of children, and in addition, particularly noteworthy for its massive involvement of parents and its innovative use of non-professionals."[59]

At a Head Start Planning Committee meeting in Detroit, John Niemeyer reported, the members "pressed Jule Sugarman [about defunding CDGM] and spoke out strongly against the decision. . . . With that meeting, the Committee's usefulness, in the eyes of the OEO decision-makers—and perhaps others above them—was ended. We were never convened again."[60]

After a series of complicated and often contentious negotiations, OEO reinstated CDGM's funding, albeit at a lower level than CDGM thought adequate. The group requested funding levels of $41 million, which OEO rejected outright. In August 1966 CDGM resubmitted a proposal for $20.3 million.[61] In December 1966 Shriver announced grants for CDGM of $5 million. This award would help 5,900 disadvantaged children in seventeen Mississippi counties.[62]

The group's supporters were disappointed by the relatively modest allocation for fiscal year 1967, but OEO believed that Mississippi already received a disproportionate share of Head Start funding. In a letter to the United Presbyterian Church, associate director Jule Sugarman wrote: "As you know, however, Mississippi is entitled under the statutory allotment formula to only $7,500,000 in Head Start funds. The Director of OEO has made an additional $22,500,000 available for Head Start in Mississippi. As a result, nearly 10% of all the Head Start operating funds for fiscal 1967 will be used in that state."[63]

Uneven Quality of Head Start Programs

From the project's inception, local programs varied greatly in type and quality. This diversity was reinforced by the fact that Head Start had no mandatory or recommended preschool curriculum.[64] Such freedom stemmed in part from strong disagreements among experts regarding necessary components of comprehensive services. For example, the Cooke committee emphasized medical, social, and nutritional services but downplayed education training; OEO staff—many of whom distrusted school systems—reinforced this relative neglect of educational services.

When OEO described Head Start to Congress in 1965, it emphasized the need for improving the "health and physical abilities of the poor, developing their self-confidence and ability to relate to others, increasing their verbal and conceptual skills, involving parents in activities with their children and providing appropriate social services for the family."[65] Interestingly, as OEO described the tasks involved, it made it clear that "professionals will do the teaching, assisted by neighborhood residents, parents and volunteer aides. They will work with four- and five-year-old children in vacant schools and community centers."[66]

Variations in quality between summer and year-round programs were especially evident. The former provided opportunities for local schools and teachers to participate in Head Start during the summer vacation months. In 1966 and 1967, schools comprised two-thirds of delegate agencies (grantees that actually administered programs). Moreover, regular teachers were a significant proportion of professionals involved in the programs. Schools and teachers were less involved in year-round programs, however. Indeed, in the full-year programs of 1965–66 and 1966–67, only about one-third of Head Start delegate agencies were schools, and fewer teachers participated.[67]

Further disparity emerged as the movement away from using regular teachers in local Head Start programs gained momentum and by 1967 more emphasis was placed on hiring nonspecialist paraprofessionals. Eveline Omwake, an early childhood educator and former member of the Advisory

Committee on Teacher Training for Project Head Start, noted that "by this time the employment function of the project was taking precedence over the educative function." Omwake felt that "the plan for replacing trained teachers with neighborhood residents reflected two assumptions: first, that to help the children it was necessary to strengthen the home and environmental forces at work in their lives; and second, that since early-childhood education had not been able to define or defend a consistent educational approach, a professional educator's approach was not a demonstrated 'must' for Head Start." She further observed that "as staffs came to be made up largely of paraprofessionals, many experienced teachers were replaced or they resigned. These teachers found it impossible to maintain constructive working relationships in the midst of a power struggle."[68]

Several of the key participants in the creation and implementation of Head Start argued that the provision of quality education services received insufficient attention. Zigler, for example, noted that "for a program that was first and foremost promoted as a way to prepare poor children to do well in school, it is ironic that the disparities in Head Start's quality were especially noticeable in the area of early childhood education. Part of the problem was that early childhood educators were in the minority on the Planning Committee."[69] As a result, Zigler felt that "to ensure that Head Start was a comprehensive program, particularly one that downplayed 'cognitive' development, we may have paid too little attention to the educational component. We were unanimous in hoping that Head Start would be something more than a traditional nursery school; unfortunately, in some communities, it turned out to be considerably less."[70] Recruiting high-quality teachers also was complicated by the fact that some OEO staff members questioned the value of hiring regular schoolteachers rather than providing opportunities for Head Start parents and local community members to staff the programs.[71]

Despite the problems and concerns confronting Head Start at its inception, it enjoyed unusually strong public and bipartisan political support. The question that remained, however, was where the federal government should house Head Start and how to most effectively improve the program in the following few years.

Evaluating Head Start

Neither the Johnson administration nor the Congress had a clear, long-term plan for the Office of Economic Opportunity—partly because the Economic

Opportunity Act contained diverse mandates and partly because it was difficult for OEO to implement and oversee many local initiatives with limited federal staff and resources. One widely shared view, however, was that OEO would develop new projects and then transfer them to agencies within Labor or Health, Education, and Welfare. Julius Richmond explained that "Mr. Shriver always articulated that it was an innovative agency, it was to develop these new things, get them started and then they'd be turned over, we assumed largely to HEW."[72]

The agency's mandate also required it to coordinate the War on Poverty. Thus, theoretically, the transferred programs would shift from OEO's direct oversight to its broader coordinating jurisdiction. In practice, however, Shriver and OEO were reluctant to transfer a popular program such as Head Start—especially in the face of mounting attacks against OEO in 1966 and 1967. Moreover, OEO was not effective in coordinating poverty-related programs in other agencies.[73]

As the administration launched its War on Poverty, federal domestic agencies introduced the Planning-Programming-Budgeting (PPB) system, a heavily quantitative and economically oriented analytic tool, into evaluation processes. The Department of Defense pioneered the PPB system in the early 1960s, and Johnson subsequently ordered it installed at other federal agencies.[74] A study of sixteen agencies found that only three had made substantial progress in incorporating PPB into their operations: OEO, HEW, and the Department of Agriculture.[75] But the PPB approach proved to be problematic in assessing War on Poverty programs in general and Head Start in particular. As Henry J. Aaron, a senior fellow at the Brookings Economic Studies program, later explained:

> Things did not work out that way for several reasons, some political, some analytical. First, certain OEO programs—especially the Community Action Program, Legal Services, and the Job Corps—were under continuous political attack. Political conflict made detached analysis and evaluation of their operations almost impossible because it supported the fear that any negative findings or qualifications of positive findings would find their way into the brief of someone bent on destroying the program.
>
> Second, evaluation of programs contained in the War on Poverty, and indeed of all government programs affecting human resources, has proven extremely difficult. In some cases the benefits from the programs cannot be measured with any precision. . . .
>
> Third, a central tenet of the poverty program was that a simultaneous attempt to deal with several manifestations of poverty at once might work

where partial methods would not. . . . Yet most evaluations had to focus on
the effectiveness of a particular, rather modest program in achieving some
special objective. . . .

Fourth, evaluation ended up being used in rather surprising ways. Head
Start received failing marks in its evaluations, but remains politically ro-
bust. The Job Corps received mixed marks and may have yielded benefits
greater than its costs; nevertheless, it was sharply curtailed. . . . Evaluations indicated that Community Action Programs had succeeded, but
CAPs became the popular symbol of the failure of the War on Poverty. . . .
This history suggests that evaluation was only one element, and a very far
from decisive one, in the political determination of whether programs
should live or die. In short, evaluation was a political instrument to be trot-
ted out when it supported one's objectives or undercut one's opponents',
and to be suppressed, if possible, when it opposed one's objectives or
strengthened one's opponents'. Far from being an instrument for even-
handed, objective deliberation, evaluation was transmuted into "forensic
social science." Moreover, the use of analysis in political debates tended to
direct attention to the issues that analysts could cope with, which were not
necessarily the central aspects of the program.[76]

Moreover, the PPB system was better suited to evaluating agencies or projects as a whole; OEO left the assessment of particular program or project aspects to its subunits.[77] But not everyone welcomed those assessments (for example, those performed on issues such as which Head Start curricula were
the most effective in helping disadvantaged children). Staff members such as
Polly Greenberg saw little need for more research and questioned the contributions of experts in general.[78] And Zigler later explained that some members of the Cooke Head Start Planning Committee also opposed evaluations
of the program: "The medical people felt that the purpose of Head Start was
to feed children, get their teeth fixed, and offer them a pleasant experience.
What was there to evaluate? It was clear Head Start would do no harm."[79]

But several other panel members, including Zigler, favored evaluations.
Julius Richmond agreed, appointing Yale University professor Edmund Gordon to direct the evaluation effort. Gordon, Bronfenbrenner, Richmond, and
Zigler worked together during the spring of 1965 to design an assessment instrument, but their efforts were hampered by a lack of suitable measures. As
a result, Zigler acknowledged, "as the chief person responsible for developing
the first measures used to evaluate Head Start that summer, I have to say that
they were a disaster. They were so badly done that the results could never be
analyzed."[80]

Shriver's insistence that all half-million students—not a more manageable sample of attendees—required assessment impeded evaluation of the 1965 summer Head Start programs. After struggling with design and implementation of the initial evaluation, Gordon subsequently funded regional centers for researching and evaluating Head Start. Some of these eventually developed useful, long-term longitudinal studies of the program.[81]

After its first chaotic summer, Project Head Start devoted considerable funding to research and evaluation: it allocated $2 million in fiscal year 1966 and $6 million in fiscal years 1967 and 1968, representing about 1 to 2 percent of the total program budget.[82] The monies were almost equally allocated among evaluation and research centers, research demonstrations, development projects, and individual research grants.[83]

George Washington University professor Sar Levitan, who authored one of the best contemporary assessments of OEO and the Head Start office, explained that much of the early evaluation work focused on basic issues of measurement. Levitan appreciated the pioneering research but pointed out that it provided limited immediate guidance for operating programs.[84]

As OEO and Project Head Start began to assess their programs, preliminary results from individual researchers also appeared. Initially, several local studies claimed that the summer programs were successful. Johns Hopkins University professor Leon Eisenberg, for example, found gains of 8 to 10 IQ points among 480 Baltimore children enrolled in the 1965 summer programs.[85] Shriver quickly distributed the *Baltimore Sun*'s account of Eisenberg's study to administration officials.[86] And in a June 1966 letter to Lady Bird Johnson, Shriver cited various local studies testifying to the success of Head Start.[87]

Despite continued public enthusiasm for the eight-week summer programs, other analysts raised increasingly serious questions about their short- and long-term effectiveness.[88] For example, a widely quoted, OEO-funded study of four New York City kindergartens by Yeshiva University researchers Max Wolff and Annie Stein reported that the benefits of participation faded six months after the first summer programs. Further, Head Start attendees fared no better on kindergarten achievement tests than children of comparable socioeconomic background who had not enrolled in the summer programs.[89] In October 1966 the *New York Times* published a story based on the New York City study with the headline "Head Start Value Found Temporary."[90] Shriver himself cited the Wolff and Stein study at the annual meeting of the Great Cities Research Council in Milwaukee, acknowledging that existing schools were "critically inadequate to meet the needs of children of poverty. This seems like a harsh judgment, but it is borne out by a recent follow-up study of Head Start children."[91]

But OEO did not always welcome criticism of Head Start. Martin Deutsch, one of the leading analysts of early childhood education, had been appointed to the program's national advisory commission. In an interview a decade later, Deutsch recalled events following his public questioning of the summer Head Start programs' effectiveness. "All over the country newspapers had headlines on a new 'miracle program' to change our school system. I gave interviews at the time, I wrote articles . . . and said this is simply not possible—this is nothing but a political game. So when I said this at the first advisory committee meeting I was asked to resign. They wanted to allow the public image that a miracle cure was possible. . . . Shriver wanted 100 percent consensus . . . two of us walked out at the time, one was Ted Sizer, who was a Dean at Harvard, and myself."[92] Some later analysts have also castigated those who challenged the success of Head Start. For example, Edward Zigler and Jeanette Valentine wrote that "particularly detrimental to the program has been the coterie of psychologists, early childhood educators, and social analysts who have regularly, albeit erroneously, proclaimed the failure of Head Start."[93]

Policy makers and the media often relied on hastily assembled and methodologically weak studies. Indeed, early works were not scientific evaluations at all but simply descriptive reports portrayed as serious and reliable analyses. Impressionistic evidence of the success or failure of Head Start and similar programs competed with the few in-depth, scientifically oriented investigations of early childhood development for media attention.[94]

On March 8, 1965, Johnson announced that OEO would institute year-round Head Start programs in the fall of that year.[95] With questions about the summer programs' efficacy mounting, one might think that the administration would phase out them out. The administration, however, faced considerable internal pressure from the Bureau of the Budget to maintain summer programs; this format was less expensive and could therefore serve more children. As a result, the number of children in summer programs actually rose slightly in 1966, decreased by 18.7 percent in 1967, and then grew by 1.5 percent in 1968.[96]

Head Start's mandate provided that 15 percent of CAP funds—$67 million in fiscal years 1965 and 1966—could be spent on research and development projects. This provision was a second major source of experimental funding. Sanford Kravitz, who was in charge of that program, focused on a few national demonstration projects that included major CAP program areas. Yet some OEO officials and local community action agencies opposed spending such large sums on R&D projects because they diverted funds from local service programs and often denied community activists a role in designing and running special endeavors. Congress responded to these critics by reducing the amount of CAP funds from 15 to 5 percent in fiscal years 1967 and 1968 as well as mandating that the projects receive advance approval by the local CAAs. The sudden reduction in R&D funds required CAP to spend most of its diminished R&D monies on existing projects and not on initiating new ones.[97]

National Evaluation of Head Start

As part of the larger federal effort to enhance evaluation via the PPB system, OEO created its own Office of Research, Planning, Programs, and Evaluation (RPP&E) in the fall of 1967, appointing Robert Levine as director. Levine and John Evans, head of OEO's evaluation unit, were impressed by neither Project Head Start's national assessment of its 1965 summer program nor the subsequent decentralized, individual program evaluations.[98] Therefore, in March 1968 RPP&E developed a request for proposals for a national evaluation of children currently in the first, second, and third grades. Using an ex post facto design, the investigation was to compare how former program participants performed on cognitive and affective measures compared to a control group of nonparticipants.[99]

The Head Start research committee of Bronfenbrenner, Gordon, and Zigler objected to a design that evaluated the program as a whole, pointing to the great variation among local programs and their quality. They also objected to the inclusion of the 1965 summer program in the design because that experience had been unusually hectic and chaotic. The committee expressed further misgivings regarding the emphasis on cognitive measures and the effort to retrospectively locate an appropriate control group of nonparticipants. As an alternative, they called for a longitudinal, random-assigned study of Head Start.[100]

Concern that OEO's evaluators were stressing the cognitive development of children was not misguided. The evaluation director, Robert Levine, appreciated the possible broad benefits of Head Start but emphasized the importance of improving educational outcomes. "Head Start may be a fine Community Action program, and the indicators are that it is. It may improve the health of kids. But it is *primarily* a program to improve children's learning abilities, and on this criterion it must finally stand or fall. If the program does not bring about educational improvement, then the other favorable effects may be brought in much more cheaply."[101]

Indeed, Shriver recalled that "because of the five years I had spent as president of the Board of Education in Chicago, I had a bias in favor of education, and originally I had thought of Head Start as an educational program."[102] Robert Cooke also later acknowledged that OEO had initially seen Head Start mainly as an educational endeavor. "When Sargent Shriver and his staff in the Office of Economic Opportunity first decided to undertake a preschool program, the primary objective was early academic enrichment."[103]

The problem was that individuals and groups varied with respect to what they thought Project Head Start should be. This is not unusual for such a diverse and comprehensive program.[104] For example, the Cooke Planning Committee downplayed the educational component, but key policy makers such as Johnson and Shriver emphasized it—especially in the mid-1960s, when they were selling the program to the American public and Congress. Later, as Shriver tried to stave off the proposed transfer of Head Start to the Office of Education in HEW, he sometimes tried to deny the educational objectives that he had championed earlier. Similarly, although it was acknowledged at that time that enhancing the education of the disadvantaged was an important aspect of Head Start for many policy makers and OEO officials, subsequent analysts (some of whom had earlier opposed efforts to increase children's IQs) downplayed the role of education by stressing the recommendations of the Cooke committee and minimizing the views and contributions of Shriver and other administration officials in late 1964 and early 1965.[105] In addition, later, when Zigler became director of the new Office of Child Development in HEW in the Nixon administration, policy guidelines issued by the agency stated that "IQ change and achievement-test scores were not the ultimate goals of Head Start."[106]

As questions about the program's efficacy increased, Congress threatened to relocate the program to a new agency. In the face of these pressures, OEO decided that it could ill afford to wait for results from a longitudinal evaluation. Moreover, owing to its disappointment with existing evaluations of Head Start, including those undertaken by the agency itself, OEO felt it imperative to quickly fund a new national assessment. It awarded the assessment contract to the Westinghouse Learning Corporation and Ohio University and gave these organizations less than one year to complete their evaluation.[107]

Preliminary results of the Westinghouse Learning Corporation's analysis were unavailable until after Nixon took office. Therefore the results had no bearing on the Johnson administration's deliberations about the program. When Westinghouse released its evaluation, the results raised questions about the ability of Head Start—and in particular its summer programs—to enable disadvantaged children to make lasting academic advances. Although critics challenged the study's methodology and interpretation, the Westinghouse Report temporarily dampened initial enthusiasm for Head Start among policy makers and the public.[108]

Even as OEO struggled to evaluate and improve Head Start in the late 1960s, it was compelled to operate under increasingly difficult circumstances. In 1965, despite the potential availability of funds, Johnson had refused to expand the agency. In the last half of the decade, the escalating costs of the Vietnam War and the White House's political reluctance to raise taxes precluded significant increases in funding for the War on Poverty. Furthermore, during its first three years of existence, OEO was annually revamped by Congress. This constant restructuring kept the agency in a perpetual state of flux. These factors, combined with the late delivery of federal funds, caused OEO to struggle for survival rather than working to improve programs.

While OEO struggled, state and municipal leaders—and the United States Congress—questioned CAP's continued efforts to help local community activists challenge the existing political establishment. For example, OEO remained determined to retain its few popular programs, such as Project Head Start, but the local Head Start programs faced opposition from within the agency and from local CAAs opposed to the privileging of that program with regard to funding and attention. In addition, OEO refused to allocate even more of its limited funds to Head Start, despite public enthusiasm for it.

Confronted by growing professional criticism of Head Start, some of its strongest supporters wondered whether OEO was really the best federal location for the program. For example, though generally unknown to those outside the Johnson administration's inner circle, frustrated members of the Cooke committee threatened to resign because of OEO's mistreatment of the program. Sugarman, in an administratively confidential May 1968 memo, informed the secretary of HEW:

> I think you should be aware that there is a substantial revolt in the Head Start planning committee chaired by Dr. Robert Cooke. They are very concerned over the way in which Head Start is being administered by OEO and the lack of attention it gets in the OEO regional offices.
>
> The point that has developed most recently, however, is an effort by the OEO research division to initiate an evaluation study based solely on cognitive growth, with the announced intention that Head Start should stand or fall on this question alone.
>
> The Committee is so disturbed that they asked me to consult with them last Friday. I advised them to make their views known quite clearly to Mr.

Harding and suggested that, if they were still not satisfied, they might seek an appointment with you.

This is an excellent group of people and it is they who are really responsible for the original conceptualization of Head Start. I think that if they were to resign en masse, as they have some inclination of doing, it would be a serious blow to the reputation of Head Start.[109]

The White House managed to avoid the public embarrassment of an open attack from staunch program advocates, but the relationship between OEO and Head Start was severely strained by the close of the Johnson administration.

The 1965 Interagency Task Force on Education

The special task force was a major tool for the administration in generating new ideas and reviewing existing programs. Johnson asked Bill Moyers to oversee the fourteen task forces created in 1964; these secret panels played a key role in developing the White House's ambitious legislative agenda for the Eighty-ninth Congress.[110] Following Moyers's July 1965 appointment as press secretary, Joe Califano assumed oversight of subsequent task forces and interagency groups.[111]

The task forces organized after 1964 focused more than their predecessors had on assessing recently enacted Great Society programs and recommending legislative and administrative adjustments to improve their operations.[112] Many of the recommendations resulted in initiatives by the Johnson administration. Moreover, the deliberations and secret reports produced by later task forces are analytically useful because they reveal both internal and interagency thinking about Great Society programs.

In 1965 Califano supervised thirteen interagency and four external task forces. Among these was the small Interagency Task Force on Education headed by Commissioner of Education Francis Keppel. For this task force Califano identified and ranked eight problem priorities requiring analysis. The third priority he listed was "development of a preschool education program, perhaps on a year round basis. (This paper should also include an analysis of the scope and effectiveness of the current OEO projects in this area.)"[113]

Keppel agreed to Califano's request to produce eight staff papers. He assigned Henry Loomis of HEW's Office of Education and Lisle Carter of OEO to draft the preschool education paper.[114] Keppel then revealed his four suggestions for the task force's agenda and assigned top priority to developing a program of nationwide assessment of educational progress. Early childhood education was not one of Keppel's four major agenda items, but it earned brief mention in his broader call for "training workers for the War on Poverty and the Elementary and Secondary Education Act."[115]

Loomis and Carter addressed Republican criticism that the administration's 1965 ESEA proposal ignored early childhood education. They also supported Democratic assertions that the final legislation allowed preschool funding under Title I. Yet questions about the way ESEA's early childhood provisions would coordinate with OEO's Head Start initiatives remained. In addressing these concerns, Loomis and Carter's short paper emphasized the value of early childhood education and noted the strong bipartisan support for preschools. Because only 42 percent of five-year-olds attended kindergartens, however, they argued that the top priority should be expanded kindergarten enrollment and that kindergarten teachers should receive better training. The costs of these proposed programs, however, were prohibitively high; Loomis and Carter estimated that providing kindergarten services for all five-year-olds from families earning less than $2,000 annually would carry an additional $235 million price tag.[116]

The Keppel Interagency Task Force on Education completed its report on October 8, 1965. Given the high cost of providing kindergarten education for all children, the task force acknowledged the importance of early education but recommended only "(1) that the Administration substantially expand OEO expenditures for preschool programs in Fiscal Year 1967 and (2) that an overall plan for the future be proposed by OEO, with the cooperation of HEW, by June of 1966."[117]

Following a late-October meeting, Califano confirmed that the administration had commissioned several additional studies, including one titled "An Overall-all Plan to Improve Pre-school Programs for the Poor [which would d]evelop proposals, including the training of teachers and other support, for an expanded kindergarten program for poor children. This should be worked out in conjunction with OEO."[118]

The resulting staff paper recommended an amendment to Title I that would provide monies for local school districts to expand and improve kindergartens for disadvantaged five-year-olds. The current Head Start Program would continue to serve three- and four-year-olds "and would be encouraged to supplement OE 5-year-old projects." The paper further recommended the "use of Title I funds to meet the follow-through requirement imposed by this [proposed] program."[119]

Although one might expect conflict between OEO and HEW regarding early childhood education, the Keppel Task Force and the late-1965 staff papers on preschool education recommended a division of responsibilities: OEO would continue to administer Head Start and HEW would use Title I money to expand support for disadvantaged students in kindergartens. This arrangement reflects in part the existing division of labor between OEO and HEW, but it also highlights participants' reluctance to reorganize the operation of the 1965 Head Start summer programs once their organization and location in the federal government had been established.

The 1966 Early Childhood Development Task Force

The Johnson administration created eleven external task forces in 1966—almost three times as many as the previous year. The Task Force on Early Childhood Development consisted of fourteen distinguished members and two consultants and was chaired by the prominent psychologist J. McVicker Hunt. Among its members were Jerome S. Bruner, John Goodlad, Edmund W. Gordon, Susan Gray, and Oscar Lewis. The group also included two members of the original Cooke Head Start Planning Committee—Robert E. Cooke and Urie Bronfenbrenner. Emerson J. Elliot of the BOB served as the executive secretary and helped the task force maintain a close working relationship with top administration staff.

In its 157-page final report, the task force produced an usually comprehensive, in-depth policy and research review of early childhood development and federal initiatives—such as Head Start—in the mid-1960s. The panelists, although they differed on some issues, agreed on the final report. As a result, the report provides a useful opportunity to view the analyses and recommendations of leading scholars and policy makers regarding young children and education.

The task force first met on October 15, 1966, and it was to report its findings to the administration in the midsummer of 1967, approximately one year after its establishment. But Johnson became so interested in the group's recommendations that he wanted the work to be completed by mid-December 1966. This abbreviation of the schedule upset many panelists, but they managed to submit their secret report—which was nonetheless widely read and influential within the administration—on December 19.[120]

At the panel's initial meeting several key administration officials shared their perspectives on early childhood education. Califano informed the members that the "President wants judgments of outsiders on 'best' programs; *they* should not consider political or budgetary feasibility. The President will judge how and when to act on the Task Force recommendations."[121] At the same meeting, Shriver urged that education monies be focused on follow-up programs and that federal dollars be targeted on poor children.[122]

Commissioner of Education Harold Howe sent the task force a memo about the problems and needs that young children face in schools. He was concerned that "thousands of children are finishing Head Start programs— where initial reports seem to show at least some significant success—and the benefits seem to fade out within a few months (to our embarrassment) as the newspapers seem quick to point out."[123] Howe focused on the task force's mandate, urging the panel to recommend kindergarten expansion and nursery school establishment in the public schools: "Nursery schools for 3- and 4-year-old children should be established in public schools for all children who can benefit from the program."[124]

While Howe praised early childhood education, he made it clear that it alone was insufficient to overcome the cultural and economic handicaps that disadvantaged children in our society experience. "Follow-through" programs in the later grades were necessary to help these students thrive in regular public schools.[125] At the same time, however, Howe opposed creating two separate systems of education—preferring to serve all children at existing public schools but after improvements had been made. "For children who have received the benefits of a comprehensive program prior to school entrance, this program must be 'followed through' within the structure of the public school both from the viewpoint of comprehensive services and quality instruction. To continue two competing educational programs would be divisive and destructive to public education."[126]

The report of the Early Childhood Development Task Force stressed that "America has entered a new epoch which has greatly enhanced the value of intellectual competence." At the same time, Americans faced a new problem: teaching children "how to cope with change."[127]

The panel noted that "mental development and competence are heavily determined by conditions encountered during the first three years and are largely set by age six unless the circumstances of life change radically." The issue of whether there is a "critical period" in human development remained unclear, but the group agreed that "solid evidence also indicates that the longer any given kind of circumstances continue to influence the very early development of organisms, the more difficult it becomes to alter the direction of their effects later." The task force further believed that "the social circumstances which a child encounters within his family are highly important for later development. They are important not only for later social and personality traits and for character, but also for intellectual competence. . . . Evidence is accumulating to indicate that the circumstances of slum rearing produce experiences that hamper the development of the young during both the prenatal and the post-natal phase in ways that damage almost every human trait of social importance."[128]

As a result of these observations, the panel called for a broad approach to helping disadvantaged young children. It simultaneously acknowledged America's failure to provide adequate assistance to these children, in part because it was not clear which forms of assistance were most helpful.[129]

Throughout its report, the panel noted prior neglect of intellectual competence and its current importance. "This new emphasis on the value of [intellectual] competence is still in the process of being appreciated. It represents a substantial shift in emphasis from that on emotional and social adjustment which has dominated the past 30 or 40 years." Although agreeing that Head Start should be improved, the task force nevertheless strongly endorsed the program. "To millions of Americans, Project Head Start has constituted the most notable achievement of the anti-poverty program. . . . Although many Head Start programs could probably be improved by sharper focus on those particular skills that the children of the poor have failed to learn, the program is the best remedy now available."[130]

The task force acknowledged the challenge that recent studies posed to claims that Head Start programs yield long-term academic gains, but it also cautioned that many of these analyses were methodologically flawed.[131] It failed, however, to caution readers about comparable methodological problems in the early studies that showed large gains in test performance among program participants. Nor did the panel chastise authors who first reported positive findings to the media before publishing them in an appropriate scientific journal. Perhaps reflecting its strong support for Head Start, the report also did not significantly criticize the program.

At the same time, it admitted that disadvantaged students should not be expected to retain what they gained from the program without continued special assistance. As part of the continuation services, the panel believed, the public schools should provide not only academic training but also comprehensive services for disadvantaged students similar to those available through Head Start.[132] To this end, it recommended that "if any additional funds for education of the disadvantaged are appropriated under the Elementary and Secondary Education Act, such funds should be earmarked specifically for 'follow through' into the kindergarten and early primary grades." The panel further suggested that "these funds should be expended for such techniques as involvement of parents, use of the teacher-pupil ratios of Head Start, use of volunteers and aides, 'ungrading' classes, increased use of innovative and individualized curricular materials, and arrangements for exchange of teachers and other personnel between preschool and the school programs for children aged 5, 6, and 7."[133]

The report went on to complain that the government provided insufficient help for children. To remedy the lack of strong, unified leadership, the panel called for the establishment of a federal-level Office for Children within HEW to be "administered by an Officer for Children equivalent in rank to the chief officers for health, education, and welfare." The Office for Children would oversee the Children's Bureau programs, Head Start, and the other proposed services. In addition, the task force called for federal grants to Community Commissions for Children, which would "initiate and organize the Centers for Children and Parents in the neighborhoods."[134]

Although the task force valued community initiatives for providing services for children, it did not trust them to set their own standards, at least not initially. "At the outset, the responsibility for determining the standards under which grants will be awarded to Community Commissions and to Centers for Children and Parents—in the neighborhoods—will reside at the Federal level. The ultimate objective, however, is to delegate a considerable part of this responsibility to the States as they demonstrate commitment to the needs of young children and initiative in developing programs recognizing the significance of development-fostering conditions."[135]

Developing a Follow-Through Program

Almost immediately after the conclusion of the 1965 summer Head Start programs, Johnson indicated his interest in a follow-through program. In an August 31 speech he announced a three-part extension of Project Head Start—including "follow-through programs for children limited to summer sessions. These will begin with this year's Head Starters: There will be special classes; there will be field trips; and other ways of sustaining the head start that these children have made."[136]

The Office of Economic Opportunity acted on this presidential directive, using the Economic Opportunity Act's broad mandate to fund some efforts to help Head Start students make the transition into mainstream educational settings. And reinforced by the Gardner Task Force on Early Childhood Development's secret recommendations, the Johnson administration continued developing a follow-through program to help Head Start students maintain their recent gains as they entered classrooms.

In his January 10, 1967, State of the Union Address, Johnson pledged to continue waging the War on Poverty by expanding the Head Start program.[137] The following month the president delivered a special message to Congress concerning children and youth in which he detailed plans for this expansion. He praised the program but acknowledged that its benefits could decline if not reinforced. To head off this possibility, Johnson called for a follow-through program.[138]

Following Johnson's calls for programs to sustain Head Start's benefits, federal officials turned to early childhood experts for help in assessing extant preschool programs. In March 1967 David P. Weikart, a researcher who had received funding from the Office of Education and was working with public schools in Ypsilanti, Michigan, offered a particularly interesting—and important—analysis. Joseph Froomkin, OE's assistant commissioner for program planning and evaluation, asked Weikart to produce a paper about preschool interventions, and Weikart began his assessment by questioning the long-term effectiveness of most preschool programs.[139]

Weikart noted that a key difference among preschool projects was the curriculum style each employed:

> Three curriculum styles represent the range of programming commonly utilized. The *traditional* nursery school methods employ watching and waiting for the child's needs to emerge and determine the timing of different activities. The primary goals are for social, emotional and motoric development. The *structured* nursery school methods employ carefully sequenced presentations of teacher-planned activities according to a specific developmental theory. The primary goals are intellectual and language development. Traditional nursery school materials and activities are frequently employed, but are used to achieve pre-determined goals. The *task-oriented* nursery school methods employ carefully sequenced presentations of teacher-planned activities to accomplish specific pre-determined goals such as reading, arithmetic, or logical thinking. New, specifically designed, task-related activities and materials are used; those of the traditional nursery school are not.[140]

He argued that the structural, or task-oriented, model appeared to be more successful in improving intellectual development than the traditional approach.[141]

Weikart voiced skepticism that extant preschool programs would have much long-term impact on children living in seriously disadvantaged environments such as city slums. He felt it necessary to develop more realistic expectations for early childhood interventions and to pursue new, more effective avenues to help children.[142]

The Johnson administration assessed Weikart's opinions carefully. In May

1967, Emerson Elliott, a key Bureau of the Budget staffer, asked J. McVicker Hunt, former chair of the Early Childhood Development Task Force, for his reaction to Weikart's memo. Hunt agreed with the overall thrust of Weikart's analysis, but he questioned the certainty of some of its conclusions and worried about the reaction of more traditional nursery school operators.[143] In addition, Hunt believed that though the task force and Weikart agreed with respect to many key issues, the task force favored follow-through programs but Weikart did not.[144] Hunt closed his letter to Emerson by defending Head Start programs—in large part because he believed (despite little evidence to support the belief) that they would naturally evolve toward the more structured, task-oriented curriculum that Weikart advocated.[145]

Even before securing congressional approval for follow-through programs, OEO funded a $2.5 million pilot follow-through project. And in June 1967, OEO transferred this program to the Division of Compensatory Education (DCE) within the Bureau of Elementary and Secondary Education (BESE) in the U.S. Office of Education.[146]

Follow Through received another endorsement in mid-1967 when the 1966 Task Force on Education, chaired by William Friday, issued its secret report to the Johnson administration. The report's major thrust recommended "substantial increases in Title I appropriations" and "encourage[d] participation of middle income children in its programs. Recent studies strongly suggest that the education of children is closely related to the 'mix' of racial and economic backgrounds of the students in the school."[147] The Friday Task Force briefly discussed early schooling for the disadvantaged, endorsing the recommendations of the Task Force on Early Child Development and calling for trying to make the benefits of early schooling more long-lasting.[148]

The new Ninetieth Congress also had to deal with preschools and the proposed Follow Through Program, but it differed significantly in composition from the Eighty-ninth Congress. This was especially true in the House, where Republicans gained forty-seven seats in the 1966 elections. The Senate remained relatively stable; Republicans gained only three seats. Despite sizable Democratic majorities in both chambers (248–187 in the House, 64–36 in the Senate), conservative southern Democrats sometimes sided with the GOP and now were able to thwart the administration's domestic initiatives.[149]

Several factors—among them frustration regarding the escalating Vietnam War and widespread ghetto rioting in the summer and fall of 1967—contributed to frequent congressional gridlocks with regard to key domestic issues. Thus, although the GOP failed to dismantle entirely some of the Great Society programs, they were able, with the assistance of conservative southern Democrats, to challenge several components of the War on Poverty.

Chapter 6 discusses the broader Republican attacks on the Johnson administration's education and poverty programs. Here I simply note events that took place during the reauthorization of the War on Poverty (S. 2388) and the enactment of the Follow Through Program. During the reauthorization process, Congress added four "national emphasis programs" (including Follow Through) to the four (Head Start, Legal Services, Comprehensive Health Services, and Upward Bound) housed already within OEO.[150]

Although the administration planned to expand Follow Through from a pilot program to a broadly available service enrolling two hundred thousand students during 1968–69 and costing $120 million, the financial pressures of the Vietnam War and mounting questions about OEO programs resulted in congressional authorization of only $12 million in new Follow Through funds for fiscal year 1969. Thus, program architects scaled the program down, redesigning it as an experimental rather than a service program.[151]

As the administration developed Follow Through in late 1967 and early 1968, Richard Snyder, assistant director of the program for HEW, asked experts in the field about difficulties with Follow Through programs as well as recommendations for evaluating them. Edward Zigler, a member of the Cooke committee, agreed with an approach that included evaluation of different types of programs.[152] He also warned about the problem of exaggerated and unrealistic expectations for Head Start and Follow Through created by professionals in the field:

> I would like to state that I am not as optimistic about changing the mentation of deprived children as are those current drum beaters who would have us believe that the child's intellect is so plastic that our only problem is the discovery of the correct remedial technology. I think that it is inappropriate for professionals to delude either themselves or the tax paying public on this issue. I do not think that it is in our power to rescind the biological law of human variability. The goals of Follow-Through should be realistic ones and we must be aware continually of the dangers inherent in overselling such efforts as Project Head Start or Follow-Through. I am very much concerned that undue optimism about such programs can quickly be replaced by undue pessimism. Allow me to point out to you that it was the disappointment in the public's mind concerning the impact of Head Start that gave rise to the Follow-Through Program. One cannot help but be fearful at the consequences should we discover that Head Start plus Follow Through does not result in long-lasting improvement in intellectual

skills. We have already witnessed the disillusionment with such highly pub-licized efforts as Higher Horizons and other programs in particular cities.[153]

Zigler explained that there is no simple panacea for disadvantaged chil-dren. Moreover, "there are many ways that the intellect is developed. Indeed, my own reading of the evidence leads me to believe that cognitive develop-ment would be aided much less by the application of one more technology than it would be by the removal of deleterious social factors, in and out of the school, that impede the natural cognitive growth of the child." Zigler also emphasized the role of motivation in fostering classroom achievement and called for an assessment of abilities that was broader than simply testing read-ing, arithmetic, and spelling. "It involves the desire of the child to remain in school, to attend to his teacher and to believe that he is part of the fabric of society rather than viewing himself as an outsider. These attitudes and views are just as important in determining the nature and quality of the child's later adult life as are those intellectual abilities tapped by intelligence and motiva-tional tests."[154]

Follow Through had been developed to assist Head Start children in mak-ing the transition into regular K-3 classrooms; the expectation was that the program would help disadvantaged children maintain the otherwise tempo-rary gains they had made in preschool programs. The severe budget cuts, however, meant that the program was redesigned as an experimental, planned variation curriculum program, and much of the intended close con-nection between Head Start and early elementary education was lost. More-over, the quality of many of the Follow Through experiments was inade-quate, and this limited the usefulness of their results in the 1970s and 1980s.[155]

The 1967 Child Development Task Force

In anticipation of the 1968 legislative session, the Johnson administration cre-ated eleven additional task forces in August 1967, including an interagency task force on child development led by William Gorham. The twenty mem-bers, who included Urie Bronfenbrenner and Nicholas Hobbes from the Hunt Task Force on Early Child Development, were charged with continuing the assessment of child development issues and making recommendations for future activities.

The Gorham Task Force on Child Development met three times in Octo-ber and sent its report to the White House on November 7, 1967. The report opened by acknowledging that its recommendations were constrained by anticipated limitations in the fiscal year 1969 budget.[156] After recommending more earmarked funds for evaluation of federal programs, the task force concluded that "at least two general conclusions have emerged from the Head Start experience so far: (a) that whole-year programs are more effective than short summer programs; (b) that involving parents as well as children in the program enhances its effectiveness." It noted that the debate about the best ways of raising IQ continued and recommended that a "major effort . . . be made to learn more about what kinds of programs can be effective in overcoming the educational handicaps of disadvantaged preschool children."[157]

The panel called for improvement in daycare and preschool services. It also stressed the need for changing federal involvement in elementary schools—including developing follow-through programs for children who had been enrolled in preschools.[158]

The Gorham Task Force began with a much more modest set of objectives than had the earlier task forces on education and child development, largely because of the federal budget limitations brought on by the accelerated Vietnam War. The administration adopted the task force's suggestions for expanded federal research and development, however, especially that of studying different models for Head Start and Follow Through programs.[159]

Congressional and Administration Debates about Transferring Head Start

The Johnson administration's Economic Opportunity Act of 1964 passed with little congressional deliberation and change. Republicans objected to the way the measure was "railroaded" through Congress, but they were unable to form policy alternatives attractive to most Democratic legislators. Attention temporarily shifted from EOA as the nation voted for a president that November. The considerably enhanced Democratic Eighty-ninth Congress supported most of the White House's 1965 initiatives, including the Elementary and Secondary Education Act.

The second session of the Eighty-ninth Congress in 1966 focused on the escalating war in Vietnam and increased inflation. Republicans found new Democratic allies in opposing some of the Great Society reforms—though Congress passed strong auto and highway safety legislation as well as a significant increase in the minimum wage.[1] It also passed legislation (H.R. 13161) authorizing more money for ESEA and transferring adult education programs from OEO to the Commissioner of Education in HEW. Concern about forced school desegregation led to provisions in the bill prohibiting busing to achieve racial balance in the schools. Congress passed legislation promoting international educa-tion in colleges as well, and it finally provided modest funds for the previ-ously enacted Teacher Corps.[2]

As Republicans and conservative Democrats challenged the War on Poverty, they also raised questions about the future location of popular pro-grams such as Head Start. Attempts were made to transfer the program from the Office of Economic Opportunity to the Office of Education in HEW. These battles were more than disagreements about turf; they were debates about the nature of Head Start and what might happen to the program in different bureaucratic settings.

Debates about the War on Poverty in 1966

In 1966 the White House called for a three-year reauthorization of the War on Poverty and suggested a $1.75 billion authorization for fiscal year 1967. Many earlier critics now accepted the need for federal antipoverty measures, but there was growing concern about the operation of OEO in general and the Community Action Program in particular.

Shriver was denounced and disrupted by militant spokespeople on behalf of the poor at a national convention on poverty in mid-April 1966 (sponsored by the Citizens' Crusade against Poverty). "Cleveland's Lillian Craig accused Shriver of eating 'luxurious meals while my children eat beans.'" And as Shriver was escorted away from the hostile demonstrators, "a member of Washington's youth organization, 'Rebels with a Cause,' shouted: 'Sargent, you retire.'"[3]

Congress, and the House in particular, questioned the administration of the OEO programs. And Democratic and Republican mayors continued to protest against what they perceived as the improper involvement of the poor in municipal decision-making by means of the community action programs. Despite efforts by Senators Joseph Clark (D-PA), Edward Kennedy (D-MA), and Robert Kennedy (D-NY) to significantly increase OEO funding and al-lowing Shriver considerable administrative discretion, Congress provided only $1.75 billion for the program and imposed a series of restrictions on how those monies could be spent.[4]

The House Subcommittee on the War on Poverty Program, chaired by Representative Adam C. Powell (D-NY), held seven days' worth of hearings on the administration's proposal (H.R. 13391). Powell, who at times un-abashedly criticized aspects of the War on Poverty, now praised the initiative as a whole. He announced two amendments—one separately funding Head

Start at $300 million annually and another limiting federal contributions to salaries of local poverty officials to $10,000. House Republicans complained that witnesses who were critical of the War on Poverty once again did not have a fair opportunity to testify at these hearings. They also accused Shriver and administration witnesses of ignoring or minimizing the disarray and ineffectiveness of OEO programs such as Head Start. When asked about the greatest success of the War on Poverty, Shriver singled out Project Head Start and cited preschool studies from Johns Hopkins University and the Mental Health Society of Staten Island that reported intellectual gains by participating children.[5]

Representative Al Quie (R-MN), an early supporter of preschool education, responded to Shriver's answer with his own enthusiastic endorsement of Head Start and called for additional funding of the program. "Mr. Shriver, I would like to commend you for the work you have done on Head Start. I agree with you that this is the most successful venture that OEO has been engaged in." Quie then criticized the earlier unwillingness of Congress to be more supportive of early childhood education. "I tried to get a special preschool program through this Congress for us to set national policy. . . . When the bill was first passed, a passing reference to preschool programs was in the report, and that's all. If you had waited for the congressional action, you wouldn't have been able to point to the successful story you have now. I feel so strongly about this, Mr. Shriver, that I would like to see the Congress provide whatever money is needed to embark on as big a preschool program as the communities are ready to develop, both summer and the all-year program."[6]

Although many members of Congress urged additional funding for Head Start, they disagreed about Shriver's order the previous fall "that no more than one-third of the community action funds could be used for Head Start." Shriver had assented to additional antipoverty monies, but he opposed devoting a higher percentage of CAP funds to Head Start because of the risk that "there wouldn't [be] money for anything else."[7]

Republican Attempts to Transfer Head Start in 1966

House members also were divided over the previous year's attempts by Republicans to earmark Title I funds for early childhood education.[8] When Representative Charles E. Goodell (R-NY) testified at the 1966 antipoverty hearings, he complained, "As I follow the community educators' records throughout the country, they have indicated to me that they had no way of coordinating poverty money to go with Head Start and the Elementary and Secondary Education Act money." As a result, Goodell wondered, "Does it really make any sense to have Head Start funded with two different programs when local people don't know how much money is going to come out of education funds and how much out of poverty? If we have a Head Start program, which we apparently all think is a good idea, we ought to fund it. Why don't we have a single, clear-cut program for Washington, with the standards set up, and let the local people run these programs as they have been running them primarily?"[9]

Democratic members opposed Republicans' suggestions to transfer control of Head Start to OE. Shriver provided arguments against combining Head Start with early childhood education programs under Title I of ESEA:

> I personally think there are a number of reasons, Congressman. First of all, Head Start . . . is available to private groups, like settlement houses, hospitals, church-related institutions, et cetera. The other program operates only through local boards of education and State boards of education.
>
> So in the wintertime [a] huge proportion of the total kids in Head Start are not in schools. They are in different kinds of places which are not possible to support under the Elementary-Secondary School Education Act. . . .
>
> The second reason is that Head Start . . . is a child development program. It is not just a preschool program. Some places prefer or may think that all that is needed is a preschool program. They may prefer to do that. It seems to me that they should have that alternative, if they wish to do it.
>
> I think that to try to force everybody in the United States to go into just one locked-step thing, which is what you would sort of describe as a Federal program, with Federal controls, I think is a mistake.[10]

Republicans strongly supported early childhood education in the 1964 OEO legislation, and they tried to mandate an even larger federal role for preschools during the 1965 debates about ESEA. Under the chairmanship of Quie, the Republican Task Force on Education released its forty-seven-page study, "A New Look at Pre-School Education, Present and Future," in mid-1966.[11]

The task force criticized the Johnson administration and OEO for poorly implementing and underfunding Head Start. It advised transfer of the program to the Office of Education. "As the original sponsors of a pre-school program, we Republicans are incensed to see Project Head Start, the most successful of all the poverty programs, become entangled in bureaucratic confusion and deprived of necessary funds. We must place the children of poverty at the very top of our list of domestic needs in America, and in that light, we strongly recommend that Project Head Start be transferred from the Office of Economic Opportunity to the Office of Education to be run under the Elementary and Secondary Education Act."[12]

The task force noted that when the legislation creating OEO was passed, the ESEA had not been enacted yet; the act now provided preschool funding. Therefore, it was time to consolidate these two early childhood education programs. "This dual funding has caused considerable confusion on the local level, but under our recommendation, their money would all come from the U.S. Commissioner of Education. We would be taking one more step toward coordinating the programs and consolidating them so that confusion and red-tape would no longer mar this very important educational undertaking."[13]

The Republicans proposed substantially increasing Head Start support by combining OEO's existing funding with monies earmarked for Title I of ESEA. "We would recommend that a sum of $650 million be provided to get a good pre-school program underway. This sum represents the total of $352 million given to Project Head Start under the Economic Opportunity Act Amendments of 1966, plus the approximately $300 million allowed to the Office of Education for aid to school districts on the basis of the number of children from low-income families, under Title I of the Elementary and Secondary Education Amendments. Under the Office of Education, Head Start applications should be given preference for full funding."[14]

In September the OEO reauthorization (H.R. 15111) was debated on the House floor. Quie offered a GOP substitute, the "Opportunity Crusade," which would have left OEO with only the Community Action Program and VISTA; the other OEO programs would have been moved into the old-line federal agencies. The Job Corps and the Neighborhood Youth Corps, for example, would go to the Labor Department; Head Start and the adult basic education program would be transferred to HEW. The House rejected Quie's substitute on a 162–203 roll-call vote.[15]

Quie's separate motion to transfer Head Start to HEW lost on a 26–45 standing vote. He did persuade the House, however, to accept an amendment requiring that at least one-third of local community action board members represent the poor and be chosen by those living in the poverty-stricken areas. The Democratic bill (H.R. 15111)—passed on September 29 on a 210–156 roll-call vote—earmarked funds for several OEO programs, including Head Start. The House bill gave Head Start statutory authority and allocated to the program at least $352 million of the authorized community action monies for fiscal year 1967.[16]

A week later, on a 49–20 roll-call vote, the Senate passed H.R. 15111, which did not earmark funds for most programs. But, on a 38–34 roll-call vote, it passed an amendment submitted by Winston L. Prouty (R-VT) mandating that at least $339 million of CAP funds be reserved for Head Start. Reacting to growing criticism of the use of some CAP funds to challenge local political power structures, the House-Senate conference reduced OEO's flexibility in spending those monies. The legislators now earmarked funds for several popular national OEO programs such as the Neighborhood Youth Corps and Head Start.[17]

While the Eighty-ninth Congress authorized a modified War on Poverty, the mounting, but often concealed, costs of the Vietnam War prevented the Johnson administration from calling for major funding increases for OEO. The *Washington Post,* usually favorable to OEO, headlined its lead editorial "OEO in Decline" on November 4, 1966. The paper challenged the president to either provide more attention and support for OEO or transfer its programs to other departments such as Labor and HEW.[18]

As discussed in chapter 5, the Republicans made sizable gains in the House in the November 1966 elections. The Ninetieth Congress, though still controlled by the Democrats, was now more Republican and conservative than its predecessor. The "conservative voting alliance" of Republicans and southern Democrats was resurrected and coalesced on 54 of the 245 roll-call votes in 1967—including victories on 38 of those 54 occasions (the largest victory total since those data first were compiled in 1957).[19]

Goodell held a two-hour discussion with Shriver on March 8, covering the poverty program in general and Head Start in particular. According to Goodell, Shriver "expressed hope that we would not move Head Start out of Community Action. His argument was that Head Start was the lever that they used to get 'the kind of Community Action you and I wanted' in areas where they had no interest in other programs such as Legal Services. He noted Percy's recent suggestion in a speech that we set up a new section in HEW with a title involving 'youth or children' and probably absorbing the Children's Bureau. He said this would be preferable to placing Head Start in OE."[20]

In that interview with Goodell, Shriver explained his role in drafting the ESEA legislation and his opposition to GOP and Office of Education efforts to designate Title I monies for preschools. "[Shriver] believes ESEA would not have passed without the Poverty Program. 'I got together and helped them write that.' Shriver claims that he originally urged OE to bar any Title I expenditures for pre-school. They refused. Shriver would welcome an amendment to accomplish this, but could not support it publicly or propose it." Shriver stated that he wanted Head Start to be situated exclusively within OEO. "There is not going to be enough money for all the other things we should do in education. Head Start should be exclusively under the Poverty Program. Perhaps later it can be transferred to another agency in HEW apart from OE."[21]

The major education battle proved to be the attempt by Quie and the GOP to change ESEA by replacing the existing categorical programs with block grants to the states. The Democrats narrowly defeated the Republican amendment—in part with assistance from Catholics who worried that their parochial schools might not continue to receive federal assistance from some of the state departments of education. When Representative Edith Green (D-OR) offered an amendment that would send Title III monies (for innovative education centers) to the states, however, the GOP votes, combined with those of southern Democrats, succeeded. Johnson signed the two-year ESEA reauthorization (H.R. 7819) on January 2, 1968.[22]

The White House feared that Republicans and southern Democrats might ally to dismantle the antipoverty programs. Representative Sam M. Gibbons (D-FL) warned the Johnson administration in January 1967 that the GOP might scuttle the programs by passing the party's earlier Opportunity Crusade bill.[23] Surprisingly, the Ninetieth Congress kept the OEO intact but allowed local public officials more control over CAAs. Whereas Congress had previously enacted the Economic Opportunity Act of 1964 on an annual basis, the 1967 legislation (S. 2388) included a two-year authorization. Congress completed work on the bill on December 11, 1967, and the president signed the legislation en route to Cam Ranh Bay, South Vietnam, twelve days later.[24]

Goodell and Quie once again introduced the GOP's 1966 antipoverty alternative—the Opportunity Crusade (H.R. 10682). The Opportunity Crusade would have abolished OEO and transferred its programs to other federal agencies. As the House opened a month's worth of hearings on the administration's bill (H.R. 8311) in June, Shriver and the Democrats defended the existing program and opposed the Republican substitute.[25]

The Senate Labor and Public Welfare Committee held hearings on reauthorizing EOA in June and July but waited until the end of August to approve the administration's bill (S. 1545)—reissued as a clean bill (S. 2388). The committee's report (S. Rept. 563) criticized the lack of coordination of antipoverty programs but endorsed OEO and refused to shift its programs to other federal entities. Pronouncing Head Start successful but noting the discontinuity between Head Start and the regular school grades, the report endorsed the administration's proposal for a follow-through program.[26]

GOP Attempts to Transfer Head Start in 1967

During the full Senate's deliberations on September 27, 1967, Peter H. Dominick (R-CO) offered an amendment that would transfer Head Start to the Office of Education in the following fiscal year. Although Dominick praised Head Start, he believed that it was not adequately coordinated with other early childhood education programs in ESEA. The administration and Congress were poised to create Follow Through, to be delegated to HEW, and Dominick wanted to place both entities in HEW. He believed that Head Start programs operated by public school systems were the most effective preschool programs. "I believe most of us would agree that Head Start, by and large, has been a pretty successful program. The interesting fact is that— if you look through the records and if you talk with the people who have been connected to it—when it has been most successful, it has been operated within the structure of the public school system. This is where it has been most successful."[27] Dominick bolstered his argument by citing widespread approval to transfer Head Start to OE. The Council of Chief State School Officers, the Great Cities for School Improvement, the National Congress of Parents and Teachers, the National Association of State Boards of Education, and the National Education Association, among others, supported the idea. Advocates of the transfer, including Senator George Murphy (R-CA), also emphasized that "Head Start was an education program."[28]

Most Senate Democrats and some of their Republican colleagues questioned the need to transfer Head Start to OE. Because almost everyone agreed that the program was the most successful component of the War on Poverty, Robert F. Kennedy (D-NY) wondered why anyone should want to change it.[29] Joseph S. Clark (D-PA) pointed out that Head Start "is not primarily an educational program. It is a comprehensive child development program, which includes, in addition to the educational component, medical and dental services, nutritional services, social services, and parental involvement."[30] Given the problems of racial prejudice in the South and many parts of the North, Clark argued, "school systems in the North or in the South, in many instances, are [not] presently capable of taking on a Head Start program, running it successfully, and preventing this really meaningful and successful experiment from being killed in the process."[31]

Another reason advanced against the transfer was that the program was an integral part of community action and especially vital to the continued survival of local CAAs. As Shriver noted during Senate hearings, "Head Start has been very helpful to us at any rate, as a community action program in getting community action started, in getting people working together. Outside of the South there are people working together who have never worked together before, were brought together because of their mutual interest in these children. From that has emanated a great many things to benefit community action." Head Start director Jule Sugarman echoed Shriver's observations: "There are literally hundreds of communities which have Head Start as the primary program for their community action agency. If they were excluded from the operation of the Head Start program, then it is very likely that they could go out of existence or lose the forward thrust that they have thus far."[32]

Opponents of the transfer cited Commissioner of Education Harold Howe's testimony at the hearings. Howe argued that OE was not ready to handle Head Start.[33] In addition, Howe had antagonized many southern senators and some northern senators by his vigorous pursuit of desegregation. As a result, members of Congress were afraid that if Howe controlled Head Start he would enforce integration of its programs even more rigorously. As Clark not so subtly reminded his colleagues: "I am pretty skeptical, frankly, about turning a program over to Harold Howe of the Office of Education, for whom I personally have great respect but who, let us face it, is a pretty controversial figure in many parts of the country at this time."[34]

On September 27 the Senate rejected Dominick's amendment to transfer Head Start by a 54–35 roll-call vote (60.7 percent opposed). Of those opposing the transfer, forty-eight were Democrats and six were Republicans; supporting the transfer were twenty-six Republicans and nine Democrats. The vote was strongly partisan: 84.2 percent of the Democrats opposed the transfer, but 81.3 percent of the Republicans favored it.[35]

Among the Democrats, only nine senators supported the transfer of Head Start to HEW, and eight of those were from the South (although fourteen other southern senators opposed the transfer). Moreover, most of the Democrats favoring the transfer were among the more conservative members of their party. Four of the six Republicans opposed to the transfer were from the Northeast (the other two were from the Midwest and the West), and most of these were considered to be among the most liberal senators.[36]

Following the defeat of Dominick's amendment, Art Dufresne, a Republican Senate staffer, discussed the Senate's concerns regarding transferring OEO's programs to OE with Dixie Barger, a Republican House staffer. He explained that some GOP senators feared that if Head Start were transferred, rather than delegated, to another agency, Democrats might argue for even more antipoverty funds (citing the money removed from the OEO budget because of the transfer). Moreover, though many Republican senators agreed with House efforts to move the program, they had reached an agreement not to offer amendments to transfer Head Start or Upward Bound if the Democrats abandoned their proposed emergency employment legislation.[37]

In the House, Quie's amendment to transfer Head Start and Upward Bound from OEO to OE was overwhelmingly rejected on a 135–33 standing vote (80.4 percent opposed) on November 15. Other GOP amendments proposed "spinning off" OEO programs. John N. Erlenborn (R-IL) suggested transferring the Jobs Corps to OE and eventually phasing out the program; its components then were to be incorporated into the vocational education program. Erlenborn's amendment was defeated by a 164–116 teller vote (58.6 percent opposed). Similarly, John R. Dellenback (R-OR) tried to move the in-school Neighborhood Youth Corps to HEW and set up new work-training programs; this was rejected by a 169–108 vote (61.0 percent opposed). The greater opposition to transferring Head Start reflected in part the feeling among many members of Congress that it was an already successful program as administered by OEO.[38]

Dominick's 1968 Attempt to Transfer Head Start

In 1968, as these legislative debates continued, the national context was changing. The mounting costs of the Vietnam War, growing campus protests, and turmoil in the inner cities contributed to diminishing public and congressional sympathy for Johnson's Great Society programs. Continuing questions about the War on Poverty in general and OEO in particular encouraged supporters of specific antipoverty programs to explore alternative federal entities that might better mobilize public and congressional assistance. The administration's inability to influence policies rose dramatically after Johnson's weak showing in the New Hampshire Democratic presidential primary and his unexpected announcement on March 31, 1968, that he would not run for reelection.

The administration sought to coordinate its preschool and day care programs in early 1968. The Gorham Task Force on Child Development had recommended that HEW take the lead in coordinating these programs and systematically evaluating their effectiveness.[39] The secretary of HEW, Wilbur Cohen, called for an interagency coordinating committee and persuaded Sugarman to run the committee in addition to becoming the new assistant director of the Children's Bureau. Cohen's suggestion was accepted and cleared by BOB and OEO.[40] Drawing on Cohen and Sugarman's work, Special Assistant to the President Joseph Califano outlined the structure of the interagency group that was to coordinate preschools and day care services.[41]

While the administration contemplated the future of early childhood care following Johnson's announcement that he would not be a candidate, some officials publicly called for a larger and more systematic education component. Commissioner of Education Howe, in an April speech to the National Education Association, praised preschool education but lamented that it benefited mainly the relative well-to-do rather than disadvantaged children.[42] He urged elementary schools to incorporate early childhood education into their programs.[43]

Howe acknowledged Head Start as a model but noted the lack of attention to teaching skills. "We have had three years with this type of early education experience—with most programs marked by a permissive quality and more emphasis on changing environment and attitudes than on the teaching of specific skills. The assumption has been that children with deprived home backgrounds can catch up *indirectly.*" He cited efforts to provide more direct cognitive training. "Now we are testing some unconventional approaches— the most significant being based on the proposition that deprivation means mainly language deprivation and that we had better set about approaching that problem *directly* at an early age with a variety of techniques, including intensive drill." He acknowledged that there was no single, scientifically proven approach yet, but he was pleased that "we are gathering evidence to help us decide what kind of preschool experience is most successful with children who have excessive catching up to do—the kind that stresses cognitive learning or the kind that operates in the tradition of the nursery school."[44]

Even while Howe publicly promoted early childhood education for public schools, he privately told Cohen, "The more I think about the possible transfer of Head Start to HEW, the more I think you should give careful consideration to putting it in OE rather than the Children's Bureau or some other division of SRS [Social Rehabilitation Service]."[45] He provided nine reasons for the transfer. Howe acknowledged fears on the part of OEO that the Office of Education was too bureaucratic to oversee an innovative program such as Head Start, but he denied that OE was not a suitable agency for the program.[46]

Cohen sent a copy of Howe's memo to Sugarman for comment. Sugarman rebutted Howe's analysis and suggested that Head Start remain with OEO. After discussing at length the inappropriateness of the proposed move, Sugarman concluded by endorsing the Children's Bureau as a possible home—if the program had to be transferred at all.[47] In a separate, attached memo written on the same day, Sugarman informed Cohen of the reactions of several other key participants who did not oppose delegating Head Start to an agency such as the Children's Bureau. For example, Sugarman reported that Richard Boone, executive director of the Citizens' Crusade against Poverty, felt that "it would be wise to act administratively before what [Boone regarded] as inevitable Congressional action. His primary concern is that there be an outside monitoring organization (OEO) which would keep the program honest."[48]

Sugarman also had been asked to provide a discussion draft of a document titled "Memorandum of Understanding between the Office of Economic Opportunity and the Department of Health, Education and Welfare Relative to the Administration of the Head Start Program under a Delegation of Authority." Sugarman wrote this document on the assumption that Head Start would be placed in the Children's Bureau rather than OE. The proposed delegation was to be issued in April 1968, but no action was taken by the administration.[49]

The administration continued soliciting internal advice regarding OEO. White House staffer Fred Bohen, for example, was asked in May about his personal views concerning OEO's future. Bohen argued for maintaining it as a smaller, independent agency within the Executive Office. Yet he thought that "nearly all of OEO's nationally administered programs should be transferred and consolidated with the organizations and programs of other agencies. . . . I would relocate nearly all the urban programs except CAP to HEW and Labor. . . . Head Start, Neighborhood Health Centers, Upward Bound, VISTA, Foster Grandparents and even Job Corps should eventually go to HEW."[50]

Despite growing internal and public concern about OEO's long-term viability, few observers expected that Head Start would be transferred to another agency in 1968—especially given the considerable opposition to that idea in the first session of the Ninetieth Congress. Rumors did circulate that either the Republicans or Democrat Edith Green might introduce an amendment to the Vocational Education Amendments of 1968 (H.R. 18366) that would transfer Head Start, but no one offered such an amendment on the floor. The House unanimously passed the bill on July 15.[51]

On the same day, the full Senate began to deliberate the legislation. The Senate bill already included a provision for the Commissioner of Education to provide contracts or grants "for the development and carrying out . . . of experimental preschool and early education programs for handicapped children." This section had been developed and inserted by Winston Prouty (R-VT).[52]

Two days later, Senators Peter Dominick and George Murphy introduced an amendment to H.R. 18366 transferring Head Start from OEO to the Office of Education in fiscal year 1970; the change would add an eighth title, "Preschool Programs for Children of Low-Income Families," to ESEA. The authorization for Head Start was to be $375 million for the first year.[53] Do-

minick praised Head Start but believed that the program could be strengthened by transferring it to OE.[54] He explained that "the amendment will improve the Head Start program and insure its long-range success by first,
greater coordination with the school system; second, specifically earmarking
funds for its use; third, writing Head Start into law by statute; and fourth,
providing safeguards and requiring a balanced program to assure participation of parents and community as well as the availability of comprehensive
benefits for these children."[55] Dominick also criticized the Democrats and
the Johnson administration for inadequately funding Head Start—in part because OEO refused to allocate more of its money for the program—despite
GOP attempts in the previous two years to earmark additional funds for it.[56]

Senator Joseph Clark, who had led the opposition to the transfer of Head
Start during that time, opposed the Dominick-Murphy amendment. One day
before Dominick formally introduced his motion, Clark quickly secured letters from OEO director Bertrand M. Harding, Cohen, and others opposing
the proposed transfer; Clark then released the letters during the Senate debate. Yet Clark, sensing the Senate's changing mood regarding the transfer of
Head Start, pleaded with his colleagues not to act right then but to reconsider
this issue later.[57]

Senator Wayne Morse (D-OR), the influential subcommittee chair who
had previously opposed the transfer, now switched his position and supported Dominick's amendment. A key reason was OEO's poor administration of antipoverty programs in general. Moreover, he was angry about what
he regarded as the Johnson administration's interference in Senate deliberations, and he called Harding's letter inappropriate.[58]

On the roll-call vote, the amendment to transfer Head Start from the
Office of Economic Opportunity to the Office of Education in HEW passed
by a substantial margin of 60–29. The motion was evenly supported by thirty
Democrats and thirty Republicans, revealing much less partisan division than
a similar amendment had engendered the previous year. Almost all GOP senators (85.7 percent) continued to favor the transfer of Head Start, but a majority of their Democratic colleagues (55.6 percent) now agreed with them.[59]

Using information from the 1967 and 1968 roll-calls of the senators as well
as the announced positions of some of those who had not formally voted,
one can analyze the characteristics of the members who switched positions
between the 1967 and 1968 amendments.[60] Thirty-three of the ninety-nine
members who were present in both 1967 and 1968 consistently favored the
transfer, and thirty opposed it.[61] Thus, approximately two-thirds of the senators did not alter their position between 1967 and 1968.

But twenty-three did switch their position. Of these, twenty-one changed from opposition to the transfer to support of it (nineteen Democrats and two Republicans); only two Democrats shifted from endorsing the transfer to opposing it. Almost all of the Democrats who changed their position in favor of the transfer came from the South or the West; the Democratic switchers were evenly distributed in terms of their general support of liberal positions as indexed by votes they had cast in accordance with the recommendations of the Americans for Democratic Action.[62]

Members of the Senate Labor and Public Welfare Committee in 1967 had opposed by the transfer of Head Start by a 10–5 margin—mainly along party lines (the Democratic members opposed the transfer 9–0; the Republicans favored it 5–1). A year later, the committee supported the transfer by a 7–6 vote (the Republicans supported it 4–1, but the Democrats were now split 5–3 in opposition to the transfer).

On the same day, Harding issued a memo to all of his employees. "I believe this is most harmful to a coordinated approach to the problems of poverty. Such action, taken without hearings or full discussions, does not provide the proper safeguards to insure dedication of the program to the best interests of the poor. For this reason, we will continue to oppose this action with all the means available to us."[63] The next day Morse angrily denounced Harding's actions and urged the White House to discipline him.[64]

As Morse criticized OEO's opposition to the Senate's action as improper, the White House staff and others debated the administration's response to the differences between the chambers regarding Dominick's amendment. White House staffer Jim Jones reported his meetings with Barefoot Sanders (the White House liaison to the House), Mike Manatos (the White House liaison to the Senate), Bert Harding, and Wilbur Cohen; each agreed that the Dominick amendment was "undesirable and that every effort should be made to eliminate it from the Voc Ed Bill in conference."[65] As Jones pointed out, the conferees were evenly divided on the issue, and it was hard to predict the final outcome. Interestingly, they also agreed that Head Start should be delegated to HEW—particularly if this transfer was necessary to defeat the Dominick amendment.[66]

A week later Wilbur Cohen reported that Edith Green planned to introduce on the House floor an amendment to the Higher Education Act that would transfer Head Start to OE. If the House accepted her amendment, Green hoped, "the more educationally oriented Conference on Higher Education Bill" might approve the transfer. Despite Morse's recent and heated warnings to Harding to resist interfering with congressional efforts to transfer Head Start, both Harding and Sanders were "working to defeat Mrs. Green on the floor."[67]

The Head Start office in Washington anticipated the possibility of renewed congressional threats to the agency's location. When OEO heard of Green's possible amendment, Head Start director Richard E. Orton mobilized the Washington office as well as regional and local program providers and supporters to persuade House members not to agree to the transfer.[68]

The unofficial but close participation of OEO officials in legislative affairs was not unusual and continued to be practiced despite periodic protests from some members of Congress. For example, according to Gaither, in the August congressional debates about appropriations, "Harding has his people preparing a series of floor speeches [to] be distributed as soon as the Senate return[ed]."[69]

Green, a member of the House-Senate conference committee on the Vocational Education bill, expressed continued interest in the proposed transfer of Head Start to OE. On August 6 she received a letter from Harold Kleiner, assistant superintendent of schools in Portland, Oregon, who was in charge of their Early Childhood Education Head Start program (she sent a copy of the letter to Howe). Kleiner criticized OEO's inept management of the Portland program.[70] He also complained that "the great instability and turnover in OEO personnel makes it almost impossible to develop a consistent program. During the last two years of our Head Start program there have been no less than seven regional Head Start directors to whom we have been responsible. Each new person in this capacity changes the ground rules so that staff people devote most of their time to making reports and satisfying conditions instead of devoting their efforts to improvement of instruction." As a result, Kleiner argued, "in the interest of a most effective Head Start program it seems most desirable to incorporate Head Start in HEW."[71]

Green asked Howe, "If 'Head Start' programs were transferred to the Office of Education is there any reason that they couldn't be coordinated effectively with the pre-school programs under Title I? Is there any reason why a Head Start program administered by a private school could not continue to be administered by that private school?"[72] The deputy commissioner of education, J. Graham Sullivan, responding for the administration, noted good coordination among the different preschool programs but warned that the Senate amendment "would probably lead to a curtailment of the involvement of private schools and other private nonprofit groups, including those of religious affiliation, in the administration of Head Start."[73]

Opponents of the Senate amendment to transfer Head Start mobilized a letter-writing campaign to the House and Senate conferees. The Child Welfare League of America, for example, wrote Quie, "If, however, Congress insists on its premature removal from OEO, despite the protests of the Department of Health, Education, and Welfare as well as that of OEO, then the League advocates that the Head Start program be administered by the Children's Bureau of HEW rather than by the Office of Education. We believe that the experience and expertise of the Children's Bureau will be better able to preserve the comprehensive character of the Head Start program."[74]

Whereas the Senate had named its conferees almost immediately, the House did not appoint them for another two months (it did so on September 24). Opponents of the proposed transfer tried to prevent Green from being on the House conference committee, fearing that she would join GOP members in favoring the transfer. Representative Carl Perkins, however, placed her on the delegation but obtained her proxy for voting in the conference.[75]

The conference report (H. Rept. 1938) on H.R. 18366 was filed on October 1, 1968. The House conferees adamantly opposed moving Head Start, and the Senate conferees reluctantly agreed. Rather than transferring the program, the legislation called for an analysis of possibilities for its future location (similar to the study of the Job Corps mandated in the same legislation).[76]

The next day the full Senate completed discussion of the Vocational Education Amendments of 1968. Dominick expressed his frustration at the conference committee's handling of his transfer proposal despite its widespread support in the Senate. He recounted the House opposition to his amendment in the conference committee.[77] Included among the Democratic proxies was that of Green, who some of the Republican members had hoped would side with them regarding such key issues as the transfer of Head Start.[78] Dominick also berated the House Democratic conferees for the "inaccurate and misleading language that is in the statement [about the Head Start amendment] of the managers on the part of the House." He concluded by stating, "In my judgment, the study language in the conference report is of doubtful value and will accomplish little."[79]

Senator Prouty, who had supported the transfer of Head Start, shed additional light on the conference process. He revealed that "we had no alternative but to reach a compromise. . . . It was only after I offered a substitute calling for a joint study by the agencies involved as to the feasibility of the transfer that we were able to compromise by instructing the President to recommend to Congress whether Head Start should remain in the Office of Economic Opportunity."[80]

The other senators spent little time discussing Head Start. Most of their attention was focused instead on a controversial provision exempting educational programs from the federal government's $6 billion reduction, as mandated in the tax bill. The proposed exemption would require deeper cuts from other programs. Despite disappointment with respect to the Head Start provision, all of the House-Senate conferees signed the final conference report—including key Republicans who favored the transfer (Senators Dominick, Murphy, and Prouty). On October 2, the Senate accepted the report on a 58–11 roll-call vote. The next day the House agreed to the conference report on a voice vote.[81]

On October 1, the same day that the conference committee issued its request for a study of the feasibility of transferring Head Start, Orton, the agency's director, recommended to Harding the appointment of a "study group . . . of persons from within and outside the government, with a majority of the latter."[82] Harding forwarded Orton's memo to the White House staff but remarked that "the list is too long and stacked pretty badly against the educational community."[83]

Three weeks later Cohen strongly urged Califano to complete the report quickly and delegate Head Start to HEW by November 15. Cohen explained that he continued to be concerned that "the Administration take all steps within its power to protect the Head Start program from adverse Congressional action. Administrative action by the President at this time is, in my judgment, most likely to lead to appropriate legislative decisions in the next Congress.[84]

The Bureau of the Budget, responding to an early October memo, created a task force to address the issues raised in the Vocation Education Amendments of 1968, section 309. The section 309 task force drafted a preliminary report on October 21.[85] The report emphasized the importance of child development, citing widely quoted but frequently misleading statistics from the early 1960s.[86] Although the task force believed that Head Start programs were successful, it acknowledged difficulties in evaluating the projects, partly because the multiple services Head Start offered. The few completed evaluations of the summer programs indicated strengths and weaknesses of the current endeavors.[87] After discussing early child development programs, the panel analyzed various proposals to assign Project Head Start to a different federal agency.[88]

If the program was to be reassigned, many of its supporters were determined that it should go to the Children's Bureau rather than to OE—which they regarded as too narrowly education-oriented. Indeed, Cohen had indicated his own preference for that location and had recruited Sugarman, former director of Head Start, to that agency in anticipation of a possible transfer.

As fighting within HEW intensified after the preliminary draft of the section 309 task force's report, the Office of Education continued to insist that it was the best location for Head Start. An eight-page memo provided documentation for this position.[89] On the other hand, Orton continued to argue that Head Start was conceived as a much broader initiative than simply an education program.[90]

Following the preliminary task force report and additional input from potential host agencies for Project Head Start, the White House debated Johnson's options regarding the proposed transfer of Head Start and Job Corps before Richard Nixon's inauguration on March 20, 1969. With the Economic Opportunity Act scheduled for reauthorization the following year, the new administration and the Ninety-first Congress would soon revisit the fate of both programs. Wilbur Cohen, Bill Wirtz, Bert Harding, Charles Zwick, Harold Howe, Jim Gaither, and Joe Califano met in mid-December to explore the various alternatives; the group told Johnson that the administration should act quickly—preferably delegating the Jobs Corps to the Labor Department and Head Start to HEW.[91]

The group suggested the possible content of a report recommending this action, based on its interpretation of OEO's intended role. Their suggestions clashed with some of the previous arguments they had made to Congress regarding the two programs. "In essence, the [proposed] report would lay out the general concept which we have expressed from the very start of OEO—that OEO's major function is to innovate, experiment and develop new approaches to the problems of poverty. Once those new approaches or programs have been tested and proven in practice, they should then be delegated to the established Departments."[92] In addition, the group said that because the report would address the two programs, it "would express the view that both the Head Start program and the Job Corps are now sufficiently well developed to be delegated to the established Departments. The report would go on to say that, in view of the change in Administrations, no delegations are being made at this time and the matter is being left to the next Administration and to the Congress."[93]

The White House decided not to dispatch a report to Congress early, however, and after Nixon's election in November 1968, Johnson continued to resist staff suggestions to send any report about Head Start and Job Corps to Congress, preferring to allow the incoming administration maximum flexibility in dealing with their future location.

Head Start and the 1968 Election

Education was not a major campaign issue in the 1968 presidential election. In 1964 Johnson had won a landslide victory over Barry Goldwater, and the Democrats had significantly increased their control in Congress. In the midterm elections, however, the GOP abandoned many of its more extreme right-wing policy positions and recaptured some of its former congressional seats. Mounting public concerns about the Vietnam War, urban riots, unrest on college campuses, and the lack of effectiveness of some Great Society programs eroded support for the Johnson administration. As a result, Republicans' prospects for capturing the White House in 1968 improved considerably.

As the presidential campaign season opened, the leading Republican contender was Governor George Romney of Michigan. An effective and popular executive, Romney had the backing of the influential New York governor Nelson Rockefeller and other liberal Republicans. Though knowledgeable about domestic issues, Romney was not as familiar with foreign affairs and issued hasty, controversial positions on Vietnam. In an ill-advised effort to extricate himself from his earlier stances regarding the Vietnam War, Romney claimed that he had been "brain-washed"—a statement that doomed his candidacy.[94]

The new front runner was Richard Nixon, who had narrowly lost his presidential bid in 1960. Two years later he had been defeated more decisively in the race for the governor's office in California and exited promising the press that it would not have Nixon to kick around anymore. After he retired from politics, he joined a prestigious and profitable law firm in New York City. But he decided to enter the presidential race in 1968 and significantly revamped his campaign style and organization. Nixon benefited from strong support among the GOP party faithful during the primaries. Turning back last-minute challenges from Ronald Reagan and Rockefeller at the Miami convention, Nixon was nominated on the first ballot and selected Maryland governor Spiro Agnew as his running mate.

Throughout the primaries and the convention, the GOP was determined to avoid the controversies and divisions that had doomed Goldwater's candidacy. Even the controversy about Vietnam was avoided by crafting an ambiguous compromise plank concerning that issue at the convention. Republicans agreed among themselves regarding education. The party platform called for tax credits and deductions to stimulate family savings for higher education expenses, expanded vocational education programs, and the creation of a national commission on education. "To treat the special problems of children from impoverished families," the GOP also advocated "expanded, better programs for preschool children."[95]

Although Johnson's popularity had dropped during his second term, few expected a serious challenge to his candidacy for reelection among the Democrats. Prominent Democrats such as Robert F. Kennedy, who opposed Johnson's Vietnam policies, refused to enter the race. Senator Eugene McCarthy (D-MN), however, launched a grass-roots antiwar attack on Johnson and entered the New Hampshire primary as a weak underdog. Despite a rather lackluster primary campaign effort, McCarthy surprised everyone and almost defeated the president in New Hampshire. When it became obvious that Johnson was about to lose the Wisconsin primary to McCarthy, the president stunned the nation by announcing on March 31 that he would not seek reelection in order to focus his energies on resolving the crisis in Vietnam.[96]

Following Johnson's withdrawal, Robert Kennedy and Vice President Hubert Humphrey joined the Democratic contest—although Humphrey decided to forego the primaries. The close race for the Democratic nomination was interrupted by the tragic assassination of Martin Luther King Jr. and the wave of racial violence that swept the nation. In June Kennedy managed to win the crucial California primary, but he was tragically assassinated on the eve of his victory there.[97]

Humphrey, who held strong liberal credentials and privately questioned the wisdom of America's continued involvement in Vietnam, was forced by the peace initiatives the administration was pursuing in Paris to publicly support Johnson's foreign policies. The Democratic Convention in Chicago was marred by antiwar activists who violently disrupted the proceedings and by the overreactions of Mayor Richard Daley and the Chicago police. Humphrey managed to win the nomination, but the disarray among the delegates and antiwar demonstrators was widely publicized on national television and lessened the likelihood that the Democrats would win in November.[98]

Unlike their Republican counterparts, the Democratic delegates could not reach a compromise regarding the Vietnam plank in its platform. This disagreement resulted in a floor fight about the issue; in the end, Democrats supported the position held by Humphrey and the administration. With respect to education, however, the convention was united. Like the Republicans, the Democrats emphasized the need for additional federal aid to education, but they endorsed tax credits for higher education. The platform also called for help for educationally disadvantaged children, "including expanded preschool programs to prepare all young children for full participation in formal education."[99]

Former Alabama governor George C. Wallace ran as a third-party presidential candidate on the American Independent ticket. The party's platform advocated increasing Social Security payments by 60 percent and improving Medicare, stressed returning more control of government programs to states and local communities, supported stronger law enforcement, and opposed federal gun control regulations. The American Independent Party called for "educational opportunity for all people regardless of race, creed, color, economic or social status," but it wanted less federal interference in local and state school programs.[100] Included in the platform was an acknowledgment of the importance of early childhood education: "The goals of the American Independent Party are to improve educational opportunity for all our citizens from early childhood through the graduate level. We believe that the improvement of educational opportunity can best be accomplished at the state and local level with adequate support from the federal government."[101]

At first it appeared that Nixon, who drew enthusiastic crowds, would have an easy victory in November. The Democrats were still divided in September, and Wallace expected to win the popular vote only in the South (and thus hoped to throw the contest to the House of Representatives). On the campaign trail, the issues of Vietnam, law and order, and civil rights continued to command the interest of the public and the media.[102]

Although education was not a major concern for most voters, both Nixon and Humphrey addressed the issue—including the topic of preschool education. In an October CBS radio address concerning education, for example, Nixon devoted considerable attention to the need for early education and the proven effectiveness of Head Start and Follow Through. He nonetheless pointed to the need to consolidate the existing federal education programs and pay attention to the whole young child.[103]

Meanwhile, the Humphrey campaign developed its own education recommendations. In October, the Vice President's Task Force on Education, chaired by Francis Keppel, issued a twenty-five-page report, "Toward Excellent Education for All Americans." The report praised the progress that had been made, including the increase in federal expenditures from $2.65 billion in fiscal year 1960 to $12.3 billion in fiscal year 1969. But it acknowledged that much remained to be accomplished—including "consolidating, coordinating, and simplifying federal education programs."[104]

The task force called for equal educational opportunities for disadvantaged and handicapped children, proposing "early childhood education for all children beginning with the more than 2 million children—ages 3 to 5—of the poor, both rural and urban, and all handicapped children who could benefit." Indeed, it felt that "the time has come to make preschools a regular part of the educational system serving disadvantaged children, and ultimately, all children."[105] Humphrey followed this report with a nine-point plan of action for excellence in education, including the recommendation to "extend the opportunity for preschool education to every child."[106]

As the campaign continued, Humphrey made inroads into Nixon's lead—

especially after Johnson announced a temporary halt to U.S. bombing in the closing days of the campaign. Although the anticipated Paris Peace Accords were thwarted by the South Vietnamese government, Humphrey benefited from the administration's initiatives. Moreover, the concerted effort by unions to mobilize members on behalf of Humphrey and against the Wallace campaign paid off—though not enough, in the end, to elect Humphrey.

In one of the closest races in recent history, Nixon received 43.4 percent of the popular vote while Humphrey garnered 42.7 percent; Wallace won 13.5 percent of the vote. In the electoral college, however, Nixon easily won with 301 votes to Humphrey's 191 votes and Wallace's 46 votes.[107] Many historically Republican voters who had sided with the Democrats in 1964 returned to the GOP in 1968, and a significant number of Johnson voters abandoned the Democrats. Yet the crucial differences remained the Vietnam War, law and order, and civil rights rather than education.[108]

The Transition to the Nixon Administration

After dropping out of the race for reelection, Johnson focused on ending the Vietnam War and completing unfinished domestic initiatives. At speech to the regional directors of the Office of Economic Opportunity on October 23, 1968, Johnson proudly recounted the administration's achievements in the War on Poverty—including helping disadvantaged young children with Head Start programs.[109]

Some administration officials, anticipating a possible GOP victory in November, had urged Johnson to transfer Head Start to the Children's Bureau before the Nixon administration arrived. They recommended that at the least the president immediately send to Congress its mandated reports concerning whether Head Start and the Jobs Corps should be transferred out of OEO to HEW and Labor, respectively. Reluctant to interfere with the Nixon administration's ability to make its own decisions, Johnson did not introduce any last-minute changes in Head Start.[110]

In the last week of his administration, Johnson delivered his final State of the Union Address to Congress; he praised the progress made in education, saying that "schools and school children all over America tonight are receiving Federal assistance to go to good schools." He also pointed to the achievements in early childhood education: "Pre-school education—Head Start—is already here to stay, and, I think, so are the Federal programs that tonight are keeping more than a million and a half of the cream of our young people in the colleges and universities of this country."[111]

In discussing the War on Poverty, however, Johnson acknowledged that Congress was likely to reorganize the OEO and transfer some of its programs to other federal units. Interestingly, he recommended a fivefold increase in job training funds, rather than calling for substantial increases for Head Start or other popular antipoverty initiatives.[112]

Nixon and the GOP had praised Head Start during the campaign. For example, in his suggestions to the Republican National Convention Committee in August regarding problems of the cities, Nixon called for improving urban schools—including funding Head Start and Follow Through. (This statement was later reissued during the fall campaign.) At the same time, however, Nixon indicated his disagreement with the Democratic antipoverty and welfare programs.[113]

Transferring Head Start to HEW

After Nixon took the oath of office on January 20, 1969, the White House was scheduled, within six weeks, to convey to the Congress the previously mandated special studies of the future administrative locations of Head Start and the Jobs Corps. Because Nixon had been critical of OEO and the War on Poverty during the campaign, some observers expected him to abolish that organization immediately and transfer its programs to other federal agencies.

Nixon's first executive order, signed on January 23, 1969, set up the Council for Urban Affairs under his new assistant for urban affairs, Daniel Patrick Moynihan, former assistant secretary of labor for policy planning and research in the Johnson administration.[114] Although Moynihan had publicly challenged the value of the Community Action Programs, he was a Head Start advocate and recommended its delegation from OEO to HEW. Although he supported early childhood education, he favored job training programs and a guaranteed income approach using the Nixon administration's Family Assistance Plan (FAP).[115]

Relying on the advice of Moynihan and the more moderate elements in his White House, Nixon sent the Ninety-first Congress a message on poverty on February 19, 1963, recommending authorization for another year; Nixon also promised to "send Congress a comprehensive proposal for the future of the poverty program, including recommendations for revising and extending the Act itself beyond its scheduled [June 30] 1970 expiration."[116] Nixon envisioned OEO's new role as conducting experimental studies rather than acting as a more traditional agency by managing its own large-scale antipoverty programs. "OEO's greatest value is as an initiating agency—devising new programs to help the poor, and serving as an 'incubator' for these programs during their initial, experimental phases. One of my aims is to free OEO itself to perform these functions more effectively, by providing for a greater concentration of its energies on its innovative role."[117]

Nixon's poverty message was accompanied by the special administrative study of Head Start.[118] He also announced that "preparations [were being] made for the delegation of Head Start to the Department of Health, Education and Welfare. Whether it should be actually transferred is a question I will take up in my later, comprehensive message, along with my proposals for a permanent status and organizational structure for OEO."[119]

Based on preliminary, unpublished results from the forthcoming Westinghouse evaluation, Nixon told Congress that Head Start was still an experimental program warranting continued support but needing considerable improvement. Given the need to strengthen and coordinate early childhood education programs, Nixon called for placing Head Start in HEW.[120]

Just as the Nixon administration was considering what to do about the poverty program, on March 18 the General Accounting Office (GAO) released its fourteen-month study of OEO's efficiency and effectiveness. The report acknowledged the difficulty of carrying out such a complex evaluation and reminded readers of the adverse circumstances that OEO faced during its early years. The CAP, according to the GAO, had "varying success in involving local residents and poor people in approximately 1,000 communities." Though "an effective advocate for the poor in many communities," it met its objectives "in lesser measure than was reasonable to expect in relation to the magnitude of the funds expended."[121] The GAO said that the Head Start programs were among the most popular OEO activities but noted that its long-term effects had not yet been measured. [122]

On April 9, 1969, the White House announced the creation of the Office of Child Development (OCD) within HEW. "This Office must take a comprehensive approach to the development of young children, combining programs which deal with the physical, social, and intellectual."[123] After citing research that emphasized the need for learning very early in life, Nixon indicated that "elementary school, kindergarten, even Head Start appear to come too late for many of those children who most need help."[124] Consequently, early childhood education should begin earlier, but before early childhood programs were implemented nationwide, more research on their effectiveness was needed.[125]

The OCD was to oversee Head Start, day care programs, and other early childhood projects located in the Children's Bureau. Secretary of Health, Education, and Welfare Robert H. Finch announced that year-round Head Start programs would be expanded and that the summer programs would be reduced. But the administration, concerned about the growing evidence that the beneficial effects might not be long-lasting, remained reluctant to support a large-scale expansion of the program. Instead, the White House proposed that the allocation for Head Start for fiscal year 1970 be $338 million—the same amount the Johnson administration had recommended.

Thus, Head Start was finally transferred from OEO to HEW but placed in a special agency set apart from the Office of Education; and although funding for Head Start was maintained, the administration called for additional research and more effective ways of helping disadvantaged children. A few in the Nixon administration suggested abolishing the program, especially after the release of the controversial evaluation of the program by Westinghouse, but Project Head Start had become too popular among the public and politicians to be abandoned.[126]

This analysis of the origins of early childhood education in the Kennedy and Johnson administrations provides a rather different perspective than do most earlier studies. The narrative is complicated because it brings together such diverse strands as changing perceptions of children, the evolution of federal education policies, and the War on Poverty across several administrations. Thoroughly documenting this complex history has also made the text more challenging. Therefore, the conclusion briefly recounts the major issues raised.

At the same time, the possible policy implications for Head Start of these earlier events are noted—particularly because participants often were reacting to the immediate challenges before them without appreciating the unintended, long-term consequences of their actions. The present debates about Head Start reveal the program's popularity but also illuminate the continued uncertainty about its original purposes, its current goals, and the proven effectiveness of its diverse projects.

The 1950s and early 1960s witnessed major changes in experts' perceptions of children's intellectual development. Previously, child development specialists and the public had believed that IQ was fixed at birth and that there was little one could do to alter it. Increasingly, however, analysts such as J. McVicker Hunt and Benjamin S. Bloom argued that a child's IQ was not solely determined biologically; environment also played a large role, especially in early childhood. These changing ideas were incorporated in several experimental programs in cities such as Nashville, New York, and Syracuse.

Although limited attention was paid immediately to the new ideas about children's IQs, these changing perceptions gradually reinforced the notion that all children were capable of learning—provided that they had an opportunity to do so. An emphasis on the deleterious effects of an impoverished childhood spurred efforts to develop preschool programs for disadvantaged Americans. A handful of experiments in early childhood education provided educators and policy makers with valuable information about how such programs might be implemented in different communities.

Americans have always seen education as a vital component of our national identity and well-being and as a key element in social reform. This commitment to public schooling continued and was enhanced following World War II. Yet periodic efforts to increase federal involvement in K-12 schools in the 1950s usually faltered as many members of Congress rejected federal interference in local education on philosophical grounds, feared that federal regulations might desegregate southern schools, or opposed providing federal assistance to private and parochial schools.

As a result of these obstacles, President John F. Kennedy failed to enact major federal school-aid legislation in 1961 and 1962. Consequently, the Bureau of the Budget explored new ways for repackaging federal assistance to K-12 schools. The resultant omnibus 1963 education bill called for a more comprehensive, but still targeted, approach to federal aid—including supporting preschool programs for disadvantaged children. Although the Kennedy administration did not emphasize early childhood education programs, it did at least mention preschools as a possible way to help young children from impoverished homes and communities.

The "discovery" of poverty in the early 1960s spurred analysts and policy makers to assist those who had not shared in the postwar economic prosperity. General concerns about poverty merged with more specific fears about juvenile delinquency and the adverse effects of rapid urban growth. Efforts to address these problems by organizations such as the Ford Foundation and the President's Committee on Juvenile Delinquency and Youth Crime led to proposals to improve the overall quality of the communities in which disadvantaged Americans lived. Responding to White House inquiries, the Council of Economic Advisers began to investigate the nature of American poverty and programs to eradicate it. Preschool programs formed a small and largely unnoticed component of this effort. In the fall of 1963, as Kennedy prepared for reelection, he decided that a major federal antipoverty initiative would be a key campaign issue.

Kennedy's assassination could have disrupted federal efforts to help disadvantaged Americans, and it is difficult to speculate how his antipoverty programs might have evolved over time had he survived. But his successor, Lyndon B. Johnson, immediately adopted Kennedy's commitment to fight poverty. Johnson was eager to be seen as continuing Kennedy's legacy, and having grown up amid poverty in Texas, he had his own interest in that undertaking. Like Kennedy, he recognized the value of poverty as a campaign issue.

Antipoverty initiatives were major components of Johnson's 1964 legislative agenda. Rather than proceeding slowly and building on the scattered but promising existing programs, Johnson announced a massive War on Poverty and pledged to win it. This bold and ambitious goal captured the public's imagination, but the federal government lacked the funds and knowledge to achieve its lofty objectives. Johnson rejected any tax increases, and the escalating costs of the Vietnam War strained the federal resources previously available. The War on Poverty led the White House to initiate large-scale programs that had not been adequately vetted for their effectiveness.

Johnson adopted Kennedy's proposed antipoverty crusade, but he did not always rely on the same staff or advice. There was considerable confusion at first as numerous advisers and diverse proposals vied for the attention of the new administration. Particularly important was Johnson's decision in February 1964 to appoint Sargent Shriver as the director of the War on Poverty. Shriver, the popular director of the Peace Corps, provided Johnson with ties to the Kennedy network as well as another talented aide to work with Congress. Shriver shared Johnson's enthusiasm for the War on Poverty as well as the president's tendency to address larger political and public concerns rather than focus on the implementation or effectiveness of individual programs. Shriver was not a disciplined administrator and had problems recruiting and maintaining a staff; his lack of management skills contributed to the administration's difficulties in organizing, implementing, and evaluating the complex and controversial War on Poverty.

As the administration crafted its Economic Opportunity Act of 1964, the bill initially focused on community action and education programs. When the draft legislation made its rounds through the federal agencies and the White House, additional provisions were incorporated and the relative importance of education was reduced. Rather than funding ten large-scale urban and rural antipoverty demonstration projects, as initially recommended, Johnson and Shriver wanted EOA to be a much larger and more ambitious initiative. Indeed, poverty was to be eliminated within a decade. Early childhood education was mentioned briefly during deliberations about EOA, yet neither Shriver nor congressional Democrats stressed preschools. Instead, they focused on providing services for disadvantaged youths and young adults.

It was the House Republicans who initially championed early childhood education. They invited Urie Bronfenbrenner to testify at the House hearings on EOA. He criticized the administration's proposal for targeting assistance to those aged sixteen to twenty-two while ignoring early childhood education. Representatives Charles Goodell and Al Quie praised Bronfenbrenner's testimony and relied on it in the GOP's minority attachment to the House committee's report. Republicans criticized the White House and congressional Democrats for ignoring the needs of young children and recommended support for preschools.

In August 1964 the Democrats passed EOA by surprisingly large margins in both the House and the Senate. The legislation continued to focus on youths and young adults but indicated that community centers could provide preschool day-care services and remedial education.

Starting in mid-1964, interest in early childhood education had been growing. A widely read article by Charles E. Silberman in *Harper's Magazine* enthusiastically recommended preschool programs. Commissioner of Education Francis Keppel, who had not emphasized early childhood education as a means of combating poverty, started advocating preschools. Only four days after the passage of EOA, the consultant Harry Levin provided the Office of Education with an assessment and endorsement of preschool programs. The influential but secret report of the Gardner Task Force on Education praised preschools and recommended that the newly created Office of Economic Opportunity oversee them. And HEW recommended expanding preschools in its 1965 legislative planning.

As attention to preschools mounted, Shriver and OEO began to explore early childhood programs in late 1964. They were aided by the staff at the Office of Education, who assisted the antipoverty agency in assessing the education components of programs proposed by applicants and developing the first summer Head Start programs. Staffers Richard Boone and Jule Sugarman of OEO also met with Robert Cooke of Johns Hopkins University to discuss early childhood education. A few weeks later, Johnson, in his annual message to Congress on January 4, 1965, announced a major federal preschool initiative. The following week he provided further details and labeled the initiative "Head Start." Initially, the administration recommended eight-week summer programs serving one hundred thousand students. These key decisions were reached and announced before Cooke's Head Start Planning Committee convened and made its recommendations.

Following the 1964 landslide victory of Johnson and congressional Democrats, the Elementary and Secondary Education Act of 1965 was quickly passed. The White House's bill recommended assistance for children aged five and older. The Republicans again criticized the administration for ignoring early childhood education. The GOP alternative, the Education Initiative Act, included Quie's proposal for $300 million in annual, direct grants to states; states would allocate monies to schools on the basis of the number of children aged three to eight living in families with less than $3,000 in income. Unlike the Democratic bill, which would have paid only a small portion of the cost of educating a Title I student, the GOP proposal fully funded the initial year and then gradually decreased federal funding to two-thirds of the overall costs.

Democrats denounced the GOP's targeting of Title I funds to early childhood education at the expense of older children; they also attacked the Republican package as providing less overall money for education than the Democratic bill. Congressional Democrats countered GOP attacks by incorporating into the House bill language permitting preschool programs—although on the whole Democrats did not stress the value of early childhood education programs during the debates. The White House's ESEA bill, with only few amendments, handily passed both chambers in April 1965.

Given the bipartisan support for preschool programs, the Johnson administration had considerable latitude in how to develop and implement Head Start. Using results from experimental early childhood education programs, scholars such as Jerome Bruner and Martin Deutsch argued for starting with a small number of well-funded Head Start projects staffed by well-trained preschool educators. Shriver acknowledged that he was not familiar with most such experiments (except those dealing with mental retardation). Responding to the administration's political and publicity needs, however, Shriver rejected the advice of most experts and the Gardner Task Force on Education by endorsing an ambitious plan to begin summer Head Start programs immediately. Part of Shriver's rationale for undertaking a large-scale initiative was, he claimed incorrectly, that congressional Republicans and conservative Democrats might try to dismantle Head Start unless a large parental constituency was created to protect the program.

Shriver also relied on his own set of advisers, led by Robert Cooke. The Cooke Head Start Planning Committee issued a widely distributed report, "Improving the Opportunities and Achievements of the Children of the Poor," which recommended that Head Start programs provide comprehensive health, social, and educational services.

Most members of the committee favored a small, high-quality pilot program in order to ascertain the most effective ways to help disadvantaged young children in different settings. Confronted with the administration's prior decision to launch a large-scale, relatively underfunded summer initiative, the Cooke committee did not question that decision publicly. As one member, Edward Zigler, recalled, the panel was reluctant to challenge Shriver's recommendation—especially because some of the key committee appointees had been closely associated with Shriver and the Kennedy Foundation and deferred to Shriver's political instincts.

The reluctance of many prominent experts to openly question the administration's major decisions about Head Start was unfortunate; it meant that political considerations not only trumped expert knowledge within White House deliberations but also hindered Congress from hearing serious reservations regarding the proposed operation of Head Start. Few on the Cooke committee really believed that an eight-week summer program would have a lasting effect on disadvantaged children, but they were reluctant to raise that concern. When a prominent outside child development expert such as Martin Deutsch publicly questioned the administration's exaggerated claims of Head Start's effectiveness, he was promptly removed from the program's national advisory committee (a different group from the planning committee). And when the Cooke committee strongly criticized Shriver and OEO for not continuing to fund the Child Development Group of Mississippi, the committee was not convened again (although some individual members were consulted on issues related to Head Start).

The little-noticed but very important decision by OEO to create inexpensive summer Head Start programs and allow them to hire inadequately trained teachers had serious long-term consequences. Experts such as Deutsch calculated that at least $1,000 per child was needed for the eight-week programs, but Jule Sugarman, deputy director of Head Start, arrived at the figure of $180 per child—an estimate Shriver and OEO accepted and widely publicized. Because Shriver and others proclaimed the summer Head Start programs successful, it was difficult later to argue that more money per student was needed, especially because this would have meant reducing the total number of children served. The conundrum became even more acute once the administration shifted to year-round programs, which cost much more per student; any effort to improve the quality of instruction now became yet more expensive and would reduce further the number of participants.

Once the decision was made to serve about half a million children in the 1965 summer Head Start projects, it immediately became clear that there were not enough qualified teachers to staff them. Other adults, including some parents of program participants, were hired as substitute teachers (and as teacher aides in other programs). Not only did use of these lower-paid substitutes help reduce overall teacher costs, but it also provided valuable employment for disadvantaged local residents.

Shriver praised the job opportunities created for local citizens, but he did not discuss the possible negative effects on disadvantaged children of being taught by inadequately prepared teachers. Local community activists also valued the jobs and resisted any efforts to require higher credentials for Head Start teachers. As a result, the use of poorly qualified teachers became commonplace for many summer and year-round Head Start projects. Ironically, although most experts and policy makers initially saw Head Start as a way to compensate for or overcome the educational and cultural limitations of the home experiences of poor children, many of these youngsters soon were to enter Head Start projects taught by semiliterate parents or neighbors rather than professionally trained teachers. This situation was difficult to change later because it would have required significantly more tax dollars to pay higher teacher salaries and would have excluded many existing Head Start teachers.

The need to process quickly the thousands of project applications meant that many low-quality summer programs were selected that ordinarily might not have been funded (more than 80 percent of the applicants were funded). But internal pressure to provide services for large numbers of children meant that many weak programs were funded—presumably either to be improved later or closed down. Moreover, OEO could not agree on a recommended set of curricula for local programs or specific program goals that had to be met. And as observers noted at that time, it was very difficult to terminate weak Head Start programs once they had been funded and acquired a local constituency.

Johnson, Shriver, and many others (including prominent GOP legislators) initially proclaimed the summer programs a great success. Project Head Start became one of the most popular Great Society programs and helped the Johnson administration to deflect the otherwise growing criticisms of the Office of Economic Opportunity. Yet there were disquieting indications that Head Start, especially the summer version, did not provide disadvantaged children with lasting benefits. Several key local evaluations questioned the program's long-term effects. Although often OEO challenged the validity of these studies, the administration almost immediately began plans for year-round Head Start programs, despite its reluctance to serve fewer children. Indeed, Johnson vetoed OEO's 1967 attempt to transfer some of its summer Head Start monies to the more expensive but more effective year-round programs.

As concerns about the children's loss of short-term academic gains from Head Start projects mounted, several White House task forces as well as other child development experts and policy makers called for more effective education services and a follow-through program to help youngsters make the transition into the regular schools. Johnson recommended the Follow Through Program, and Congress authorized it in 1967. Follow Through was slated to be a major federal service program, but the escalating costs of the Vietnam War reduced its proposed budget dramatically. As a result, Follow Through was reconfigured as a small experimental demonstration program— but it was neither well-designed nor carefully implemented.

The idea of developing Follow Through was another important early childhood education innovation by the Johnson administration. The program was delegated to be administered by the Office of Education rather than OEO. Follow Through provided an opportunity for these two agencies to coordinate their programs and develop more effective ways to ease the transition of disadvantaged children into the schools.

Unfortunately, despite the many millions of dollars and twenty-five years devoted to Follow Through, the program failed to accomplish most of its objectives. The demonstration programs did not provide the type of scientifically rigorous and practically useful information its founders had envisioned. Nor did Head Start and Follow Through manage to coordinate their efforts or diminish the divisions between Head Start providers and K-3 educators. Most educators and policy makers today do not even remember Follow Through or profit from the experiences of this project. Yet periodic calls for developing new initiatives to bring Head Start and K-3 education programs closer together continue.

The November 1966 elections increased Republican representation in Congress, especially in the House, and reestablished a powerful working coalition between Republicans and conservative Southern Democrats. As a result, some observers expected that the new Ninetieth Congress might repeal many of the Great Society programs—including OEO, which was increasingly viewed as wasteful and ineffective.

Republicans did propose dismantling OEO and transferring most of its programs elsewhere. But they continued to praise Project Head Start, which they nonetheless wanted to move to the Office of Education in order to coordinate it with the early childhood education programs under Title I of ESEA. Some GOP legislators also complained that Head Start was not receiving adequate attention and financial support within OEO. They attacked Shriver and OEO's Community Action Program for refusing to allocate even more of the available antipoverty monies for Head Start.

Shriver and most Democratic legislators insisted that Head Start belonged in OEO and saw it as an essential element of local community action programs. They also felt that public schools were poorly administered and that transferring Head Start to OE would eliminate the comprehensive and innovative aspects of the program. Indeed, many OEO staffers had an almost visceral opposition to the educational components of Head Start.

But not everyone in the Johnson administration opposed the transfer. Secretary of Health, Education, and Welfare Anthony Celebrezze and his assistant secretary, Wilbur Cohen, for example, wanted Head Start placed in HEW—though not necessarily in the Office of Education. On the other hand, Commissioner of Education Harold Howe argued forcefully that Head Start belonged in OE and that the education component of the program should be enhanced. And even Johnson secretly contemplated moving the program to HEW in late 1965. Publicly, however, administration officials maintained a united front and insisted that Head Start was thriving in OEO and should be kept there.

Republican efforts to transfer Head Start failed in 1966 and 1967, and their prospects did not look any better for 1968. But in that year a move by Senator Peter Dominick to amend the Vocational Education Act to transfer Head Start unexpectedly passed the Senate—in large part because of support from influential Democratic senators such as Wayne Morse who denounced OEO's ineffectiveness.

The administration, led by Shriver and the Head Start staff, managed to persuade the House-Senate conference committee to drop Dominick's amendment, but it became increasingly clear that it was only a matter of time before the program would be transferred. Johnson's decision to abandon his reelection bid in March 1968 and the prospect of a Republican takeover of the White House in November encouraged Head Start supporters to seek an alternative agency for their program. Given the continued hostility of many Head Start proponents to the public school systems in general and to the Office of Education in particular, agencies such as the Children's Bureau and a proposed office for children in HEW were seen as possible sites.

Following the narrow election of Richard Nixon and the leaking of the preliminary negative results from the controversial Westinghouse Corporation's evaluation of Head Start, there was considerable fear for the future of the program. The Nixon administration continued to support it but moved it into the new Office of Child Development in HEW. More emphasis was placed on how to improve the long-term effectiveness of Head Start, and the Nixon administration, like its predecessor, looked to Follow Through and other experimental demonstration programs to complement and improve Head Start projects.

Despite its contentious history, Head Start was a good idea. Earlier experimental preschool programs suggested that disadvantaged children might be helped by early childhood education projects (especially those that provided comprehensive health, social, and education services). Critics of K-3 public education correctly pointed to the need for better schools, and they were justified in questioning the operation and leadership of the Office of Education in the 1950s.

At the same time, however, opponents of linking Head Start to the elementary grades lost an opportunity to encourage public schools to provide broader and more comprehensive services for K-3 students—something that even some Republicans (such as Al Quie) favored. They also may have underestimated the potential willingness of the Office of Education, under more dynamic and innovative leaders such as Francis Keppel and Harold Howe, to work with states and local communities to improve K-3 education. If more Head Start projects had been part of the regular public school system, perhaps the pay and qualifications of preschool teachers would have been set at higher levels. And might the growing opposition to academic instruction in many Head start projects have been reversed? Such reform efforts certainly would have been difficult to achieve in the short term, but focusing public attention on the academic, social, and health outcomes of disadvantaged preschool and K-3 students might have been an important step in the right direction.

Politics is an inevitable part of policy-making—but political expediency should not dominate decision-making. Ignoring the advice of experts and available research for the sake of temporary political gains is not a wise tradeoff—especially when it affects the lives of so many disadvantaged children. No one doubts that in the 1960s most political leaders sincerely wanted to eliminate poverty and help those most in need. But some decision makers allowed their own enthusiasm for large-scale, politically popular programs to outweigh the need to first develop and implement pilot projects that would discover more effective ways to help the poor and disadvantaged in practice.

Rather than starting slowly and providing sufficient funds for high-quality preschool services, which almost all experts recommended, the Johnson administration and OEO, with the quiet acquiescence of some experts, sponsored large numbers of low-quality, underfunded early childhood education projects. These projects did not provide sufficiently strong nor lasting benefits by themselves to help disadvantaged young children overcome their circumstances. The administration's 1966 Early Childhood Development Task Force warned about the limitations of the current Head Start programs and called for more emphasis on the intellectual development of young children. Yet by prematurely declaring Head Start programs effective and frequently ignoring expert criticism, OEO inadvertently downplayed the need to develop more effective programs. As a consequence, the failure by OE and OEO to cooperate more closely to design, implement, and evaluate more scientifically rigorous and useful demonstration projects for Project Follow Through meant that educators and policy makers in the 1970s and 1980s did not have the necessary information to improve early childhood education programs.

The Johnson administration temporarily bolstered public and political support for OEO and its controversial Community Action Program by immediately providing low-cost but low-quality Head Start services for half a million disadvantaged children. These children did not receive the high-quality but more expensive preschool programs initially proposed by many early childhood educators and endorsed by some far-sighted Democratic and Republican policy makers. The education and well-being of millions of disadvantaged Americans may have been unintentionally shortchanged. And rather than saving money, taxpayers paid more in the long run because disadvantaged children were not given a real opportunity to become equal and productive citizens.

INTRODUCTION

1. Linda Jacobson, "Senate Committee Backs Head Start Plan," *Education Week,* November 5, 2003, p. 28.

2. For a good introduction to the current debates about Head Start, see Edward Zigler and Sally J. Styfco, eds., *The Head Start Debates* (Baltimore: Paul H. Brookes, 2004).

3. Edward Zigler and Susan Muenchow, *Head Start: The Inside Story of America's Most Successful Educational Experiment* (New York: Basic Books, 1992).

4. Edward Zigler and Jeanette Valentine, eds., *Project Head Start: A Legacy of the War on Poverty* (New York: Free Press, 1979) (hereafter *Project Head Start*). For a very useful collection of excerpts about the war on poverty, including Head Start, see Michael L. Gillette, *Launching the War on Poverty: An Oral History* (New York: Twayne, 1996).

5. See, e.g., the fine contemporary study by Sar A. Levitan, *The Great Society's Poor Law: A New Approach to Poverty* (Baltimore: Johns Hopkins University Press, 1969), pp. 133–63.

6. Barbara Beatty, *Preschool Education in America: The Culture of Young Children from the Colonial Era to the Present* (New Haven: Yale University Press, 1995). Many of the later histories do not provide much insight into the early policymaking deliberations of the Kennedy and Johnson administrations, either. See, e.g., Catherine J. Ross, "Early Skirmishes with Poverty: The Historical Roots of Head Start," in *Project Head Start,* pp. 21–49; Josh Kagan, "Empowerment and Education: Civil Rights, Expert-Advocates, and Parent Politics in Head Start, 1964–1980," *Teachers College Record* 104 (April 2002): 516–62.

7. Originally, Scott Stossel was asked to ghostwrite Shriver's autobiography; as the project progressed and Shriver was diagnosed as being in the early stages of Alzheimer's disease, the book evolved into an authorized but scholarly biography of Shriver based on considerable secondary sources as well as unpublished manuscript documents. The book generally is very useful and well written, but the chapter concerning Head Start relies heavily on interviews and

records from only a few of the participants, ignoring much of the other available information. Scott Stossel, *Sarge: The Life and Times of Sargent Shriver* (Washington, DC: Smithsonian Books, 2004), pp. xxi–xxx, 416–30.

8. See, e.g., Bob Herbert, "A Muscular Idealism," *New York Times*, April 23, 2004, p. A23.

9. This program was intended to facilitate the transition of Head Start students into the regular public schools; Follow Through was created in the second half of the 1960s and immediately transferred to the Office of Education in HEW.

10. This manuscript is a revised version of a report that provides additional documentation: Maris A. Vinovskis, "Origins of the Head Start Program in the Kennedy and Johnson Administrations," Final Report to the Spencer Foundation's Small Grants Program (December 2003).

CHAPTER ONE

1. Diane Ravitch, *The Troubled Crusade: American Education, 1945–1980* (New York: Basic Books, 1983).

2. Robert A. Divine, *The Sputnik Challenge: Eisenhower's Response to the Soviet Satellite* (New York: Oxford University Press, 1993).

3. Eugene Eidenberg and Roy D. Morey, *An Act of Congress: The Legislative Process and the Making of Education Policy* (New York: Norton, 1969).

4. U.S. Bureau of the Census, *Historical Statistics of the United States, Colonial Times to 1970*, bicentennial edition, pt. 1 (Washington, DC: U.S. Government Printing Office, 1975), ser. F25.

5. On the economic and social advances made during the 1950s see David Halberstam, *The Fifties* (New York: Villard Books, 1993); William O'Neill, *American High: The Years of Confidence, 1945–1960* (New York: Free Press, 1986); James T. Patterson, *Grand Expectations: The United States, 1945–1974* (New York: Oxford University Press, 1996), pp. 311–74.

6. Sheldon H. Danziger, Robert H. Haveman, and Robert D. Plotnick, "Antipoverty Policy: Effects on the Poor and the Nonpoor," in *Fighting Poverty: What Works and What Doesn't*, ed. Sheldon H. Danziger and Daniel H. Weinberg (Cambridge: Harvard University Press, 1986), p. 56.

7. Allison Davis, *Social-Class Influences upon Learning* (Cambridge: Harvard University Press, 1948); Frank Riessman, *The Culturally Deprived Child* (New York: Harper and Row, 1962).

8. Geoffrey Perret, *Jack: A Life Like No Other* (New York: Random House, 2001), pp. 247–51.

9. Harry M. Caudill, *Night Comes to the Cumberlands: A Biography of a Depressed Area* (Boston: Little, Brown, 1962).

10. Michael Harrington, *The Other America: Poverty in the United States* (Baltimore: Penguin Books, 1964). Although Harrington's book was not an immediate best-seller, a laudatory review in the *New Yorker* attracted considerable attention. Dwight MacDonald, "The Invisible Poor," *New Yorker*, January 19, 1963, 82–132.

11. Harrington, *Other America*, pp. 9, 21.

12. Ibid., pp. 20, 135, 156.

13. Ibid., pp. 155–70.

14. David L. Featherman and Maris A. Vinovskis, "Growth and Use of Social and Behavioral Science in the Federal Government since World War II," in *Social Science and Policy-Making: A Search for Relevance in the Twentieth Century*, ed. David L. Featherman and Maris A. Vinovskis (Ann Arbor: University of Michigan Press, 2001), pp. 40–82; Alice O'Connor, *Poverty Knowledge:*

Social Science, Social Policy, and the Poor in Twentieth-Century U.S. History (Princeton: Princeton University Press, 2001), pp. 139–95.

15. Judith D. Auerbach, *In the Business of Child Care: Employer Initiatives and Working Women* (New York: Praeger, 1988); Victoria L. Getis and Maris A. Vinovskis, "History of Child Care in the United States before 1950," in *Child Care in Context: Cross-Cultural Perspectives,* ed. Michael E. Lamb, Kathleen J. Sternberg, Carl-Philip Hwang, and Anders G. Broberg (Hillsdale, NJ: Lawrence Erlbaum, 1992), pp. 185–206; Margaret O'Brien Steinfels, *Who's Minding the Children? The History and Politics of Day Care in America* (New York: Simon and Schuster, 1973); Judith Sealander, *The Failed Century of the Child: Governing America's Young in the Twentieth Century* (Cambridge: Cambridge University Press, 2003), pp. 222–58.

16. U.S. Department of Health, Education, and Welfare, Social and Rehabilitation Service, U.S. Children's Bureau, *The Story of the White House Conference on Children and Youth* (Washington, DC: U.S. Government Printing Office, 1967), p. 4.

17. Sonya Michel, *Children's Interests / Mothers' Rights: The Shaping of America's Child Care Policy* (New Haven: Yale University Press, 1999); Elizabeth Rose, *A Mother's Job: The History of Day Care, 1890–1960* (New York: Oxford University Press, 1999).

18. Sheila Rothman, "Other People's Children," *Public Interest* 30 (1973): 11–27; Steinfels, *Who's Minding the Children?*

19. Rose, *A Mother's Job.*

20. Ibid.

21. Virginia Kerr, "One Step Forward—Two Steps Back: Child Care's Long American History," in *Child Care, Who Cares? Foreign and Domestic Infant and Early Childhood Development,* ed. Pamela Roby (New York: Basic Books, 1973), pp. 151–71.

22. Federal Works Agency, WPA, *Report on Progress of the WPA Program* (Washington, DC: U.S. Government Printing Office, 1938–1941); Getis and Vinovskis, "History of Child Care"; Steinfels, *Who's Minding the Children?*

23. Rose, *A Mother's Job.*

24. Susan Elizabeth Riley, "Caring for Rosie's Children: Child Care, American Women and the Federal Government in the World War II Era" (Ph.D. diss., University of California, Berkeley, 1996); Rose, *A Mother's Job;* William M. Tuttle Jr., *Daddy's Gone to War* (New York: Oxford University Press, 1993); Emilie Stoltzfus, *Citizen, Mother, Worker: Debating Public Responsibility for Child Care after the Second World War* (Chapel Hill: University of North Carolina Press, 2003).

25. Kristen Nawrotzki, Anna Mills Smith, and Maris A. Vinovskis, "Social Science Research and Early Childhood Education: An Historical Analysis of Developments in Head Start, Kindergartens, and Day Care," in *The Social Sciences Go to Washington: The Politics of Knowledge in the Postmodern Age,* ed. Hamilton Cravens (New Brunswick: Rutgers University Press, 2004), pp. 155–80; Anna Smith, "Seeds of Conflict: A Second Look at World War II Day Care Policy," paper presented at the Policy History Conference, St. Louis, Missouri, May 27–30, 1999.

26. Auerbach, *In the Business of Child Care;* Getis and Vinovskis, "History of Child Care"; Rose, *A Mother's Job.*

27. Michel, *Children's Interests / Mothers' Rights;* Rose, *A Mother's Job;* Smith, "Seeds of Conflict."

28. U.S. Bureau of the Census, *Historical Statistics,* pt. 1, ser. H421.

29. Barbara Beatty, *Preschool Education in America: The Culture of Young Children from the Colonial Era to the Present* (New Haven: Yale University Press, 1995); Nawrotzki, Smith, and Vinovskis, "Social Science Research."

30. For an excellent discussion of early childhood experts and their views of children's IQ,

see Hamilton Cravens, *Before Head Start: The Iowa Station and America's Children* (Chapel Hill: University of North Carolina Press, 1993). On the evolution of the field of child development, see Robert R. Sears, *Your Ancients Revisited: A History of Child Development* (Chicago: University of Chicago Press, 1975); Alice Boardman Smuts, "Science Discovers the Child, 1893–1935: A History of the Early Scientific Study of Children" (Ph.D. diss., University of Michigan, 1995).

31. Cravens, *Before Head Start*, pp. 72–105, 185–216.

32. Ibid., pp. 185–216.

33. Donald O. Hebb, *The Organization of Behavior: A Neuropsychological Theory* (New York: Wiley, 1949).

34. J. McVicker Hunt, *Intelligence and Experience* (New York: Ronald Press, 1961).

35. J. McVicker Hunt, "The Implications of Changing Ideas on How Children Develop Intellectually," in *Foundations of Early Childhood Education: Readings*, ed. Michael S. Auleta (New York: Random House, 1969), p. 60. The essay was reprinted from a 1964 essay that appeared in *Children.*

36. Ibid., pp. 68, 73.

37. Benjamin S. Bloom, *Stability and Change in Human Characteristics* (New York: Wiley, 1964), pp. 207–8.

38. Ibid., p. 216.

39. See, e.g., Samuel J. Braun and Esther P. Edwards, *History and Theory of Early Childhood Education* (Belmont, CA: Wadsworth, 1972); Edmund W. Gordon and Doxy A. Wilkerson, *Compensatory Education for the Disadvantaged: Preschool through College* (New York: College Entrance Examination Board, 1966); Joe L. Frost, ed., *Early Childhood Education Discovered: Readings* (New York: Holt, Rinehart, and Winston, 1968); Fred M. Hechinger, ed., *Pre-school Education Today: New Approaches to Teaching Three-, Four-, and Five-Year-Olds* (New York: Doubleday, 1966); Robert D. Hess and Roberta Meyer Bear, eds., *Early Education: Current Theory, Research, and Action* (Chicago: Aldine, 1968); Evelyn Weber, *Early Childhood Education: Perspectives on Change* (Belmont, CA: Wadsworth, 1970).

40. Hechinger, *Pre-school Education Today.*

41. Edward Zigler and Karen Anderson, "An Idea Whose Time Had Come: The Intellectual and Political Climate for Head Start," in *Project Head Start: A Legacy of the War on Poverty*, ed. Edward Zigler and Jeanette Valentine (New York: Free Press, 1979), pp. 3–19.

42. Peter Marris and Martin Rein, *Dilemmas of Social Reform: Poverty and Community Action in the United States* (New York: Atherton, 1967); Harold Silver and Pamela Silver, *An Educational War on Poverty: American and British Policy-Making, 1960–1980* (Cambridge: Cambridge University Press, 1991), pp. 39–48.

CHAPTER TWO

1. Sol Cohen, ed., *Education in the United States: A Documentary History* (New York: Random House, 1974), 2:809.

2. Roger L. Williams, *The Origins of Federal Support for Higher Education: George W. Atherton and the Land-Grant College Movement* (University Park: Pennsylvania State University Press, 1991).

3. Donald R. Warren, *To Enforce Education: A History of the Founding Years of the United States Office of Education* (Detroit: Wayne State University Press, 1974).

4. For analyses of the evolution of federal aid to education, see Homer D. Babbidge Jr. and

Robert M. Rosenweig, *The Federal Interest in Higher Education* (New York: McGraw-Hill, 1962); Sidney W. Tiedt, *The Role of the Federal Government in Education* (New York: Oxford University Press, 1966).

5. James L. Sundquist, *Politics and Policy: The Eisenhower, Kennedy, and Johnson Years* (Washington, DC: Brookings Institution Press, 1968), pp. 155–220.

6. These figures are calculated from U.S. Office of Education data as reported in Congressional Quarterly Service, *Congress and the Nation, 1945–1964: A Review of Government and Politics in the Postwar Years* (Washington, DC: Congressional Quarterly, 1965), p. 1199.

7. Sundquist, *Politics and Policy*, pp. 155–220.

8. Ibid.

9. These figures are calculated from U.S. Office of Education data as reported in Congressional Quarterly Service, *Congress and the Nation, 1945–1964*, p. 1199.

10. These figures are calculated from U.S. Office of Education data as reported in ibid. The relative share of all federal education monies for vocational-technical training, adult education, agricultural extension services, library assistance, and other aid dropped from 36 percent to 19 percent.

11. Sundquist, *Politics and Policy*, pp. 155–220.

12. Congressional Quarterly Service, *Congress and the Nation, 1945–1964*, p. 30.

13. Theodore H. White, *The Making of the President, 1960* (New York: Atheneum, 1961).

14. Congressional Quarterly, *Almanac, 86th Congress, 2nd Session, 1960*, vol. 16 (Washington, DC: Congressional Quarterly, 1960), pp. 771–75; White, *Making of the President*.

15. Sundquist, *Politics and Policy*, p. 464.

16. Congressional Quarterly, *Almanac, 1960*, p. 234.

17. Frank J. Munger and Richard F. Fenno Jr., *National Politics and Federal Aid to Education* (Syracuse, NY: Syracuse University Press, 1962), pp. 92–93; Sundquist, *Politics and Policy*, pp. 443–48.

18. Congressional Quarterly, *Almanac, 1960*, p. 799.

19. William O'Hara, *John F. Kennedy on Education* (New York: Teachers College Press, 1965), pp. 14–15.

20. *New York Herald Tribune*, September 25, 1960, pp. 1, 38.

21. Kennedy's Los Angeles speech of November 2, 1960, quoted in Sundquist, *Politics and Policy*, p. 187.

22. Quoted in ibid.

23. *New York Herald Tribune*, September 25, 1960, p. 38.

24. Quoted in O'Hara, *John F. Kennedy on Education*, p. 84.

25. Congressional Quarterly Service, *Congress and the Nation, 1945–1964*, p. 39.

26. Allen J. Matusow, *The Unraveling of America: A History of Liberalism in the 1960s* (New York: Harper and Row, 1984), pp. 27–28.

27. Congressional Quarterly Service, *Congress and the Nation, 1945–1964*, p. 40.

28. Robert Dallek, *An Unfinished Life: John F. Kennedy, 1917–1963* (Boston: Little, Brown, 2003), pp. 26–68.

29. Lawrence John McAndrews, "Broken Ground: John F. Kennedy and the Politics of Education" (Ph.D. diss., Georgetown University, 1985), 1:30–67. The thesis later was published as Lawrence J. McAndrews, *Broken Ground: John F. Kennedy and the Politics of Education* (New York: Garland, 1991).

30. Wilbur Cohen characterized Ribicoff as "self-centered and egotistical." Edward D. Berkowitz, *Mr. Social Security: The Life of Wilbur J. Cohen* (Lawrence: University Press of Kansas, 1995), p. 139.

31. Congressional Quarterly, *Almanac, 87th Congress, 1st Session, 1961,* vol. 17 (Washington, DC: Congressional Quarterly, 1961), pp. 945–52.

32. Larry Berman, *The Office of Management and Budget and the Presidency, 1921–1979* (Princeton: Princeton University Press, 1979); Hugh Davis Graham, *The Uncertain Triumph: Federal Education Policy in the Kennedy and Johnson Years* (Chapel Hill: University of North Carolina Press, 1984), pp. 13–25.

33. James W. Giglio, *The Presidency of John F. Kennedy* (Lawrence: University Press of Kansas, 1991), pp. 23–44.

34. The Education Task Force was chaired by Frederick Hovde, president of Purdue University. It also included Russell Thackery, executive secretary of the Land Grant Colleges Association; Benjamin Willis, superintendent of the Chicago Schools; Alvin Eurich, vice president of the Ford Foundation; Francis Keppel, dean of the Harvard School of Education; and John Gardner, president of the Carnegie Corporation. M. B. Schnapper, *New Frontiers of the Kennedy Administration: The Texts of the Task Force Reports Prepared for the President* (Washington, DC: Public Affairs Press, 1961), p. 65.

35. The expenditure for the larger cities was targeted somewhat more specifically for "support of research and experimental programs in the special problems of these urban schools, for the planning and construction of facilities, for the acquisition of land sites, for the improvement of programs of community service by the schools, and for the strengthening of guidance and job placement programs for pupils over 16 years of age." Ibid., pp. 65–66.

36. Ibid., pp. 66–69.

37. At the same time that the Education Task Force was making its recommendations, the BOB was helping to prepare a legislative agenda for the new administration. Graham, *Uncertain Triumph,* pp. 11–13.

38. Quoted in Hugh Douglas Price, "Race, Religion, and the Rules Committee: The Kennedy Aid-to-Education Bills," in *The Uses of Power,* ed. Alan F. Westin (New York: Harcourt and Brace, 1962), p. 22.

39. See, e.g., the campaign statements that Kennedy made against aid to parochial schools, *New York Herald Tribune,* September 25, 1960, pp. 1, 38.

40. Giglio, *Presidency of John F. Kennedy,* p. 97.

41. *Public Papers of the Presidents of the United States: John F. Kennedy, 1961* (Washington, DC: U.S. Government Printing Office, 1962), p. 107.

42. Although the administration might have preferred to model its legislation more along the lines suggested by the Hovde Education Task Force or the BOB recommendations, McNamara's staff made it clear that the closer the proposal was to the previous S. 8, the more likely it was to receive a quick, positive response. Graham, *Uncertain Triumph,* pp. 13–18.

43. When the administration's bill was released, it contained a surprise—impact aid for school construction and operation was to be made permanent, but the amount of money for it would be reduced by one-half. Congressional Quarterly, *Almanac, 1961,* p. 212; Graham, *Uncertain Triumph,* pp. 18–20.

44. *Public Papers of the Presidents of the United States: John F. Kennedy,* p. 109.

45. Sorensen and Ribicoff were to secretly try to negotiate a compromise with the Catholic leadership. Theodore C. Sorensen, *Kennedy* (New York: Harper and Row, 1965), pp. 360–61.

46. Hugh Douglas Price, "Schools, Scholarships, and Congressmen: The Kennedy Aid-to-Education Program," in *The Centers of Power,* ed. Alan F. Westin (New York: Harcourt, Brace, and World, 1964), pp. 53–105. Throughout the Kennedy and Johnson administrations, Adam Clayton Powell played a key but often troublesome role in education and antipoverty initiatives.

Charles V. Hamilton, *Adam Clayton Powell, Jr.: The Political Biography of an American Dilemma* (New York: Collier, 1991).

47. Congressional Quarterly, *Almanac, 1961*, pp. 218–22.

48. Ibid., pp. 222–24; Sundquist, *Politics and Policy*, pp. 187–95.

49. On the fight to revamp the Rules Committee, see Price, "Race, Religion, and the Rules Committee," pp. 13–20.

50. A college aid bill (H.R. 7215) establishing loans for classroom construction and student scholarships was also turned back. Efforts were made to revive a revised version of the measure (H.R. 8900), but they failed, and the matter was set aside until 1962. Congressional Quarterly, *Almanac, 1961*, pp. 244–46.

51. Ibid., pp. 224–25; Price, "Race, Religion, and the Rules Committee."

52. McAndrews, "Broken Ground," 1:189–221.

53. Congressional Quarterly, *Almanac, 1961*, p. 225.

54. Quoted in ibid., p. 216.

55. *New York Times*, September 1, 1961, p. 1. Some scholars who have studied the situation, however, doubt that the outcome would have been different if Kennedy had been more involved. The divisions within Congress were too strong to have been overcome by any White House intervention. See, e.g., Irving Bernstein, *Promises Kept: John F. Kennedy's New Frontier* (New York: Oxford University Press, 1961), pp. 218–45. Others, such as Hugh Davis Graham, are less sympathetic to Kennedy because they feel that he had not worked very hard on behalf of his 1961 education initiatives. Graham, *Uncertain Triumph*, pp. 24–25. For another useful, balanced overview and appraisal, see Sundquist, *Politics and Policy*, pp. 193–95.

56. McAndrews, "Broken Ground," 1:244–46, 251.

57. Price, "Race, Religion, and the Rules Committee," pp. 66–67.

58. Congressional Quarterly, *Almanac, 1961*, p. 214.

59. Graham, *Uncertain Triumph*, pp. 26–27.

60. Congressional Quarterly Service, *Almanac, 87th Congress, 2nd Session, 1962*, vol. 18 (Washington, DC: Congressional Quarterly, 1962), p. 863.

61. Ibid., pp. 886–89.

62. Ibid., pp. 231–38; Graham, *Uncertain Triumph*, pp. 28–38.

63. Congressional Quarterly, *Almanac, 1962*, p. 230; Bernstein, *Promises Kept*, pp. 235–36; Sundquist, *Politics and Policy*, p. 193.

64. Congressional Quarterly, *Almanac, 1962*, p. 230.

65. Graham, *Uncertain Triumph*, pp. 39–40.

66. Staff Memorandum, "Background data relating to a new Federal program in education," Bureau of the Budget (November 8, 1962), p. 5, available in RG51, ser. 61.1, Subject Files of the Director, Bureau of the Budget, 1961–68, box 67, folder "A Federal Program for Education, November 1962," National Archives, College Park, Maryland.

67. Ibid.

68. George J. Hecht to President John F. Kennedy, "Bipartisan Citizen's Committee for Federal Aid for Public Elementary and Secondary Education," November 9, 1962, in Wilbur Cohen Papers, box 144, folder 10, Wisconsin Historical Society, Madison.

69. Graham, *Uncertain Triumph*, pp. 42–43.

70. Concerns about early education were not a major issue in 1962. For example, a columnist's short review of leading trends in education made no mention of preschool programs. Fred M. Hechinger, "The Leading Trends in Education," *New York Times*, western edition, January 4, 1963, p. 6.

71. Graham, *Uncertain Triumph*, pp. 43–44.

72. Congressional Quarterly Service, *Almanac, 88th Congress, 1st Session, 1963*, vol. 19 (Washington, DC: Congressional Quarterly, 1963), pp. 1029–30.

73. John D. Morris, "Kennedy Wins House Rules Fight as 88th Congress Opens Session; 15-Man Committee Kept, 235–196," *New York Times*, western edition, January 10, 1963, p. 1.

74. Tom Wicker, "Kennedy Places Tax Legislation First on His List," *New York Times*, western edition, January 3, 1963, pp. 1, 4; E. W. Kenworthy, "The Congress Seems Likely to Put Limits Again on the Scope of Executive Leadership," *New York Times*, western edition, January 7, 1963, pp. 1, 11.

75. Congressional Quarterly Service, *Almanac, 1963*, p. 941.

76. "School Aid Plan to Cost 6 Billion," *New York Times*, western edition, January 19, 1963, p. 4.

77. "Highlights of the Budget," *New York Times*, western edition, January 18, 1963, p. 4.

78. Congressional Quarterly Service, *Almanac, 1963*, p. 976.

79. Ibid., p. 978.

80. "The Education Message," *New York Times*, western edition, February 1, 1963, p. 8.

81. "School Aid Bill Ready This Week," *New York Times*, western edition, January 28, 1963, p. 1. See also Marjorie Hunter, "President Asks Broad Program to Aid Education," *New York Times*, western edition, January 30, 1963, pp. 1, 4.

82. Congressional Quarterly Service, *Almanac, 1963*, pp. 189–94.

83. Ibid., p. 192.

84. Ibid., pp. 188–89; Sundquist, *Politics and Policy*, pp. 207–10.

85. Congressional Quarterly Service, *Almanac, 1963*, pp. 188–89.

86. Waldemar Nielson, *The Big Foundations* (New York: Columbia University Press, 1972).

87. Alice O'Connor, "Community Action, Urban Reform, and the Fight against Poverty," *Journal of Urban History* 22 (July 1996): 586–625.

88. In the ten-year period from 1951 to 1960, the Ford Foundation spent at least 41 percent of its total of $1.3 billion in grants on domestic education. Ford Foundation, *Annual Report, 1960* (New York: Ford Foundation, 1960), p. 10.

89. Peter Marris and Martin Rein, *Dilemmas of Social Reform: Poverty and Community Action in the United States* (New York: Atherton Press, 1967), pp. 14–20.

90. The initial grant of $871,000 went to seven participating school systems, eventually expanded to ten cities. In the initial discussion of the program in the annual report, no mention was made of early childhood education programs. Ford Foundation, *Annual Report, 1960*, p. 10. On the Ford Foundation and domestic programs in the 1960s, see Alice O'Connor, "The Ford Foundation and Philanthropic Activism in the 1960s," in *Philanthropic Foundations: New Scholarship, New Possibilities*, ed. Ellen Condliffe Lagemann (Bloomington: Indiana University Press, 1999), pp. 169–94.

91. Marris and Rein, *Dilemmas of Social Reform*, pp. 16–17.

92. Quoted in ibid.

93. Richard A. Cloward and Lloyd E. Ohlin, *Delinquency and Opportunity: A Theory of Delinquent Gangs* (New York: Free Press, 1960).

94. O'Connor, "Community Action."

95. Ford Foundation, *Annual Report, 1962* (New York: Ford Foundation, 1962), p. 34.

96. Ford Foundation, *Annual Report, 1963* (New York: Ford Foundation, 1963), p. 24.

97. Ford Foundation, *Annual Report, 1965* (New York: Ford Foundation, 1965), pp. 13, 23.

98. Kai Bird, *The Color of Truth: McGeorge Bundy and William Bundy, Brothers in Arms* (New

York: Simon and Schuster, 1998), pp. 376–95; Gregory K. Raynor, "'The Ford Foundation's War on Poverty: Private Philanthropy and Race in New York City, 1948–1968," in *Philanthropic Foundations: New Scholarship, New Possibilities,* ed. Ellen Condliffe Lagemann (Bloomington: Indiana University Press, 1999), pp. 195–228.

99. Ford Foundation, *Annual Report, 1969* (New York: Ford Foundation, 1969), p. 3.

100. James Gilbert, *A Cycle of Outrage: America's Reaction to the Juvenile Delinquent in the 1950s* (New York: Oxford University Press, 1986).

101. Sundquist, *Politics and Policy,* pp. 115–21.

102. Marris and Rein, *Dilemmas of Social Reform,* pp. 20–24.

103. Cloward and Ohlin, *Delinquency and Opportunity,* pp. 210–11.

104. Ibid., pp. 102–3.

105. Daniel Knapp and Kenneth Polk, *Scouting the War on Poverty: Social Reform Politics in the Kennedy Administration* (Lexington, MA: Lexington Books, 1971), pp. 25–63.

106. One of the reasons that there was little opposition to the measure in either chamber was that the legislation was vaguely worded and most members of Congress did not appreciate the possible implications of the calls for more community involvement. Moreover, the total amount authorized and appropriated was very small. Ibid., pp. 61–62.

107. Congressional Quarterly, *Almanac, 1961,* p. 204.

108. Knapp and Polk, *Scouting the War on Poverty,* pp. 69–72.

109. Ibid., pp. 65–107; Marris and Rein, *Dilemmas of Social Reform,* pp. 24–25.

110. Marris and Rein, *Dilemmas of Social Reform,* pp. 25–55.

111. Arthur M. Schlesinger Jr., *A Thousand Days: John F. Kennedy in the White House* (New York: Houghton Mifflin, 1965), p. 1008.

112. Marris and Rein, *Dilemmas of Social Reform,* p. 56.

113. Ibid., p. 63.

114. Ibid., pp. 63–64.

115. Some of the key people in the foundation-funded preschool programs later also staffed Project Head Start. For example, Jeanette Stone worked in a New Haven preschool and then worked with Project Head Start to develop its curriculum guidelines. Jeanette Galambos Stone, "General Philosophy: Preschool Education within Head Start," in *Project Head Start: A Legacy of the War on Poverty,* ed. Edward Zigler and Jeanette Valentine (New York: Free Press, 1979), pp. 163–74.

116. Giglio, *Presidency of John F. Kennedy,* pp. 117–18.

117. Carl M. Brauer, "Kennedy, Johnson, and the War on Poverty," *Journal of American History* 69, no. 1 (June 1982): 98–119; Giglio, *Presidency of John F. Kennedy,* pp. 135–40; Alice O'Connor, *Poverty Knowledge: Social Science, Social Policy, and the Poor in Twentieth-Century U.S. History* (Princeton: Princeton University Press, 2000), pp. 143–46; Herbert Stein, *The Fiscal Revolution in America* (Chicago: University of Chicago Press, 1969).

118. Sundquist, *Politics and Policy,* p. 112.

119. Giglio, *Presidency of John F. Kennedy,* p. 119; Sundquist, *Politics and Policy,* pp. 134–37.

120. Richard Reeves, *President Kennedy: Profile of Power* (New York: Simon and Schuster, 1993), pp. 479–80; Schlesinger, *Thousand Days,* pp. 1009–13. There is considerable confusion among participants concerning whether Kennedy actually read the Harrington book. For example, Charles Schultze, assistant director of the BOB, said in an oral interview that Kennedy had actually read the book and that it had a major impact on him. Michael L. Gillette, *Launching the War on Poverty: An Oral History* (New York: Twayne, 1996), p. 3.

121. Walter W. Heller, memorandum to Anthony J. Celebrezze, "An attack on poverty," October 30, 1963, in Wilbur Cohen Papers, box 149, folder 5, Wisconsin Historical Society, Madison.

122. Michael S. March, memorandum to the director, "Progress Report of the 'Selective Service' and 'Opportunity' Projects," October 29, 1963, quoted in Julie Roy Jeffrey, *Education for Children of the Poor: A Study of the Origins and Implementation of the Elementary and Secondary Education Act of 1965* (Columbus: Ohio State University Press, 1978), pp. 32–33.

123. Walter W. Heller, memorandum to the Secretary of Agriculture, Secretary of Commerce, et al., "1964 Legislative Programs for 'Widening Participation in Prosperity'—An Attack on Poverty," November 5, 1963, p. 1, in Wilbur Cohen Papers, box 149, folder 5, Wisconsin Historical Society, Madison.

124. Ibid., p. 3, emphasis in original.

125. Ibid., appendix A, p. 1.

126. Ibid., pp. 2–3, emphasis in original.

127. John Bibby and Roger Davidson, *On Capitol Hill: Studies in the Legislative Process* (New York: Holt, Rinehart, and Winston, 1967), pp. 223–27.

128. Secretary of HEW, memorandum to Walter Heller, "1964 Legislative Programs for 'Widening Participation in Prosperity'—An Attack on Poverty," November 19, 1963, p. 1, in Wilbur Cohen Papers, box 149, folder 5, Wisconsin Historical Society, Madison.

129. Ibid., p. 9.

130. Ibid.

131. Sorensen, *Kennedy*, p. 753.

132. Schlesinger, *Thousand Days*, p. 1012.

133. The *New York Times* article (October 20, 1963) by Homer Bigart and Ted Sorensen took the lead in mobilizing relief programs for that area. Gillette, *Launching the War on Poverty*, p. 3

134. Reeves, *President Kennedy*, pp. 655–56.

135. Gillette, *Launching the War on Poverty*, p. 15; Schlesinger, *Thousand Days*, p. 1012.

CHAPTER THREE

1. Vaughn Davis Bornet, *The Presidency of Lyndon B. Johnson* (Lawrence: University Press of Kansas, 1983), pp. 12–16.

2. Kermit Gordon, the BOB's director, described the interagency work to date as a series of interesting but largely unrelated program suggestions rather than a coherent and compelling agenda for the 1964 congressional session. Michael L. Gillette, *Launching the War on Poverty: An Oral History* (New York: Twayne, 1996), p. 16.

3. Ibid.; Lyndon Baines Johnson, *The Vantage Point: Perspectives of the Presidency, 1963–1969* (New York: Holt, Rinehart and Winston, 1971), pp. 69–70; Rowland Evans and Robert Novack, *Lyndon B. Johnson: The Exercise of Power* (New York: Signet Books, 1968), pp. 354–79.

4. Perhaps the best and most in-depth (though highly critical) analyses of Johnson's Texas experiences are Robert A. Caro, *The Years of Lyndon Johnson: The Path to Power* (New York: Knopf, 1982); Robert A. Caro, *The Years of Lyndon Johnson: Means of Ascent* (New York: Knopf, 1990).

5. John Bibby and Roger Davidson, *On Capitol Hill: Studies in the Legislative Process* (New York: Holt, Rinehart and Winston, 1967), p. 227.

6. William M. Capron and Burton Weisbrod, memorandum to Walter W. Heller, "Attack on Poverty," December 2, 1963, p. 6, in Wilbur Cohen Papers, box 149, folder 5, Wisconsin Historical Society, Madison.

7. Ibid., pp. 10, 13, 15, emphasis in original.

8. Ibid., pp. 18, 19.

9. William B. Cannon, "Draft of Material for Insertion in CEA Memo to Sorensen," December 17, 1963, in Legislative Background—War on Poverty, box 1, folder "Bureau of the Budget Papers on Poverty," Lyndon Baines Johnson Library, Austin, Texas.

10. Walter W. Heller, memorandum to Theodore Sorensen, "Poverty Program," December 20, 1963, p. 1, in Wilbur Cohen Papers, box 149, folder 5, Wisconsin Historical Society, Madison, emphasis in original.

11. Ibid., attachment A, p. 1.

12. Ibid., attachment A, pp. 1–3.

13. Ibid., attachment B, p. 1.

14. Gillette, *Launching the War on Poverty,* p. 23.

15. Quoted in Edward D. Berkowitz, *Mr. Social Security: The Life of Wilbur J. Cohen* (Lawrence: University Press of Kansas, 1995), p. 197.

16. Johnson, *Vantage Point,* p. 74.

17. Ibid., p. 75. But other participants, such as OEO's director of public affairs, Herbert J. Kramer, felt that Johnson was "wary of community action" in practice. Gillette, *Launching the War on Poverty,* p. 192. See also the remarks by Yarmolinsky in ibid., pp. 73–74.

18. Congressional Quarterly Service, *Almanac, 88th Congress, 2nd Session, 1964,* vol. 20 (Washington, DC: Congressional Quarterly, 1964), p. 862.

19. Ibid.

20. Ibid. The initial costs of the War on Poverty were easily accommodated in the federal budget, and therefore the public was not called on to make major financial sacrifices to help the poor. As the costs of the Vietnam War escalated, the public and politicians did not appear ready to raise taxes even more in order to accelerate the War on Poverty. John C. Donovan, *The Politics of Power,* 2d ed. (Indianapolis: Pegasus, 1973), pp. 111–41. The larger War on Poverty in Shriver's plans went well beyond OEO. It also included transfer payments and a negative income tax. Sargent Shriver, memorandum to the President, "National Anti-Poverty Plan," October 20, 1965, Welfare, EX WE9, box 26, Lyndon Baines Johnson Library, Austin, Texas.

21. David Zarefsky, *President Johnson's War on Poverty: Rhetoric and History* (University: University of Alabama Press, 1986).

22. White House, *Economic Report of the President Together with the Annual Report of the Council of Economic Advisers, 1964* (Washington, DC: U.S. Government Printing Office, 1964), pp. 6–70.

23. Ibid., pp. 75–76.

24. Berkowitz, *Mr. Social Security,* p. 198. Moreover, HEW was not alone in opposing a separate agency in the White House. Attorney General Robert Kennedy, for example, wrote Johnson in mid-January endorsing the War on Poverty. On the basis of his earlier experiences with the President's Committee on Juvenile Delinquency and the President's Study Group on a Domestic Peace Corps, Kennedy wrote that "it would be neither necessary nor desirable to place some super-authority over the Departments. This would be building another layer of government. It would come between the President and the Cabinet officers reporting directly to him." Robert Kennedy, memorandum to the President, "Anti-Poverty Program," January 16, 1964, p. 2, in Office Files of Bill Moyers, box 39, folder "poverty, no. 2," Lyndon Baines Johnson Library, Austin, Texas.

25. Hirst Sutton, memorandum to Kermit Gordon, "Unresolved issues confronting education project grants," January 8, 1964, quoted in Julie Roy Jeffrey, *Education for Children of the Poor:*

A Study of the Origins and Implementation of the Elementary and Secondary Education Act of 1965 (Columbus: Ohio State University Press, 1978), p. 42.

26. Jeffrey, *Education for Children of the Poor*, pp. 42–43.

27. Following Kennedy's assassination, Sorensen was not as involved with legislative details as he had been earlier. Berkowitz, *Mr. Social Security*, pp. 199–200.

28. Bibby and Davidson, *On Capitol Hill*, pp. 227–30.

29. "Title II—Educational Improvement in Low Income Areas," draft bill, January 30, 1964, p. 8, in Wilbur Cohen Papers, box 149, folder 6, Wisconsin Historical Society, Madison. The January 24, 1964, version of that legislation by HEW proposed that the bill be passed separately. "A Bill to Improve Educational Opportunities in Urban and Rural Areas with High Concentrations of Families with Low Incomes and with Attendant Special Educational Deficiencies and Needs," draft, January 24, 1964, in Office Files of Henry H. Wilson, box 4, folder "poverty," Lyndon Baines Johnson Library, Austin, Texas.

30. Jeffrey, *Education for Children of the Poor*, p. 45.

31. For a favorable biography of Sargent Shriver released when he was being considered as a possible vice-presidential candidate in 1964, see Robert A. Liston, *Sargent Shriver: A Candid Portrait* (New York: Farrar, Straus, 1964). A new and much better scholarly biography is Scott Stossel, *Sarge: The Life and Times of Sargent Shriver* (Washington, DC: Smithsonian Books, 2004). It was important for Johnson to provide continuity with the Kennedy administration and persuade the Kennedy political network to support him during the 1964 election. On Johnson's early appointment strategies, see Richard L. Schott and Dagmar S. Hamilton, *People, Positions, and Power: The Political Appointments of Lyndon Johnson* (Chicago: University of Chicago Press, 1983).

32. Two others were seriously considered for the post: Terry Sanford, governor of North Carolina, and Richard Lee, mayor of New Haven, Connecticut. Bibby and Davidson, *On Capitol Hill*, p. 230. For the telephone discussion between Johnson and Shriver about the appointment, see Michael R. Beschloss, *Taking Charge: The Johnson White House Tapes, 1963–1964* (New York: Simon and Schuster, 1997), pp. 202–5.

33. Gillette, *Launching the War on Poverty*, pp. 31–35.

34. Ibid., pp. 31–32.

35. Bibby and Davidson, *On Capitol Hill*, pp. 230–31. Shriver insisted that he had not been hostile to the idea of community action, saying that he favored the idea from the beginning: "In fact, community action—which the people in community action thought was so revolutionary—was something that we had been running in the Peace Corps for four years before it ever got into the War on Poverty." Gillette, *Launching the War on Poverty*, p. 35.

36. Gillette, *Launching the War on Poverty*, p. 52.

37. Ibid.

38. Quoted in Sar A. Levitan, "The Design of Antipoverty Strategy," in *Aspects of Poverty*, ed. Ben B. Seligman (New York: Thomas Crowell, 1968), p. 266.

39. Gillette, *Launching the War on Poverty*, pp. 59–60.

40. Ibid., p. 57.

41. "A bill to mobilize the human and financial resources of the Nation to combat poverty in the United States," draft, February 24, 1964, p. 16, in office files of Bill Moyers, box 39, folder "poverty, no. 1," Lyndon Baines Johnson Library, Austin, Texas.

42. "A bill to mobilize the human and financial resources of the Nation to combat poverty in the United States," [second] draft, March 2, 1964, p. 16, in office files of Bill Moyers, box 39, folder "poverty, no. 1," Lyndon Baines Johnson Library, Austin, Texas.

43. Jeffrey, *Education for Children of the Poor*, pp. 48–49.

44. U.S. Congress, Senate, Select Subcommittee on Poverty, *The War on Poverty. . . . A Compilation of Materials Relevant to S. 2642*, Document no. 86, 88th Cong., 2nd Sess. (Washington, DC: U.S. Government Printing Office, 1964), p. 54.

45. Jeffrey, *Education for Children of the Poor*, p. 29.

46. Congressional Quarterly Service, *Almanac, 1964*, pp. 875–76.

47. Ibid., p. 875.

48. Bibby and Davidson, *On Capitol Hill*, pp. 238–48.

49. Jeffrey, *Education for Children of the Poor*, pp. 49–54.

50. Samuel Halperin, memorandum to Francis Keppel, "Anti-poverty hearings," April 15, 1964, in Wilbur Cohen Papers, box 149, folder 1, Wisconsin Historical Society, Madison.

51. Testimony of Urie Bronfenbrenner, in U.S. Congress, House, Subcommittee on the War on Poverty Program, *Hearings on the Economic Opportunity Act of 1964*, pt. 3, April 23, 1964, 88th Cong., 2nd Sess. (Washington, DC: U.S. Government Printing Office, 1964), p. 1337.

52. Ibid.

53. Ibid. Surprisingly, when Bronfenbrenner recalled his involvement with the creation of Head Start, he did not mention his testimony before Congress. Urie Bronfenbrenner, excerpted in *Project Head Start: The Legacy of the War on Poverty*, ed. Edward Zigler and Jeanette Valentine (New York: Free Press, 1979), pp. 77–89.

54. Quie had met Bronfenbrenner earlier and was familiar with his work on early childhood education in the Soviet Union. U.S. Congress, House, Subcommittee on the War on Poverty Program, *Hearings on the Economic Opportunity Act of 1964*, pp. 1346–54.

55. Jack T. Conway, "Statement of Jack T. Conway before House Education and Labor Committee," April 28, 1964, p. 1, in Adam Yarmolinsky Papers, box 87, folder "OEO Poverty Legislation," John F. Kennedy Library, Boston.

56. Congressional Quarterly Service, *Almanac, 1964*, pp. 215–21. A copy of H.R. 1050 is available in Adam Yarmolinsky Papers, box 87, folder "OEO," John F. Kennedy Library, Boston.

57. Landrum had been a cosponsor of the 1959 Landrum-Griffin bill, which placed restrictions on unions, and he was widely perceived as a conservative enemy of labor. For useful recollections of the passage of the OEO legislation, see Gillette, *Launching the War on Poverty*, pp. 113–41.

58. U.S. Congress, House, Committee on Education and Labor, *Economic Opportunity Act of 1964*, Report no. 1458, 88th Cong., 2nd Sess. (Washington, DC: U.S. Government Printing Office, 1964), p. 2.

59. Ibid., p. 10.

60. Ibid., p. 70.

61. Ibid., p. 71.

62. Ibid., p. 92.

63. Bibby and Davidson, *On Capitol Hill*, pp. 243–44.

64. See, e.g., U.S. Congress, Senate, Select Committee on Poverty, *Hearings on the Economic Opportunity Act of 1964*, June 17, 18, 23, and 25, 1964, 88th Cong., 2nd Sess. (Washington, DC: U.S. Government Printing Office, 1964), pp. 82, 169, 171, 209, 214, 290–91. Interestingly, although Bronfenbrenner's public testimony regarding early childhood education had a major impact on Republican House members, in the Senate Bronfenbrenner's written testimony, given after the public hearings, went unnoticed. Prepared statement by Urie Bronfenbrenner, U.S. Congress, Senate, Select Committee on Poverty, *Hearings on the Economic Opportunity Act of 1964*, June 25, 1964, pp. 355–57.

65. U.S. Congress, Senate, Committee on Labor and Public Welfare, *Economic Opportunity*

Act of 1964, Report no. 1218, 88th Cong., 2nd Sess. (Washington, DC: U.S. Government Printing Office, 1964), p. 7.

66. Ibid., p. 20.

67. Ibid.

68. Ibid., pp. 69, 85.

69. Ibid., pp. 87–91.

70. Bibby and Davidson, *On Capitol Hill*, pp. 245–47.

71. The legislative details of the House and Senate authorizations are from Congressional Quarterly Service, *Almanac, 1964*, pp. 208–28.

72. Charles E. Silberman, "Give Slum Children a Chance: A Radical Proposal," *Harper's Magazine*, May 1964, pp. 37, 38.

73. Ibid., p. 39.

74. Ibid., p. 40.

75. Ibid.

76. U.S. Congress, House, Subcommittee on the War on Poverty Program, *Hearings on the Economic Opportunity Act of 1964*, April 28, 1964, 88th Cong., 2nd Sess. (Washington, DC: U.S. Government Printing Office, 1964), p. 1552. Moorhead's statement appears to have been provided for the record after the April 28 hearing on OEO.

77. Francis Keppel, "Poverty: Target for Education," February 15, 1964, speech delivered before the American Association of School Administrators, Atlantic City, New Jersey, p. 11, in RG12, Records of the Office of Education, Office Files of the Commissioner of Education, 1939–1980, box 168, folder "Speeches and Articles of Francis Keppel, January 1964–May 28, 1964, Economic Opportunity Act of 1964," in National Archives, College Park, Maryland.

78. Quoted in a memorandum from Harry Levin to Francis Keppel, "Preschool Programs for Disadvantaged Children," August 24, 1964, p. 3 in RG12, Records of the Office of Education, Office Files of the Commissioner of Education, 1939–1980, box 125, folder "LL7-1, Economic Opportunity Act of 1964," National Archives, College Park, Maryland. Whether responding to Silberman's *Harper's* article or simply reiterating the brief mentions of the possibility of preschool programs under Title II, Shriver, in a June 24 speech to the NAACP, also stated: "First of all, we intend through Title Two, which is called 'Community Action,' to make it possible for localities, communities, and school districts to start nursery schools. These nursery schools will make sure that young people—especially people from the minority groups—when they arrive in the first grade, will be able to profit from education." Quoted in ibid.

79. Ibid., pp. 1, 4.

80. Ibid., p. 26.

81. Francis Keppel, "How Should We Educate the Deprived Child?" October 23, 1964, speech delivered at the Council for Basic Education, Washington, DC, pp. 7–8, in RG12, Records of the Office of Education, Office Files of the Commissioner of Education, 1939–1980, box 169, folder "Articles and Speeches by Francis Keppel, January 1965–February 1965," National Archives, College Park, Maryland.

82. Ibid., pp. 12–13.

83. Philip Reed Rulon, *The Compassionate Samaritan: The Life of Lyndon Baines Johnson* (Chicago: Nelson-Hall, 1981).

84. Caro, *Years of Lyndon Johnson: The Path to Power.*

85. Lyndon B. Johnson, "Address before a Joint Session of the Congress," November 27, 1963, in *Public Papers of the Presidents of the United States: Lyndon B. Johnson, 1963–64* (Washington, DC: U.S. Government Printing Office, 1965), 1:8–10.

86. James L. Sundquist, *Politics and Policy: The Eisenhower, Kennedy, and Johnson Years* (Washington, DC: Brookings Institution Press, 1968), pp. 155–220.

87. Robert Dallek, *Flawed Giant: Lyndon Johnson and His Times, 1961–1973* (New York: Oxford University Press, 1998).

88. Quoted in Berkowitz, *Mr. Social Security,* p. 197.

89. Wilbur J. Cohen, staff memorandum, "Outline of a Proposed Poverty Program," to the Director of the Bureau of the Budget and the Chairman, Council of Economic Advisers, January 10, 1964, Legislative Background, War on Poverty, box 1, Bureau of the Budget Papers on Poverty, Lyndon Baines Johnson Library, Austin, Texas.

90. Lyndon B. Johnson, "Annual Budget Message to the Congress, Fiscal Year 1965," January 21, 1964, in *Public Papers of the Presidents of the United States: Lyndon B. Johnson, 1963–64* (Washington, DC: U.S. Government Printing Office, 1965), 1:189.

91. Congressional Quarterly Service, *Almanac, 1964,* pp. 259–67.

92. Lyndon B. Johnson, "Remarks at the 1964 Democratic Congressional Dinner," March 19, 1964, in *Public Papers of the Presidents of the United States: Lyndon B. Johnson, 1963–64* (Washington, DC: U.S. Government Printing Office, 1965), 1:399.

93. Lyndon B. Johnson, "Remarks at the University of Michigan," May 22, 1964, in *Public Papers of the Presidents of the United States: Lyndon B. Johnson, 1963–64* (Washington, DC: U.S. Government Printing Office, 1965), 1:706.

94. Hugh Davis Graham, *The Uncertain Triumph: Federal Education Policy in the Kennedy and Johnson Years* (Chapel Hill: University of North Carolina Press, 1984), pp. 61–66. For additional discussions of the Gardner Task Force, see Hugh Davis Graham, "The Transformation of Federal Education Policy," in *Exploring the Johnson Years,* ed. Robert A. Divine (Austin: University of Texas Press, 1981), pp. 155–84; Philip Kearney, "The 1964 Presidential Task Force on Education and the ESEA of 1965" (Ph.D. diss., University of Chicago, 1967).

95. On the Johnson task forces, see Norman C. Thomas and Harold Wolman, "Policy Formulation in the Institutionalized Presidency: The Johnson Task Forces," in *The Presidential Advisory System,* ed. Thomas E. Cronin and Sanford D. Greenberg (New York: Harper and Row, 1969), pp. 124–43; Norman C. Thomas and Harold L. Wolman, "The Presidency and Policy Formulation: The Task Force Device," *Public Administration Review* 29 (September–October 1969): 459–71; Nathan Glazer, "On Task Forcing," *Public Interest* (Spring 1969): 40–45.

96. Barbara Biber, "Recommendations Paper: Preschool Education," August 1964, p. 3, Task Force on Education, July 9, 1964–August 30, 1964, RG51, box 36, National Archives, College Park, Maryland.

97. Ibid., p. 12.

98. John I. Goodlad, "Toward the Improvement of Childhood Education," August 10, 1964, pp. 1–2, Task Force on Education, July 9, 1964–August 30, 1964, RG51, box 36, National Archives, College Park, Maryland.

99. Ibid., p. 2.

100. Memorandum, "Education," October 23, 1964, Task Force on Education, September 23, 1964–December 16, 1964, RG51, box 37, National Archives, College Park, Maryland.

101. Memorandum, "List of Major Legislation under Consideration in Agencies, Department of Health, Education, and Welfare," October 27, 1964, Task Force on Education, September 23, 1964–December 16, 1964, RG51, box 37, National Archives, College Park, Maryland.

102. John W. Gardner, "Report of the President's Task Force on Education," November 14, 1964, p. ii, Task Force on Education, September 23, 1964–December 16, 1964, RG51, box 37, National Archives, College Park, Maryland.

103. Ibid., p. 7.

104. Ibid.

105. Ibid., p. 11.

106. Mary C. Brennan, *Turning Right in the Sixties: The Conservative Capture of the GOP* (Chapel Hill: University of North Carolina Press, 1995); Gregory L. Schneider, *Cadres for Conservatism: Young Americans for Freedom and the Rise of the Contemporary Right* (New York: New York University Press, 1999).

107. Congressional Quarterly Service, *Almanac, 1964*, p. 1079. For an analysis of Goldwater and his campaign, see Rick Perlstein, *Before the Storm: Barry Goldwater and the Unmaking of the American Consensus* (New York: Hill and Wang, 2001).

108. Congressional Quarterly Service, *Almanac, 1964*, p. 1087.

109. Ibid., p. 1085.

110. Ibid., pp. 1110–11; Evans and Novack, *Lyndon B. Johnson*, pp. 458–87.

111. Congressional Quarterly Service, *Almanac, 1964*, p. 1106.

112. Sargent Shriver, "Statement of Sargent Shriver before the Democratic Platform Committee, August 18, 1964," p. 2, in Adam Yarmolinsky Papers, box 87, folder "OEO Platform," John F. Kennedy Library, Boston.

113. Theodore H. White, *The Making of the President, 1964* (New York: Atheneum, 1965), p. 331.

114. Ibid., passim.

115. Norman H. Nie, Sidney Verba, and John R. Petrocik, *The Changing American Voter* (Cambridge: Harvard University Press, 1976); Gerald Pomper, *Voters' Choice: Varieties of American Electoral Behavior* (New York: Dodd and Mead, 1975).

116. This is based on a perusal of speeches and comments made by Johnson during the 1964 campaign in *Public Papers of the Presidents: Lyndon B. Johnson, 1963–64* (Washington, DC: U.S. Government Printing Office, 1965), vols. 1–2.

117. Lyndon B. Johnson, *My Hope for America* (New York: Random House, 1964).

118. Hubert H. Humphrey, *War on Poverty* (New York: McGraw Hill, 1964), p. 124.

119. Congressional Quarterly Service, *Almanac, 1964*, pp. 1021–23.

CHAPTER FOUR

1. Lyndon B. Johnson, "Remarks upon Signing the Economic Opportunity Act," August 20, 1964, in *Public Papers of the Presidents of the United States: Lyndon B. Johnson, 1963–64* (Washington, DC: U.S. Government Printing Office, 1965), 2:989.

2. Sar A. Levitan, *The Great Society's Poor Law: A New Approach to Poverty* (Baltimore: Johns Hopkins University Press, 1969), pp. 50, 52. Levitan's book provides an excellent contemporary overview of the organization and operation of OEO. This section draws heavily on his useful chapter "Housekeeping."

3. On the organization of OEO, see Emmette S. Redford and Marlan Blissett, *Organizing the Executive Branch: The Johnson Presidency* (Chicago: University of Chicago Press, 1981), pp. 77–106.

4. Lyndon B. Johnson, "Remarks at the Swearing in of Sargent Shriver as Director, Office of Economic Opportunity," October 16, 1964, in *Public Papers of the Presidents of the United States: Lyndon B. Johnson, 1963–64* (Washington, DC: U.S. Government Printing Office, 1965), 2:1360.

5. Shriver was anxious to keep his job as director of the Peace Corps, but on June 2, 1965, the

Senate passed an amendment to the Peace Corps authorization bill requiring him to give up one of his jobs. Although he might have been able to hold on to both jobs legally, the Johnson administration felt that his having dual responsibilities now became a liability, and he resigned as the director of the Peace Corps. Richard L. Schott and Dagmar S. Hamilton, *People, Positions, and Power: The Political Appointments of Lyndon Johnson* (Chicago: University of Chicago Press, 1983), pp. 114–16.

6. Jule M. Sugarman, "Transcript of Oral History Interview," March 14, 1969, tape 1, p. 9, Lyndon Baines Johnson Library, Austin, Texas.

7. Robert A. Liston, *Sargent Shriver: A Candid Portrait* (New York: Farrar and Straus, 1964), pp. 151–74.

8. Norbert A. Schlei, "Transcript of Oral History Interview," May 15, 1980, p. 38, Lyndon Baines Johnson Library, Austin, Texas.

9. Yarmolinsky had agreed to work on the Poverty Task Force on the understanding that he would be appointed as the deputy director once the program had been passed. Adam Yarmolinsky, "Transcript of Oral History Interview," July 13, 1970, tape 1, p. 6, Lyndon Baines Johnson Library, Austin, Texas.

10. Levitan, *Great Society's Poor Law*, p. 76. After speaking to Johnson during the negotiations concerning the legislation, Shriver agreed not to recommend Yarmolinsky in order to appease southern conservatives. Schott and Hamilton, *People, Positions, and Power*, p. 117.

11. Schlei, "Transcript of Oral History Interview," May 15, 1980, p. 38. For the view that not naming Yarmolinsky as the deputy director of OEO had serious long-term consequences, see Robert A. Levine, *The Poor Ye Need Not Have with You: Lessons from the War on Poverty* (Cambridge: MIT Press, 1970), p. 51.

12. Jack T. Conway, "Transcript of Oral History Interview," August 13, 1980, Lyndon Baines Johnson Library, Austin, Texas.

13. Quoted in Schott and Hamilton, *People, Positions, and Power*, p. 120.

14. Quoted in ibid., p. 121.

15. Although Harding was never personally close to Shriver, he felt that he had a "very warm, but professional relationship." Quoted in ibid., p. 123.

16. Levine, *The Poor Ye Need Not Have with You*, p. 72.

17. Shriver tried to resign in 1966 but was persuaded to stay. Scott Stossel, *Sarge: The Life and Times of Sargent Shriver* (Washington, DC: Smithsonian Institution Press, 2004), pp. 460–61.

18. Joseph A. Califano Jr., *Inside: A Public and Private Life* (New York: Public Affairs, 2004), pp. 180–81.

19. Bertrand Harding, "Transcript of Oral History Interview," November 20, 1968, tape 1, p. 3, Lyndon Baines Johnson Library, Austin, Texas.

20. Levitan, *Great Society's Poor Law*, pp. 72–80.

21. Ibid., pp. 56–58.

22. Ibid., pp. 67–72.

23. Joseph A. Califano Jr., *The Triumph and Tragedy of Lyndon Johnson: The White House Years* (New York: Simon and Schuster, 1991), p. 80. For a useful analysis of the complex relationship between Shriver and Robert F. Kennedy over the years, see Stossel, *Sarge*.

24. Califano, *Triumph and Tragedy*, p. 80.

25. Joseph Califano, memorandum to the President, December 18, 1965, p. 1, Welfare, EX WE9, Lyndon Baines Johnson Library, Austin, Texas.

26. Redford and Blissett, *Organizing the Executive Branch*, pp. 97–104, 195–204.

27. Califano, *Triumph and Tragedy*, p. 80.

28. Levitan, *Great Society's Poor Law*, pp. 58–59.

29. Ibid., pp. 90–94.

30. Ibid., pp. 9–11. Congressional hostility toward the political activities of local community action agencies also played a role in limiting OEO's budget. When there was additional money for antipoverty initiatives, it often went to other units such as the Department of Labor rather than to OEO. Levine, *The Poor Ye Need Not Have with You*, pp. 63–72.

31. Lyndon B. Johnson, "Special Message to the Congress Proposing a Nationwide War on the Sources of Poverty, March 16, 1964," *Public Papers of the Presidents of the United States: Lyndon B. Johnson, 1963–64* (Washington, DC: U.S. Government Printing Office, 1965), 1:378.

32. Quoted in Levitan, *Great Society's Poor Law*, p. 110.

33. James C. Gaither, "Transcript of Oral History Interview," May 12, 1980, tape 1, p. 2, Lyndon Baines Johnson Library, Austin, Texas.

34. Michael L. Gillette, *Launching the War on Poverty: An Oral History* (New York: Twayne, 1996), p. 195.

35. Schott and Hamilton, *People, Positions, and Power*, pp. 124–26. Berry continued to oppose some OEO policies, such as transferring two job training programs to the Labor Department in 1966. John C. Donovan, *The Politics of Poverty*, 2d ed. (Indianapolis: Pegasus, 1973), pp. 89–91.

36. These figures are calculated from Levitan, *Great Society's Poor Law*, p. 95.

37. Ibid., pp. 120–22.

38. Ibid., p. 123.

39. Julie Roy Jeffrey, *Education for Children of the Poor: A Study of the Origins and Implementation of the Elementary and Secondary Education Act of 1965* (Columbus: Ohio State University Press, 1978), pp. 48–49.

40. Norbert A. Schlei, "Transcript of Oral History Interview," May 15, 1980, tape 1, p. 43, Lyndon Baines Johnson Library, Austin, Texas.

41. Christopher Weeks, "Transcript of Oral History Interview," September 28, 1981, tape 1, pp. 1–5, Lyndon Baines Johnson Library, Austin, Texas.

42. Testimony of Urie Bronfenbrenner, U.S. Congress, House, Subcommittee on the War on Poverty Program, *Hearings on the Economic Opportunity Act of 1964*, pt. 3, April 23, 1964, 88th Congress, 2nd Sess. (Washington, DC: U.S. Government Printing Office, 1964), p. 1337.

43. Congressional Quarterly Service, *Almanac, 88th Congress, 2nd Session, 1964*, vol. 20 (Washington, DC: Congressional Quarterly, 1964), pp. 215–21.

44. Albert H. Quie, press release, August 6, 1964, p. 1, U.S. House of Representatives, in Albert H. Quie Papers, 146.I.9.12(F), box 12, folder "Poverty No. 2," Manuscript Collection, Minnesota Historical Society, St. Paul.

45. Harry Levin, memorandum to Francis Keppel, "Preschool Programs for Disadvantaged Children," August 24, 1964, in RG12, Records of the Office of Education, Office Files of the Commissioner of Education, 1939–1980, box 125, folder LL7-1, "Economic Opportunity Act of 1964," National Archives, College Park, Maryland.

46. Peter P. Muirhead, memorandum to Francis Keppel, June 11, 1964, p. 4, in RG12, Records of the Office of Education, Office Files of the Commissioner of Education, 1939–1980, box 125, folder LL9-5, National Archives, College Park, Maryland.

47. Francis Keppel, memorandum to Douglass Cater, December 15, 1964, in RG12, Records of the Office of Education, Office Files of the Commissioner of Education, 1939–1980, box 187, folder "OE Legislative Program 1965," National Archives, College Park, Maryland.

48. Sugarman mentions that "in the fall of 1964 there was a small group of people who were brought to Washington to look at the question of what might be done to develop programs for

young children. It was in some senses a sort of abortive effort. They prepared a piece of paper which didn't get a great deal of attention in the agency. But I suppose it had enough of an impact that Mr. Shriver soon began to talk to a number of other people about the possibilities of a major effort in the area." Jule M. Sugarman, "Transcript of Oral Interview," March 14, 1969, tape 1, p. 12, Lyndon Baines Johnson Library, Austin, Texas.

49. Note that in a collection of his speeches covering the period through June 1964, Shriver discussed the Peace Corps, the War on Poverty, and education. There were three brief mentions of early childhood education, but his focus was more on older youth than young children. Sargent Shriver, *Point of Lance* (New York: Harper and Row, 1964).

50. On the history of mental retardation, see James W. Trent Jr., *Inventing the Feeble Mind: A History of Mental Retardation* (Berkeley: University of California Press, 1994). The Joseph P. Kennedy Jr. Foundation was created to honor the death of the eldest Kennedy son during World War II. For an in-depth analysis of the Kennedy Foundation and mental retardation, see Edward Shorter, *The Kennedy Family and the Story of Mental Retardation* (Philadelphia: Temple University Press, 2000). On the politics of mental retardation in the 1960s and 1970s, see Daniel A. Felicetti, *Mental Health and Retardation Politics: The Mind Lobbies in Congress* (New York: Praeger, 1975).

51. Eunice Kennedy Shriver, "Hope For Retarded Children," *Saturday Evening Post*, September 22, 1962, 71–74.

52. Shorter, *Kennedy Family*, p. 89.

53. For an analysis of the President's Task Force on Mental Retardation, see Edward D. Berkowitz, "The Politics of Mental Retardation during the Kennedy Administration," *Social Science Quarterly* 61, no. 1 (June 1980): 128–43.

54. President's Panel on Mental Retardation, *Report of the Task Force on Prevention, Clinical Services, and Residential Care* (Washington, DC: U.S. Department of Health, Education, and Welfare, 1962), p. 12.

55. Ibid., p. 13.

56. Ibid., pp. 13–14.

57. Sargent Shriver, excerpted in *Project Head Start: A Legacy of the War on Poverty*, ed. Edward Zigler and Jeanette Valentine (New York: Free Press, 1979), p. 50 (hereafter cited as *Project Head Start*).

58. Edward Zigler and Susan Muenchow, *Head Start: The Inside Story of America's Most Successful Educational Experiment* (New York: Basic Books, 1992), pp. 4–6; Liston, *Sargent Shriver.*

59. Shriver did acknowledge in mid-1964 that pursuant to Community Action regulations nursery schools could be established to help disadvantaged children, especially those from minority groups, prepare to enter the first grade. Levin to Keppel, "Preschool Programs for Disadvantaged Children," p. 3.

60. Shriver, in *Project Head Start*, p. 51. Some of the members of the mental retardation panel also played key roles on the Cooke Head Start Planning Committee. Edward Davens, excerpted in *Project Head Start*, pp. 99–91. Naturally, they tend to emphasize the importance of the recommendations of the mental retardation panel to the origins of Head Start; yet they seem to be unaware of the importance of other early childhood education programs to some key policy makers—especially members of the antipoverty and education task forces.

61. Shorter, *Kennedy Family*, pp. 52–77.

62. Bruner had recommended that only twenty-five hundred children be taught that first summer because of the limited number of qualified teachers. Shriver was depressed by this answer because he had anticipated serving at least ten thousand to twenty-five thousand pupils. Shriver, in *Project Head Start*, pp. 54–55.

63. Polly Greenberg, *The Devil Has Slippery Shoes: A Biased Biography of the Child Development Group of Mississippi (CDGM); A Story of Maximum Feasible Poor Parent Participation* (New York: Macmillan, 1969; Washington, DC: Youth Policy Institute, 1990), pp. 811–12; Polly Greenberg, "The Origins of Head Start and the Two Versions of Parent Involvement: How Much Parent Participation in Early Childhood Programs and Services for Poor Children?" in *Critical Perspectives on Project Head Start: Revisioning the Hope and Challenge*, ed. Jeanne Ellsworth and Lynda J. Ames (Albany: State University of New York Press, 1998), pp. 57–58.

64. Sargent Shriver, memorandum to Bill Moyers and Myer Feldman, "The War on Poverty: Proposals," November 21, 1964, p. 3 in Wilbur Cohen Papers, box 165, folder 4, Wisconsin Historical Society, Madison.

65. Ibid.

66. Office of Programs for Education of the Disadvantaged, "Periodic Report #1 (December 4–December 10, 1964)," in RG12, Records of the Office of Education, Office Files of the Commissioners of Education, 1939–1980, box 215, folder "Economic Opportunity Act—Programs for the Education of the Disadvantaged," p. 1, National Archives, College Park, Maryland.

67. Office of Programs for Education of the Disadvantaged, "Periodic Report #2 (December 11–December 17, 1964)," in RG12, Records of the Office of Education, Office Files of the Commissioners of Education, 1939–1980, box 215, folder "Economic Opportunity Act—Programs for the Education of the Disadvantaged," p. 1, National Archives, College Park, Maryland.

68. Fredric Bresnick, "Report of the Educational Components Funded under Title II-A," December 31, 1964, pp. 7–8, included with the Office of Programs for Education of the Disadvantaged, "Periodic Report #6 (January 8–January 14, 1965)," in RG12, Records of the Office of Education, Office Files of the Commissioners of Education, 1939–1980, box 215, folder "Economic Opportunity Act—Programs for the Education of the Disadvantaged," National Archives, College Park, Maryland.

69. Jule M. Sugarman, "Transcript of Oral Interview," March 14, 1969, tape 1, p. 13, Lyndon Baines Johnson Library, Austin, Texas.

70. Shorter, *Kennedy Family*, pp. 52–108.

71. Zigler and Muenchow, *Head Start*, p. 8.

72. There is some controversy about who actually came up with the idea of calling the program "Head Start." Ibid., p. 8.

73. Sugarman, excerpted in *Project Head Start*, p. 114. There is a tendency, especially among child developmentalists, to credit Cooke with much of the initial thinking and impetus for Head Start. See, e.g., Urie Bronfenbrenner, excerpted in in *Project Head Start*, pp. 79–80. Yet this ignores much of the other work that was occurring on behalf of early childhood education in the Johnson administration and the fact that the decision to go ahead had been reached before Cooke's committee issued its report in February 1965. Cooke and his committee did play an important role, however, in helping shape Head Start programs.

74. Sugarman, in *Project Head Start*, p. 114.

75. Lyndon Baines Johnson, "Annual Message to the Congress on the State of the Union," January 4, 1965, in *Public Papers of the Presidents of the United States: Lyndon B. Johnson, 1965* (Washington, DC: U.S. Government Printing Office, 1966), 1:7.

76. Lyndon Baines Johnson, "Special Message to the Congress: 'Toward Full Educational Opportunity,'" January 12, 1965, in *Public Papers of the Presidents of the United States: Lyndon B. Johnson, 1965* (Washington, DC: U.S. Government Printing Office, 1966), 1:26.

77. Ibid., 1:27.

78. "Head Start," *Washington Post,* January 16, 1965, p. A12.

79. Lady Bird Johnson, *A White House Diary* (New York: Holt, Rinehart, Winston, 1970), p. 219.

80. Shriver, in *Project Head Start,* p. 54.

81. Douglass Cater, memorandum to Lawrence O'Brien, February 1, 1965, p. 1, in Welfare, WE9-1, box 45, folder WE9-1, 11/23/63–12/31/66, Lyndon Baines Johnson Library, Austin, Texas.

82. Zigler and Muenchow, *Head Start,* pp. 17–23. The committee disagreed about some key issues during its deliberations. For example, Myron Wegman, a specialist in pediatrics and public health at the University of Michigan, questioned the emphasis on the medical components of Head Start because he was concerned that duplication and waste might occur. Myron E. Wegman, excerpted in *Project Head Start,* pp. 109–12.

83. Bronfenbrenner, in *Project Head Start,* pp. 81–82. Cooke acknowledged the opposition to a large-scale summer program but felt that it was better in the long run that the program had expanded rapidly. Robert E. Cooke, introduction to *Project Head Start,* xxv.

84. Zigler and Muenchow, *Head Start,* p. 22.

85. Robert Cooke, memorandum to Sargent Shriver, "Improving the Opportunities and Achievements of the Children of the Poor," February 1965, p. 1, in RG51, Records of the Office of Management and Budget, box 45, Project Head Start Planning Committee, National Archives, College Park, Maryland.

86. Ibid., emphasis in original.

87. Ibid., p. 6.

88. Ibid., p. 5.

89. James L. Hymes Jr., excerpted in *Project Head Start,* p. 97.

90. D. Keith Osborn, excerpted in *Project Head Start,* p. 107.

91. Zigler and Muenchow, *Head Start,* p. 23.

92. Apparently, Shriver had first attempted to persuade Myron Wegman of the University of Michigan to become the director of Head Start; Wegman declined the offer but agreed to serve on the program's planning committee. Wegman, in *Project Head Start,* pp. 109–12.

93. Sugarman, in *Project Head Start,* p. 116. On the debate about the extent of Richmond's early involvement in the program, see Julius B. Richmond, "An Early Administrator's Perspective on Head Start," in *The Head Start Debates,* ed. Edward Zigler and Sally J. Styfco (Baltimore: Paul H. Brookes, 2004), pp. 103–9.

94. Zigler and Muenchow, *Head Start,* pp. 31–32.

95. Jule Sugarman, interview with Susan Muenchow, September 21, 1990, quoted in ibid., p. 29.

96. Office of Economic Opportunity, *The First Step . . . on a Long Journey, April 1965* (Washington, DC: Office of Economic Opportunity, 1965), p. 60.

97. On the politics of ESEA's passage, see Eugene Eidenberg and Roy D. Morey, *An Act of Congress: The Legislative Process and the Making of Education Policy* (New York: Norton, 1969); Hugh Davis Graham, *The Uncertain Triumph: Federal Education Policy in the Kennedy and Johnson Years* (Chapel Hill: University of North Carolina Press, 1984).

98. As one Democratic Education and Labor Committee member put it: "The bill itself was really categorical aids with categories broad enough to resemble general aid. We made the categories so broad that the aid splattered over the face of the entire school system and could be called general aid in principle while politically remaining categorical aids." Quoted in Eidenberg and Morey, *Act of Congress,* pp. 90–91.

99. On the development of the child-benefit approach, see ibid., pp. 78–88; Graham, *Uncertain Triumph*, pp. 77–78.

100. Stephen K. Bailey and Edith K. Mosher, *ESEA: The Office of Education Administers a Law* (Syracuse, NY: Syracuse University Press, 1968), pp. 48–60.

101. Gerald Grant, "School Bill Change Is Firmly Opposed by Administration," *Washington Post*, March 7, 1965, p. A6.

102. Even some Democrats complained privately that they were being asked to rubberstamp the administration's bill and pass it hurriedly without any changes. Elsie Carper and Gerald Grant, "President Promises Educators All-Out Effort on School-Aid Bill," *Washington Post*, March 2, 1965, p. A1.

103. Congressional Quarterly Service, *Almanac, 89th Congress, 1st Session . . . 1965*, vol. 21 (Washington, DC: Congressional Quarterly, 1966), pp. 283–87; Eidenberg and Morey, *Act of Congress*, pp. 104–7; Elsie Carper, "2 Republicans Join Vote for Education Aid Bill," *Washington Post*, March 3, 1965, p. A1.

104. The lack of attention to ESEA and early childhood education reflected the absence of a discussion of this issue in many of the standard accounts of ESEA passage. Bailey and Mosher, *ESEA;* Graham, *Uncertain Triumph*. Eidenberg and Morey do mention the GOP's emphasis on preschools in its proposed alternative but do not analyze the more detailed House floor debates about preschools. Eidenberg and Morey, *Act of Congress*, pp. 111–13.

105. Albert H. Quie, press release, August 6, 1964, p. 1, U.S. House of Representatives, in Albert H. Quie Papers, 146.I.9.12(F), box 12, folder "Poverty No. 2," Manuscript Collection, Minnesota Historical Society, St. Paul.

106. Albert H. Quie, "Report of the Republican Task Force on Education: A New Look at Pre-school Education, Present and Future," introduction for the Republican Task Force on Education, n.d. [1966], in Albert H. Quie Papers, 146.I.9.5(B), box 148, folder "Republican Task Force on Education: A New Look at Pre-school Education," Manuscript Collection, Minnesota Historical Society, St. Paul. The quotation refers to an earlier study by the Republican Task Force on Education.

107. U.S. Congress, House, Committee on Education and Labor, *Elementary and Secondary Education Act of 1965*, Report No. 143, 89th Cong., 1st Sess. (Washington, DC: U.S. Government Printing Office, 1965), p. 72. The *Washington Post* reported the GOP criticism of the "bill for 'virtually ignoring' pre-school training": "GOP Report Calls Education Bill Spurious, Wasteful," *Washington Post* March 10, 1965, p. A2.

108. Several of the key House Republicans involved with education issues had decided to include a preschool provision as part of the proposed GOP alternative bill at a February 5 meeting. Eidenberg and Morey, *Act of Congress*, pp. 110–14.

109. Elsie Carper, "House GOP Offers School Bill Alternative," *Washington Post*, March 9, 1965, pp. A1, A15.

110. Eidenberg and Morey, *Act of Congress*, pp. 110–19.

111. Wilbur J. Cohen, memorandum to Francis Keppel, "Suggested Amendments to Elementary and Secondary Bill for Possible Discussion with Mr. Perkins," p. 1, in Wilbur Cohen Papers, box 152, folder 3, Wisconsin Historical Society, Madison.

112. Cohen wrote to Robert Kennedy: "It is very urgent that I see you as soon as possible regarding the elementary and secondary education bill. The House subcommittee will make its report to the full committee on Wednesday, and will probably act on the bill on Thursday. We will try very hard to get the House bill passed through the Senate without having to go to a conference, if this is at all possible. Consequently I should talk with you immediately about any

problems or amendments before the situation gets so complicated that the whole bill gets lost as did the higher education bill a couple of years ago." Wilbur J. Cohen to Senator Robert F. Kennedy, February 15, 1965, p. 1, in Wilbur Cohen Papers, box 152, folder 3, Wisconsin Historical Society, Madison.

113. Wilbur J. Cohen, memorandum to the President, "Senator Robert Kennedy's Suggestions on Elementary and Secondary Education Bill," February 23, 1965, p. 1, in Wilbur Cohen Papers, box 152, folder 2, Wisconsin Historical Society, Madison.

114. Ibid., pp. 1–2.

115. U.S. Congress, *Congressional Record: Proceedings and Debates of the 89th Cong., 1st Sess.*, vol. III, pt. 5, House, March 24, 1965 (Washington, DC: U.S. Government Printing Office, 1965), p. 5738.

116. Ibid., p. 5739.

117. Ibid., p. 5740.

118. Ibid.

119. U.S. Congress, *Congressional Record: Proceedings and Debates of the 89th Cong., 1st Sess.*, vol. III, pt. 5, House, March 25, 1965, p. 6018.

120. 124 Ibid., p. 6019.

121. Ibid., pp. 6016–20. The tax-related portions of the broader GOP bill had not been addressed by the Ways and Means Committee and were considered germane to the ESEA bill being discussed. Therefore, Quie separated his early childhood proposal from the larger Republican education alternative and offered it as a substitute for Title I of ESEA.

122. Ibid., p. 6018.

123. Ibid., p. 6017.

124. U.S. Congress, *Congressional Record*, March 24, 1965, p. 5742.

125. Elsie Carper, "LBJ Gains Victory in School Vote," *Washington Post*, March 27, 1965, pp. A1, A4.

126. Eidenberg and Morey, *Act of Congress*, pp. 150–55.

127. The White House urged acceptance of the House bill without any amendments, but some senators objected and planned to offer changes anyway. "Humphrey Predicts Speedy Passage of Education Aid Bill," *Washington Post*, March 31, 1965, p. A5.

128. Cohen to the President, "Senator Robert Kennedy's Suggestions," pp. 1–2.

129. U.S. Congress, Senate, Committee on Labor and Public Welfare, *Elementary and Secondary Education Act of 1965*, 89th Cong., 1st Sess., Report no. 146 (Washington, DC: U.S. Government Printing Office, 1965), pp. 13–14; Cohen to the President, "Senator Robert Kennedy's Suggestions," pp. 1–2.

130. Although Republican members wrote a minority report, it mainly criticized the opposition of the Democrats to any amendments whatsoever; the Senate Republicans, unlike their House counterparts, did not accuse the Democrats of ignoring preschool education. U.S. Congress, Senate, Committee on Labor and Public Welfare, *Elementary and Secondary Education Act of 1965*, pp. 81–85.

131. U.S. Congress, *Congressional Record: Proceedings and Debates of the 89th Cong., 1st Sess.*, vol. III, pt. 6, House, April 9, 1965, pp. 7617–19.

132. Eidenberg and Morey, *Act of Congress*, pp. 145–67.

133. Lyndon Baines Johnson, "Remarks in Johnson City, Tex., upon Signing the Elementary and Secondary Education Bill," April 11, 1965 in *Public Papers of the Presidents of the United States: Lyndon B. Johnson, 1965* (Washington, DC: U.S. Government Printing Office, 1965), 1:413.

134. Other historical studies of education have ignored the discussions of Head Start and

preschools during the debates about authorization of ESEA. See, e.g., see Julius B. Richmond, Deborah J. Stipek, and Edward Zigler, "A Decade of Head Start," in *Project Head Start,* 135–52.

CHAPTER FIVE

1. Office of the White House Press Secretary, "'The White House Made Public Today the Following Letter from the President to the President of the Senate and the Speaker of the House of Representatives," February 17, 1965, p. 1, Office Files of Bill Moyers, box 2, folder "Poverty Program Letter," Lyndon Baines Johnson Library, Austin, Texas.

2. Jule M. Sugarman, excerpted in *Project Head Start: A Legacy of the War on Poverty,* ed. Edward Zigler and Jeanette Valentine (New York: Free Press, 1979), p. 117 (hereafter cited as *Project Head Start*).

3. Community Action Program, Office of Economic Opportunity, *Project Head Start: An Opportunity for the Child and for the Community; A Statement of Purpose; A Guide to What You Can Do* (Washington, DC: Office of Economic Opportunity, 1965), p. 7. Some participants felt that the first lady exaggerated the extent of ignorance of young, disadvantaged children. For example, she claimed that many of these preschool children did not even know their own names; Zigler, on the other hand, thought that they did know their names but sometimes were too shy to share them with strangers. Edward Zigler and Susan Muenchow, *Head Start: The Inside Story of America's Most Successful Educational Experiment* (New York: Basic Books, 1992), pp. 24–25.

4. Lyndon B. Johnson to Hubert H. Humphrey, President of the Senate, and to John W. McCormack, Speaker of the House of Representatives, in *Public Papers of the Presidents of the United States: Lyndon B. Johnson, 1965* (Washington, DC: U.S. Government Printing Office, 1966), 1:201.

5. Community Action Program, *Project Head Start: An Opportunity,* pp. 3, 13.

6. Ibid., p. 13.

7. Ibid., pp. 17–18.

8. Interestingly, the cover of the OEO pamphlet shows a young child playing with letters of the alphabet, but the text contains no discussion of the need to teach Head Start children their alphabet or other early literacy skills. Indeed, in a long list of things that volunteers are encouraged to do, no specific mention is made of helping children learn their alphabet. Community Action Program, *Project Head Start: An Opportunity,* pp. 23–24.

9. Ibid., p. 22.

10. Ibid.

11. Ibid., p. 26.

12. For example, staff at the Office of Programs for the Education for Disadvantaged noted that "this unit continued to be concerned with the advance OEO planning for the eight-week pre-school summer program for 100,000 children. This program has been given the name of 'Project Head-Start.'" Office of the Commissioner of Education, "Programs for Education of the Disadvantaged," report no. 6 (January 8–14, 1965), in RG12, Records of the Office of Education, Office of the Commissioner of Education, box 215, folder "Economic Opportunity Act—Programs for the Education of the Disadvantaged," National Archives, College Park, Maryland.

13. Zigler and Muenchow, *Head Start,* pp. 29–31.

14. Polly Greenberg, *The Devil Has Slippery Shoes: A Biased Biography of the Child Development Group of Mississippi (CDGM); A Story of Maximum Feasible Poor Parent Participation* (New York: Macmillan, 1969; Washington, DC: Youth Policy Institute, 1990), p. 41.

15. Jule Sugarman, "Transcript of Oral Interview," March 14, 1969, tape 1, pp. 17–18, Lyndon Baines Johnson Library, Austin, Texas.

16. Michael L. Gillette, *Launching the War on Poverty: An Oral History* (New York: Twayne, 1996), p. 222.

17. Lyndon B. Johnson, "Remarks on Project Head Start," May 18, 1965, in *Public Papers of the Presidents of the United States: Lyndon B. Johnson, 1965* (Washington, DC: U.S. Government Printing Office 1966), 1:56. As in other instances, Johnson greatly exaggerated the effects of the eight-week program, seeing in it the difference between a productive life and one spent in welfare institutions for these children.

18. Unlike the 1955 White House Conference on Education, which was more than a year in preparation, the 1965 conference was put together in about two months. As a result, there were complaints about the uneven quality of the commissioned papers and the process for selecting the participants. See the GOP memorandum, "The White House Conference on Education," n.d., in Albert H. Quie Papers, 146.I.12.11(B), Manuscript Collections, Minnesota Historical Society, St. Paul.

19. J. W. Getzels, "Pre-school Education," in U.S. Congress, Senate, Subcommittee on Education, Committee on Labor and Public Welfare, *White House on Education: A Milestone for Educational Progress*, 89th Cong., 1st Sess. (Washington, DC: U.S. Government Printing Office, 1965), p. 118.

20. Ibid., p. 122.

21. Ibid., pp. 122–23.

22. [?] Becker, notes on the preschool education session, July 21, 1965, in Albert H. Quie Papers, 146.I.12.11(B), Manuscript Collections, Minnesota Historical Society, St. Paul.

23. Ibid.

24. Sar A. Levitan, *The Great Society's Poor Law: A New Approach to Poverty* (Baltimore: Johns Hopkins University Press, 1969), pp. 139, 146.

25. Ibid., p. 140.

26. Sargent Shriver, memorandum to President Lyndon B. Johnson, June 9, 1965, Welfare, WE 9–1, box 45, Lyndon Baines Johnson Library, Austin, Texas.

27. Lyndon B. Johnson, "Remarks on Announcing Plans to Extend Project Head Start," August 31, 1965, in *Public Papers of the Presidents of the United States: Lyndon B. Johnson, 1965* (Washington, DC: U.S. Government Printing Office, 1966), 1:953–54.

28. Robert E. Cooke to the President, December 28, 1965, p. 1, in Welfare, WE9-1, box 46, 10/21/65–6/3/66, Lyndon Baines Johnson Library, Austin, Texas.

29. Zigler and Muenchow, *Head Start*, pp. 40–41, emphasis in original.

30. Johnson, "Remarks on Announcing Plans to Extend Project Head Start," p. 954.

31. Charles L. Schultze, memorandum to the President, "Summer Head Start Program," March 18, 1967, White House Central Files, EX FG11-15, box 125, Lyndon Baines Johnson Library, Austin, Texas.

32. Ibid.

33. Sargent Shriver to Richard T. Hanna, January 24, 1968, Welfare, WE9-1, box 47, Lyndon Baines Johnson Library, Austin, Texas.

34. Jule M. Sugarman to Rosendo Gutierrez, February 21, 1967, Welfare, WE9-1, box 47, Lyndon Baines Johnson Library, Austin, Texas.

35. Levitan, *Great Society's Poor Law,* p. 139.

36. Ibid., pp. 139–40, 146.

37. Ibid., p. 142.

38. The Bureau of the Census used the designation "subprofessionals" in its compilations. One of the reviewers of this manuscript saw the use of the term as possibly derogatory. Therefore, in the text, "paraprofessionals" was substituted for "subprofessionals."

39. Levitan, *Great Society's Poor Law,* p. 143.

40. For a good example of how the mainstream media viewed OEO after the first year, see "Shriver and the War on Poverty," *Newsweek,* September 13, 1965, pp. 22–29.

41. Kenneth Clark and Jeannette Hopkins, *A Relevant War against Poverty: A Study of Community Action Programs and Observable Change* (New York: Harper and Row, 1970); John C. Donovan, *The Politics of Poverty* (New York: Pegasus, 1967); Jennifer Frost, *"An Interracial Movement of the Poor": Community Organizing and the New Left in the 1960s* (New York: New York University Press, 2001); Daniel P. Moynihan, *Maximum Feasible Misunderstanding: Community Action in the War on Poverty* (New York: Free Press, 1970); Stephen M. Rose, *The Betrayal of the Poor: The Transformation of Community Action* (Rochester, VT: Schenkman, 1972).

42. James C. Gaither, "Transcript of Oral Interview," May 12, 1980, tape 1, pp. 2–3, 9–10, Lyndon Baines Johnson Library, Austin, Texas.

43. Sargent Shriver, excerpted in *Project Head Start,* pp. 59–60.

44. Julius Richmond, "Transcript of Oral Interview," October 5, 1981, tape 1, pp. 23–24, Lyndon Baines Johnson Library, Austin, Texas.

45. Jule M. Sugarman, "Transcript of Oral Interview," March 14, 1969, tape 1, p. 24, Lyndon Baines Johnson Library, Austin, Texas.

46. For differing views of the relation between Head Start and CAAs, see Kathryn R. Kuntz, "A Lost Legacy: Head Start's Origins in Community Action," in *Critical Perspectives on Project Head Start: Revisioning the Hope and Challenge,* ed. Jeanne Ellsworth and Lynda J. Ames (Albany: State University of New York Press, 1998), pp. 1–48; Carolyn Harmon, "Was Head Start a Community Action Program?" in *The Head Start Debates,* ed. Edward Zigler and Sally J. Styfco (Baltimore: Paul H. Brookes, 2004), pp. 85–101.

47. Shriver, in *Project Head Start,* pp. 60–61. On Alinsky's reactions to OEO and Shriver, see Sanford D. Howitt, *Let Them Call Me Rebel: Saul Alinsky, His Life and Legacy* (New York: Vintage, 1989), pp. 472–82.

48. Quoted in Polly Greenberg, "Three Core Concepts of the War on Poverty: Their Origins and Significance in Head Start," in *The Head Start Debates,* ed. Edward Zigler and Sally J. Styfco (Baltimore: Paul H. Brookes, 2004), pp. 80–81.

49. The 825-page book, a reprint and expansion of the original 1969 volume, provides an in-depth analysis and documentation of the Mississippi Head Start program from CDGM's perspective. Greenberg, *The Devil Has Slippery Shoes,* though a useful and eloquent account, should be read critically in order to ascertain exactly what was happening. For a useful reading concerning Head Start community action, for example, see Harmon, "Was Head Start a Community Action Program?"

50. On the civil rights conflicts in Mississippi in the mid-1960s, see Doug McAdam, *Freedom Summer* (New York: Oxford University Press, 1988); Sally Belfrage, *Freedom Summer* (Charlottesville: University of Virginia Press, 1995); Charles M. Payne, *I've Got the Light of Freedom: The Organizing Tradition and the Mississippi Freedom Struggle* (Berkeley: University of California Press, 1995).

51. Paul B. Johnson, telegram to President Lyndon B. Johnson, February 23, 1966, Welfare, WE 9–1, box 46, Lyndon Baines Johnson Library, Austin, Texas.

52. Gillette, *Launching the War on Poverty,* p. 282.

53. Ibid., pp. 282–83. Unfortunately, there is no in-depth analysis of the Mississippi Head

Start episode that has tried to present an objective account. But observers for and against CDGM and Shriver's actions have devoted considerable attention to the episode. When Polly Greenberg, one of the staunchest proponents of CDGM, wrote her admittedly biased but moving account, she was proud of the fact that as an OEO staffer she strongly advocated funding for CGDM because "it seemed urgent that ordinary OEO staff members such as I persuade 'radical' leaders to get into the Head Start business, to join their conservative, liberal, and reactionary brothers." Greenberg, *The Devil Has Slippery Shoes*, pp. 10–11. Moreover, Greenberg acknowledged that "our uncredentialed and credentialed teachers alike could scarcely read, write, and spell" (p. 168).

54. For details of OEO's indictment of CDGM's operation, see Theodore M. Berry to Rev. J. F. McRee, October 2, 1966, in Sargent Shriver Papers, box 1, folder "CDGM No. 3," John F. Kennedy Library, Boston.

55. Shriver, in *Project Head Start*, pp. 61–62. The CDGM issued a detailed response to the various allegations against it. Child Development Group of Mississippi, "Accusations and Answers," [1966?], Welfare, WE9-1, box 46, Lyndon Baines Johnson Library, Austin, Texas.

56. For a discussion of MAP, see "MAP Distortions," *Washington Post*, October 17, 1966, p. A20.

57. *New York Times*, October 19, 1966, p. C35.

58. John C. Donovan, *The Politics of Poverty*, 2d ed. (Indianapolis: Pegasus, 1973), pp. 81–88.

59. Citizens' Crusade against Poverty, *News*, 1966, p. 2, in Citizens' Crusade against Poverty Collection, box 7, folder "CCAP, News Releases, 1966," Walter Reuter Library, Detroit.

60. John H. Niemeyer, excerpted in *Project Head Start*, p. 105.

61. Child Development Group of Mississippi, "Fact Sheet," [1966?], Welfare, WE9-1, box 46, Lyndon Baines Johnson Library, Austin, Texas.

62. Office of Economic Opportunity, "CDGM to Continue Head Start in Mississippi," December 16, 1966, Welfare, WE9-1, box 28, Lyndon Baines Johnson Library, Austin, Texas.

63. Jule M. Sugarman to Kenneth Neigh, December 16, 1966, Welfare, WE9-1, box 28, Lyndon Baines Johnson Library, Austin, Texas.

64. Louise B. Miller, "Development of Curriculum Models in Head Start," in *Project Head Start*, pp. 195–220.

65. Office of Economic Opportunity, *The First Step . . . on a Long Journey*, April 1965 (Washington, DC: Office of Economic Opportunity, 1965), p. 59.

66. Ibid. p. 60.

67. Levitan, *Great Society's Poor Law*, pp. 150–52.

68. Eveline B. Omwake, "Assessment of the Head Start Preschool Education Effort," in *Project Head Start*, p. 223.

69. Zigler and Muenchow, *Head Start*, p. 41.

70. Ibid.

71. Greenberg, *The Devil Has Slippery Shoes*.

72. Julius B. Richmond, "Transcript of Oral History Interview," October 5, 1981, tape 1, p. 45, Lyndon Baines Johnson Library, Austin, Texas.

73. Bertrand M. Harding, "Transcript of Oral History Interview," in Michael L. Gillette, *Launching the War on Poverty: An Oral History* (New York: Twayne, 1996), p. 365.

74. David L. Featherman and Maris A. Vinovskis, "Growth and Use of Social and Behavioral Science in the Federal Government since World War II," in *Social Science and Policy-Making: A Search for Relevance in the Twentieth Century*, ed. David L. Featherman and Maris A. Vinovskis (Ann Arbor: University of Michigan Press, 2001), pp. 40–82; Walter Williams and John W.

Evans, "The Politics of Education: The Case of Head Start," *Annals of the American Academy of Political and Social Science* 385 (September 1969): 118–32. On the role of the policy analysts in the federal government, see Arnold Meltsner, *Policy Analysts in the Bureaucracy* (Berkeley: University of California Press, 1976).

75. Edwin L. Harper, Fred A. Kramer, and Andrew M. Rouse, "Implementation and Use of PPB in Sixteen Federal Agencies," *Public Administration Review* 29 (November–December, 1969): 623–32.

76. Henry J. Aaron, *Politics and the Professors: The Great Society in Perspective* (Washington, DC: Brookings Institution, 1968), pp. 31–32.

77. Although the PPB system did help with specific parts of OEO, on the whole it did not have much of an impact in the agency. Robert A. Levine, *Public Planning: Failure and Redirection* (New York: Basic Books, 1972), pp. 145–50.

78. Greenberg, *The Devil Has Slippery Shoes.*

79. Zigler and Muenchow, *Head Start,* p. 48.

80. Ibid., p. 50.

81. Ibid., pp. 50–51. Myron Wegman, a member of the Head Start Planning Committee, criticized the manpower and energy spent on unnecessary record-keeping and use of meaningless medical data. Myron E. Wegman, excerpted in *Project Head Start,* pp. 109–12.

82. Levitan, *Great Society's Poor Law,* p. 139.

83. Head Start had established thirteen of these centers; they were located at universities specializing in child development.

84. Levitan, *Great Society's Poor Law,* pp. 149–50.

85. U.S. Congress, House, Committee on Education and Labor, *1966 Amendments to the Economic Opportunity Act of 1964,* pt. 2, 90th Cong., 2nd Sess. (Washington, DC: U.S. Government Printing Office, 1966), pp. 1131–41.

86. Wilbur J. Cohen, memorandum to Donald Harting, "Newspaper Article re: Head Start," December 1965, in Wilbur Cohen Papers, box 107, folder 3, Wisconsin Historical Society, Madison.

87. "The Office of Economic Opportunity during the Administration of President Lyndon B. Johnson, November 1963–January 1969," 1:241–42, in "Administrative History: Office of Economic Opportunity," Lyndon Baines Johnson Library, Austin, Texas.

88. Robert A. Levine, *The Poor Ye Need Not Have with You: Lessons from the War on Poverty* (Cambridge: MIT Press, 1970), pp. 143–47.

89. Max Wolff and Annie Stein, "Six Months Later: A Comparison of Children Who Had Head Start, Summer 1965, with Their Classmates in Kindergarten," Research and Evaluation Office, Project Head Start, OEO, 1966, available in ERIC (ED015025).

90. "The Office of Economic Opportunity during the Administration of President Lyndon B. Johnson, November 1963–January 1969," 1:249.

91. Quoted in ibid.

92. Quoted in Harold Silver and Pamela Silver, *An Educational War on Poverty: American and British Policy-Making, 1960–1980* (Cambridge: Cambridge University Press, 1991), p. 86. Loyalty to Johnson and his programs became increasingly important over time—especially later, when protesters of the Vietnam War challenged the administration. Richard L. Schott and Dagmar S. Hamilton, *People, Positions, and Power: The Political Appointments of Lyndon Johnson* (Chicago: University of Chicago Press, 1983), pp. 9–33.

93. Edward Zigler and Jeanette Valentine, preface to *Project Head Start,* p. ix. Interestingly, a decade later Zigler acknowledged that the overall program was not very effective at that time

and that the poor results from about one-third of the programs would have canceled out the good results from the better third of the programs. Zigler and Muenchow, *Head Start,* p. 154.

94. Silver and Silver, *Educational War on Poverty,* pp. 114–43; Williams and Evans, "Politics of Evaluation."

95. Lyndon B. Johnson to Hubert H. Humphrey, President of the Senate, and to John W. McCormack, Speaker of the House of Representatives, in *Public Papers of the Presidents of the United States: Lyndon B. Johnson, 1965* (Washington, DC: U.S. Government Printing Office, 1966), 1:201.

96. Levitan, *Great Society's Poor Law,* p. 139.

97. Ibid., pp. 126–27.

98. Levine, *The Poor Ye Need Not Have with You,* pp. 143–47.

99. Williams and Evans, "Politics of Evaluation."

100. Zigler and Muenchow, *Head Start,* p. 62. For a useful discussion of the importance of longitudinal, random assignment studies, see Frederick Mosteller and Robert Boruch, eds., *Evidence Matters: Randomized Trials in Education Research* (Washington, DC: Brookings Institution Press, 2002).

101. Levine, *The Poor Ye Need Not Have with You,* p. 144, emphasis in original.

102. Shriver, in *Project Head Start,* p. 57.

103. Robert E. Cooke, introduction to *Project Head Start,* p. xxiv.

104. Sheldon H. White and Deborah A. Phillips, "Designing Head Start: Roles Played by Developmental Psychologists," in *Social Science and Policy-Making: A Search for Relevance in the Twentieth Century,* ed. David L. Featherman and Maris A. Vinovskis (Ann Arbor: University of Michigan Press, 2001), pp. 83–118.

105. See, e.g., Julius B. Richmond, Deborah J. Stipek, and Edward Zigler, "A Decade of Head Start," in *Project Head Start,* pp. 135–52. The confusion about the program's objectives was often mirrored at the local level. June Solnit Sale, "Implementation of a Head Start Preschool Education Program: Los Angeles, 1965–1967," in *Project Head Start,* pp. 175–94.

106. Omwake, "Assessment of the Head Start Preschool Education Effort," p. 234.

107. Although OEO recognized the limitations of the study, it believed that the study would still produce sufficiently reliable and useful results. Williams and Evans, "Politics of Evaluation."

108. On the debates about the Westinghouse–Ohio University evaluation, see Victor G. Cicirelli, John W. Evans, and Jeffrey S. Schiller, "The Impact of Head Start: A Reply to the Report Analysis," *Harvard Educational Review* 40 (1970): 105–29; Marshall S. Smith and Joan S. Bissell, "Report Analysis: The Impact of Head Start," *Harvard Educational Review* 40 (1970): 51–104; Westinghouse Learning Corporation, "The Impact of Head Start: An Evaluation of the Effects of Head Start on Children's Cognitive and Affective Development," Ohio University Report to the Office of Economic Opportunity, Contract no. B89–4536, 1969 (available in ERIC as ED036321); Zigler and Muenchow, *Head Start,* pp. 60–72.

109. Jule M. Sugarman, memorandum to the Secretary, "Head Start," May 27, 1968, in Wilbur Cohen Papers, box 107, folder 5, Wisconsin Historical Society, Madison.

110. On the use of task forces in the Johnson administration, see Norman C. Thomas, "The Presidency and Policy Formulation: The Task Force Device," *Public Administration Review* 29 (September–October, 1969): 459–71; Adam Yarmolinsky, "Ideas into Programs," *Public Interest* no. 2 (Winter 1966): 70–79; Nathan Glazer, "On Task Forcing," *Public Interest* no. 15 (Spring 1969): 40–45; Norman C. Thomas and Harold L. Wolman, "Policy Formulation in the Institutionalized Presidency: The Johnson Task Forces," in *The Presidential Advisory System,* ed. Thomas E. Cronin and Sanford D. Greenberg (New York: Harper and Row, 1969), pp. 124–43.

111. For details on Califano's role on the Johnson White House staff, see Joseph A. Califano Jr., *The Triumph and Tragedy of Lyndon Johnson* (New York: Simon and Schuster, 1991); Joseph A. Califano Jr., *Inside: A Public and Private Life* (New York: Public Affairs, 2004), pp. 151–88.

112. Hugh Davis Graham, *The Uncertain Triumph: Federal Education Policy in the Kennedy and Johnson Years* (Chapel Hill: University of North Carolina Press, 1984), pp. 110–31.

113. Joseph A. Califano, memorandum to Anthony J. Celebrezze, July 28, 1965, p. 2, in Wilbur Cohen Papers, box 185, folder 12, Wisconsin Historical Society, Madison. For an in-depth discussion of the Keppel Interagency Task Force on Education and its impact on subsequent legislation, see Robert Eugene Hawkinson, "Presidential Program Formulation in Education: Lyndon Johnson and the 89th Congress" (Ph.D. diss., University of Chicago, 1977), pp. 191–247.

114. Francis Keppel, memorandum to the Secretary, August 4, 1965, in Wilbur Cohen Papers, box 185, folder 9, Wisconsin Historical Society, Madison.

115. Francis Keppel, draft memorandum to Joseph A. Califano Jr., August 9, 1965, p. 4, in Wilbur Cohen Papers, box 185, folder 12, Wisconsin Historical Society, Madison; Graham, *Uncertain Triumph*, pp. 115–16.

116. Hawkinson, "Presidential Program Formulation," pp. 241–42.

117. Ibid.

118. Joseph A. Califano, memorandum to John W. Gardner, October 27, 1965, p. 2, in Wilbur Cohen Papers, box 185, folder 12, Wisconsin Historical Society, Madison.

119. Francis Keppel, memorandum to Joseph Califano, "Area 8—An Overall Plan to Improve Pre-school Programs for the Poor," November 29, 1965, Wilbur Cohen Papers, box 185, folder 12, Wisconsin Historical Society, Madison.

120. Graham, *Uncertain Triumph*, pp. 141–45.

121. "Notes on Organizational Meeting of Task Force on Early Childhood," October 15, 1966, in RG51, Records of the Office of Management and Budget, box 5, folder 5, National Archives, College Park, Maryland.

122. Ibid.

123. Harold Howe II, "Views of Problems and Needs for Young Children," memorandum to Task Force on Early Childhood, n.d., p. 1, in RG51, Records of the Office of Management and Budget, box 5, folder 5, National Archives, College Park, Maryland.

124. Ibid., pp. 1, 15.

125. Ibid., pp. 4–6.

126. Ibid., pp. 2, 11.

127. Task Force on Early Childhood Development, "A Bill of Rights: Report of the President's Task Force on Early Childhood Development," January 14, 1967, p. 51, in RG51, Records of the Office of Management and Budget, box 5, folder 5, National Archives, College Park, Maryland. An earlier version was completed in December 1966, but this final version was more carefully edited and documented.

128. Ibid., pp. 3, 28, 39–40.

129. Ibid., p. 93.

130. Ibid., pp. 52, 120–21.

131. Ibid., p. 122.

132. Ibid., pp. 124–25.

133. Ibid., pp. 12, 13.

134. Ibid., pp. 3, 7, 8.

135. Ibid., p. 9.

136. Lyndon Baines Johnson, "Remarks on Announcing Plans to Extend Project Head Start,"

August 31, 1965, in *Public Papers of the Presidents of the United States: Lyndon B. Johnson, 1965* (Washington, DC: U.S. Government Printing Office, 1966), 2:467.

137. Congressional Quarterly Service, *Almanac, 90th Congress, 1st Session, 1967,* vol. 23 (Washington, DC: Congressional Quarterly, 1968), p. 4-A.

138. Ibid., p. 55-A.

139. David P. Weikart, "Results and Implications from Preschool Intervention Programs," May [?] 1967, p. 1, in RG51, Records of the Office of Management and Budget, box 5, folder "Early Childhood Task Force 1967," National Archives, College Park, Maryland. For an autobiographical account of Weikart's involvement in early childhood education, see David P. Weikart, *How High / Scope Grew: A Memoir* (Ypsilanti, MI: High / Scope Press, 2004).

140. Weikart, "Results and Implications," p. 2.

141. Ibid., p. 3.

142. Ibid., p. 11.

143. J. McVicker Hunt to Emerson J. Elliot, May 24, 1967, pp. 1–2, in RG51, Records of the Office of Management and Budget, box 5, folder on Early Childhood Task Force 1967, National Archives II, College Park, Maryland.

144. Ibid., pp. 1–2.

145. Ibid., p. 3.

146. Maris A. Vinovskis, *History and Education Policymaking* (New Haven: Yale University Press, 1999), pp. 90–92.

147. Task Force on Education, "Report of the Task Force on Education," June 30, 1967, p. 11, in Task Force Reports, Lyndon Baines Johnson Library.

148. Ibid., p. 19.

149. Congressional Quarterly Service, *Congress and the Nation, 1965–1968* (Washington, DC: Congressional Quarterly, 1969), 2:7.

150. Quoted in Robert L. Egbert, Marijane E. England, and Rosalind Alexander-Kasparik, "Glance Back at Follow Through's Beginnings," in *Follow Through: A Bridge to the Future,* ed. Betty J. Mace-Matluck (Austin, TX: Southwest Educational Development Laboratory, 1992), pp. 11–12.

151. Vinovskis, *History and Education Policymaking,* pp. 89–114.

152. Edward Zigler to Richard Snyder, January 4, 1968, p. 1, in RG51, Records of OMB, Records of the Budgetary Administration in the Department of Health, Education, and Welfare, Fiscal Years 1962–1969, General Series, box 45, folder "Follow Through #1," National Archives, College Park, Maryland.

153. Ibid., pp. 1–2.

154. Ibid., pp. 2, 3.

155. For analyses of Follow Through, see Betty J. Mace-Matluck, ed., *Follow Through: A Bridge to the Future* (Austin, TX: Southwest Educational Development Laboratory, 1992); Richard Elmore, "Follow Through: Decision-Making in a Large-Scale Social Experiment" (Ph.D. diss., Harvard University Graduate School of Education, 1976); Carol Doernberger and Edward Zigler, "Project Follow Through: Intent and Reality," in *Head Start and Beyond: A National Plan for Extended Childhood Intervention,* ed. Edward Zigler and Sally J. Styfco (New Haven: Yale University Press, 1993), pp. 43–72; W. Ray Rhine, ed., *Making Schools More Effective: New Directions from Follow Through* (New York: Academic Press, 1981); Vinovskis, *History and Educational Policymaking,* pp. 89–114.

156. Task Force on Child Development, "Report of the Task Force on Child Development," November 7, 1967, p. 1, in Wilbur Cohen Papers, Wisconsin Historical Society, Madison.

157. Ibid., p. 12.

158. Ibid., pp. 13–16, 20–24.

159. Vinovskis, *History and Education Policymaking*, pp. 89–114.

CHAPTER SIX

1. Congressional Quarterly Service, *Almanac, 89th Congress, 2nd Session, 1966*, vol. 22 (Washington, DC: Congressional Quarterly, 1967), pp. 69–86.

2. Ibid., pp. 286–310.

3. Eve Edstrom, "Boos Drive Shriver out of Meeting," *Washington Post*, April 15, 1966, pp. A1, A6. See also "Poor People Give Shriver Awful Time," *New York Times*, April 15, 1966, pp. 1, 18.

4. John C. Donovan, *The Politics of Poverty*, 2d ed. (Indianapolis: Pegasus, 1973), pp. 62–80.

5. U.S. Congress, House, Subcommittee on the War on Poverty Program, *Hearings on the 1966 Amendments to the Economic Opportunity Act of 1964*, Part 1, 89th Cong., 2nd Sess. (Washington, DC: U.S. Government Printing Office, 1966), p. 186.

6. Ibid., pp. 188–89.

7. Ibid., p. 194.

8. Ibid., pp. 197–98.

9. Ibid., pp. 198, 201.

10. Ibid., p. 202.

11. U.S. House, Republican Task Force on Education, "A New Look at Pre-school Education, Past and Present," 1966[?], in Albert H. Quie Papers, box 148, 146.I.19.5 (B), folder "Republican Task Force on Education: A New Look at Pre-school Education, Past and Future," Minnesota Historical Society, St. Paul. The report does not have a date; from the text and the footnotes it appears to have been released in mid-1966, perhaps in July or August; the forty-seven-page report was produced on legal-sized paper.

12. Ibid., p. 42.

13. Ibid.

14. Ibid.

15. Congressional Quarterly Service, *Almanac, 1966*, pp. 258–61.

16. Ibid., pp. 258, 260–61.

17. Ibid., pp. 263, 264–65.

18. Donovan, *Politics of Poverty*, p. 92.

19. Congressional Quarterly Service, *Almanac, 90th Congress, 1st Session, 1967*, vol. 23 (Washington, DC: Congressional Quarterly Service, 1968), p. 76.

20. Charles E. Goodell, memorandum to Albert H. Quie, "Two-hour discussion with Sargent Shriver, Wednesday, March 8, 1967," March 9, 1967, pp. 2–3, 146.I.19.4F, in Albert H. Quie Papers, Manuscripts Collection, Minnesota Historical Society, St. Paul.

21. Ibid., p. 3.

22. Congressional Quarterly Service, *Almanac, 1967*, pp. 611–26.

23. Gibbons noted that "there are presently 171 members who remain in Congress who voted for this proposal [the Opportunity Crusade bill] last year. When you add to this number the 47 additional Republicans that we now have in Congress, you can see that they would have an easy time in reaching a majority in carrying this proposal, in fact, you would only need the defection of 2 or 3 more Southern Democrats or absentees to carry the day." Samuel M. Gibbons to Joseph

A. Califano Jr., January 25, 1967, p. 1, in Presidential Task Forces, subject file "Gaither," box 32, folder "Transfer of OEO Programs," Lyndon Baines Johnson Library, Austin, Texas.

24. Congressional Quarterly Service, *Almanac, 1967*, pp. 1058–84.

25. Ibid., pp. 1073–75.

26. Ibid., pp. 1064–67.

27. U.S. Congress, *Congressional Record*, vol. 113, pt. 20, September 27, 1967 (Washington, DC: U.S. Government Printing Office, 1967), p. 27071.

28. Ibid., pp. 27071–72. For a useful discussion of Head Start and school superintendents at the 1967 congressional hearings, see Kathryn R. Kuntz, "A Lost Legacy: Head Start's Origins in Community Action," in *Critical Perspectives on Project Head Start: Revisioning the Hope and Challenge*, ed. Jeanne Ellsworth and Lynda J. Ames (Albany: State University of New York Press, 1998), pp. 1–48. Kuntz's overall thesis regarding the centrality of community action in Head Start's origin and early development, however, is not persuasive. See Carolyn Harmon, "Was Head Start a Community Action Program? Another Look at an Old Debate," in *The Head Start Debate*, ed. Edward Zigler and Sally J. Styfco (Baltimore: Paul H. Brookes, 2004), pp. 85–101.

29. U.S. Congress, *Congressional Record*, vol. 113, pt. 20, September 27, 1967, p. 27078–79.

30. Ibid., p. 27074. Robert Kennedy was another Democratic leader who argued for a broader view of Head Start: "Head Start, for example, is not just an education program. As I said earlier, it seeks to develop the child in relation to his family and the world around him, and a critical part of this is parental involvement." Ibid., p. 27085.

31. Ibid., p. 27074.

32. Ibid., pp. 27074, 27075.

33. Ibid., p. 27079.

34. Congressional Quarterly Service, *Almanac, 1967*, pp. 1073–75.

35. Ibid., p. 1071.

36. This information was calculated from the roll-call data and member characteristics provided in ibid., p. S-46; see Congressional Quarterly Service, *Almanac, 90th Congress, 2nd Session, 1968*, vol. 24 (Washington, DC: Congressional Quarterly, 1968), pp. 31–32, 46, 826, 833, 872.

37. Dixie Barger, memorandum to Albert H. Quie and Charles E. Goodell, "Conversation with Art Dufresne, Senator Prouty's Office," p. 1, 146.I.19.4F, in Albert H. Quie Papers, Manuscripts Collection, Minnesota Historical Society, St. Paul.

38. Congressional Quarterly Service, *Almanac, 1967*, p. 1081.

39. Task Force on Child Development, "Report of the Task Force on Child Development," November 7, 1967, in Wilbur Cohen Papers, Wisconsin Historical Society, Madison.

40. James Gaither, memorandum to Joseph Califano, March 21, 1968, in Presidential Task Forces, subject file "Gaither," box 30, folder "Head Start Transfer," Lyndon Baines Johnson Library, Austin, Texas.

41. Joseph Califano, memorandum to Wilbur Cohen, April 10, 1968, pp. 1–2, in Presidential Task Forces, subject file "Gaither," box 30, folder "Head Start Transfer," Lyndon Baines Johnson Library, Austin, Texas.

42. Howe was scheduled to deliver the speech in person in Houston, but he had to stay in Washington to testify at an appropriation meeting. The typed speech was read to the NEA audience.

43. Harold Howe II, "Picking up the Options," speech given at the annual meeting of the Department of Elementary School Principals, NEA, Houston, Texas, April 1, 1968, p. 5, in Presidential Task Forces, subject file "Gaither," box 30, folder, "Head Start Transfer," Lyndon Baines Johnson Library, Austin, Texas.

44. Ibid., pp. 5–6, emphasis in original.

45. Harold Howe II, memorandum to Wilbur J. Cohen, "Possible transfer of Head Start to HEW," April 1, 1968, in Presidential Task Forces, subject file "Gaither," box 30, folder "Head Start Transfer," Lyndon Baines Johnson Library, Austin, Texas.

46. Ibid., pp. 1–2.

47. Jule M. Sugarman, memorandum to Wilbur J. Cohen, "Head Start—Commissioner Howe's memorandum dated April 1, 1968," April 10, 1968, pp. 1–5, 7, in Wilbur J. Cohen Papers, box 107, folder 15, Wisconsin Historical Society, Madison.

48. Jule M. Sugarman, memorandum to Wilbur J. Cohen, "Attached materials," April 10, 1968, p. 1, in Wilbur J. Cohen Papers, box 107, folder 15, Wisconsin Historical Society, Madison.

49. "Memorandum of Understanding between the Office of Economic Opportunity and the Department of Health, Education and Welfare Relative to the Administration of the Head Start Program under a Delegation of Authority," discussion draft, April 9, 1968, in Wilbur J. Cohen Papers, box 107, folder 15, Wisconsin Historical Society, Madison.

50. Fred Bohen, memorandum to Joe Califano, May 6, 1968, p. 2, in Presidential Task Forces, subject file "Gaither," box 32, folder "Transfer of OEO Programs," Lyndon Baines Johnson Library, Austin, Texas.

51. Congressional Quarterly Service, *Almanac, 1968*, pp. 500–502.

52. U.S. Congress, *Congressional Record*, vol. 114, pt. 16, July 15, 1968, p. 21285.

53. The old ESEA Title VIII was to be renamed Title IX. U.S. Congress, *Congressional Record*, vol. 114, pt. 17, July 17, 1968, p. 21721–24.

54. Ibid., p. 21724.

55. Ibid., p. 21724.

56. Ibid., p. 21725.

57. Ibid., pp. 21726–28.

58. Ibid., p. 21730.

59. This information was calculated from the roll-call data and member characteristics provided in Congressional Quarterly Service, *Almanac, 1968*, pp. 31–32, 46, 826, 833, 872, S-38.

60. In 1967, eighty-nine members voted on the transfer amendment and eleven did not; however, we do know how six of those would have voted because of their stated position on the vote; similarly, in 1968, eighty-nine members voted on the transfer amendment and eleven did not; we know how three of those would voted because of their stated position on the vote. One member, Robert Kennedy, had been assassinated by the time of the vote and had not been replaced. As a result, in the comparisons of the 1967 and 1968 votes, he was not included in the calculations. In 1967 Robert Kennedy had voted against the transfer of Head Start.

61. Among the Republicans, twenty-eight supported the transfer in both votes and four opposed it; among the Democrats, twenty-six opposed the transfer on both votes and nine supported it.

62. Two Democratic supporters of the 1967 amendment were absent for the 1968 vote, and four members who were absent in 1967 now supported the transfer (two Democrats and two Republicans). Three Democratic opponents of the transfer in 1967 missed the 1968 vote; only one Democrat who was absent in 1967 voted against the transfer in 1968. One member missed both the 1967 and the 1968 vote, and Robert Kennedy, who opposed the transfer in 1967, was not present in the Senate in 1968 to vote on the amendment.

63. U.S. Congress, *Congressional Record*, vol. 114, pt. 17, July 17, 1968, p. 22030.

64. Ibid.

65. Jim Jones, memorandum to Jim Gaither, July 18, 1968, p. 1, in Presidential Task Forces,

subject file "Gaither," box 30, folder "Head Start Transfer," Lyndon Baines Johnson Library, Austin, Texas.

66. Ibid., p. 2.

67. Jim Gaither, memorandum to Joe Califano, "OEO Problems," July 25, 1968, p. 1, in Presidential Task Forces, subject file "Gaither," box 30, folder "Head Start Transfer," Lyndon Baines Johnson Library.

68. Edward Zigler and Jeanette Valentine, eds., *Project Head Start: A Legacy of the War on Poverty* (New York: Free Press, 1979), p. 130.

69. Jim Gaither, memorandum to Joe Califano, "OEO Legislative Problems," August 6, 1968, p. 2, in Presidential Task Forces, subject file "Gaither," box 30, folder "Head Start Transfer," Lyndon Baines Johnson Library, Austin, Texas.

70. Harold Kleiner to Edith Green, August 6, 1968, p. 1, in Presidential Task Forces, subject file "Gaither," box 30, folder "Head Start Transfer," Lyndon Baines Johnson Library, Austin, Texas.

71. Ibid., pp. 1–2.

72. Edith Green to Harold Howe II, August 12, 1968, p. 1, in Presidential Task Forces, subject file "Gaither," box 30, folder "Head Start Transfer," Lyndon Baines Johnson Library, Austin, Texas.

73. J. Graham Sullivan to Edith Green, August 30, 1968, p. 2, in Presidential Task Forces, subject file "Gaither," box 30, folder "Head Start Transfer," Lyndon Baines Johnson Library, Austin, Texas.

74. Joseph H. Reid to Albert H. Quie, September 27, 1968, 146.I.10.14F, in Albert H. Quie Papers, Manuscripts Collection, Minnesota Historical Society, St. Paul.

75. Office of Economic Opportunity, "The Office of Economic Opportunity during the Administration of President Lyndon B. Johnson, November 1963–January 1969," MS, 1:646–47, in Administration History, Office of Economic Opportunity, box 1, in Presidential Task Forces, subject file "Gaither," Lyndon Baines Johnson Library, Austin, Texas.

76. U.S. Congress, *Congressional Record*, vol. 114, pt. 22, October 1, 1968, pp. 29012–13.

77. Ibid., p. 29158.

78. Office of Economic Opportunity, "Office of Economic Opportunity during the Administration of President Lyndon B. Johnson," 1:646–47.

79. U.S. Congress, *Congressional Record*, vol. 114, pt. 22, October 1, 1968, p. 29158.

80. Ibid.

81. Congressional Quarterly Service, *Almanac, 1968*, p. 504.

82. Richard E. Orton, memorandum to Acting [OE] Director, "Study Group—Head Start," October 1, 1968, p. 1, in Presidential Task Forces, subject file "Gaither," box 30, folder "Head Start Transfer," Lyndon Baines Johnson Library, Austin, Texas.

83. Bertrand M. Harding, memorandum to James Gaither, October 4, 1968, p. 1, in Presidential Task Forces, subject file "Gaither," box 30, folder "Head Start Transfer," Lyndon Baines Johnson Library, Austin, Texas.

84. Wilbur Cohen, memorandum to Joseph A. Califano, "Head Start," October 24, 1968, pp. 1–2, in Wilbur Cohen Papers, box 107, folder 5, Wisconsin Historical Society, Madison.

85. Charles J. Zwick, memorandum to Joseph A. Califano, "Head Start," November 29, 1968, p. 1 in Presidential Task Forces, subject file "Gaither," box 209, folder "Head Start and Job Corps," Lyndon Baines Johnson Library, Austin, Texas.

86. Section 309 Task Force, "Preliminary Report," section titled "The Importance of Child Development," p. 1, in Presidential Task Forces, subject file "Gaither," box 209, folder "Head Start and Job Corps," Lyndon Baines Johnson Library, Austin, Texas.

87. Ibid., pp. 11–12.

88. Ibid., "Summary," pp. 1–2.

89. U.S. Office of Education, memorandum to Head Start Task Force, "Assignment of Responsibility for Head Start," November 13, 1968, in Wilbur Cohen Papers, box 112, folder 2, Wisconsin Historical Society, Madison.

90. Richard E. Orton, memorandum to Head Start Task Force, "Head Start," November 12, 1968, pp. 1–2, in Wilbur Cohen Papers, box 112, folder 2, Wisconsin Historical Society, Madison.

91. Joseph Califano, memorandum to the President, December 20, 1968, pp. 1–2, in Presidential Task Forces, subject file "Gaither," box 30, folder "Head Start Transfer," Lyndon Baines Johnson Library, Austin, Texas.

92. Ibid., p. 2.

93. Ibid.

94. On the 1968 election, see Lewis Chester, Godfrey Hodgson, and Bruce Page, *An American Melodrama: The Presidential Campaign of 1968* (New York: Viking Press, 1969); Theodore H. White, *The Making of the President, 1968* (New York: Atheneum, 1969).

95. Congressional Quarterly Service, *Almanac, 1968*, p. 989.

96. Chester, Hodgson, and Page, *American Melodrama;* White, *Making of the President, 1968.*

97. C. David Heyman, *RFK: A Candid Biography of Robert Kennedy* (New York: Dutton, 1998); Arthur M. Schlesinger Jr., *Robert Kennedy and His Times* (New York: Ballantine, 1978).

98. Chester, Hodgson, and Page, *American Melodrama;* White, *Making of the President, 1968.*

99. Congressional Quarterly Service, *Almanac, 1968*, p. 989.

100. Ibid., p. 1049.

101. Ibid.

102. Chester, Hodgson, and Page, *American Melodrama;* White, *Making of the President, 1968.*

103. Nixon-Agnew Campaign Committee, *Nixon Speaks Out: Major Speeches and Statements by Richard M. Nixon in the Presidential Campaign of 1968* (New York: Nixon-Agnew Campaign Committee, 1968), pp. 188–89.

104. Vice President's Task Force on Education, "'Toward Excellent Education for All Americans," October 1968, p. 9, in Francis Keppel Papers, box 51, folder "Humphrey Task Force on Education, no. 1," John F. Kennedy Library, Boston.

105. Ibid., p. 11.

106. Democratic National Committee, "Vice President Humphrey Proposes Nine Point Plan of Action for Excellence in Education," News Release, October 7, 1968, p. 1, in Francis Keppel Papers, box 51, folder "Humphrey Task Force on Education, no. 1," John F. Kennedy Library, Boston.

107. Congressional Quarterly Service, *Congress and the Nation,* vol. 2, *1965–1968* (Washington, DC: Congressional Quarterly Service, 1969), p. 29.

108. For detailed political scientific analyses of the 1968 election, see Richard W. Boyd, "Popular Control of Public Policy: A Normal Vote Analysis of the 1968 Election," *American Political Science Review* 66, no. 2 (June 1972): 429–49; Philip E. Converse, Warren E. Miller, Jerold G. Rusk, and Arthur C. Wolfe, "Continuity and Change in American Politics: Parties and Issues in the 1968 Election," *American Political Science Review* 63, no. 4 (December 1969): 1083–105.

109. Lyndon B. Johnson, "Remarks to Assistant and Regional Directors of the Office of Economic Opportunity," October 23, 1968, in *Public Papers of the Presidents of the United States: Lyndon B. Johnson, 1968–69* (Washington, DC: U.S. Government Printing Office, 1970), 2:1061–62.

110. For details about the recommendations for early action on Head Start, see chapter 5.

111. Congressional Quarterly, *Almanac, 91st Congress, 1st Session, 1969,* vol. 25 (Washington, DC: Congressional Quarterly, 1970), p. 2-A.

112. Ibid., p. 3-A.

113. Nixon-Agnew Campaign Committee, *Nixon Speaks Out*, pp. 192–94.

114. Richard Nixon, "Statement on Signing Executive Order Establishing the Council for Urban Affairs," January 23, 1969, in *Public Papers of the Presidents of the United States: Richard Nixon, 1969* (Washington, DC: U.S. Government Printing Office, 1971), pp. 11–12.

115. On Moynihan's service in the Nixon administration, see Godfrey Hodgson, *The Gentleman from New York, Daniel Patrick Moynihan: A Biography* (Boston: Houghton Mifflin, 2000). On Moynihan's views of OEO and the War on Poverty, see Daniel P. Moynihan, *Maximum Feasible Misunderstanding: Community Action in the War on Poverty* (New York: Free Press, 1969).

116. Congressional Quarterly, *Almanac, 1969*, p. 33-A.

117. Ibid.

118. U.S. Congress, House, Committee on Education and Labor, *President of the United States, Head Start Report*, 91st Cong., 1st Sess., House Doc. no. 91–75 (Washington, DC: U.S. Government Printing Office, 1969).

119. Congressional Quarterly, *Almanac, 1969*, p. 33-A.

120. Ibid.

121. Quoted in Kenneth W. Munden, "The Office of Economic Opportunity in the Nixon Administration," OEO, May 1973, p. 32, in Community Services Administration, A1, entry 15, box 107, National Archives, College Park, Maryland.

122. Ibid., p. 34.

123. Richard Nixon, "Statement Announcing the Establishment of the Office of Child Development," April 9, 1969, in *Public Papers of the Presidents of the United States: Richard Nixon, 1969* (Washington, DC: U.S. Government Printing Office, 1971), p. 271.

124. Ibid.

125. Ibid.

126. Edward Zigler and Susan Muenchow, *Head Start: The Inside Story of America's Most Successful Educational Experiment* (New York: Basic Books, 1992), pp. 56–75. On education policies in the early part of the Nixon administration, see Chester E. Finn Jr., *Education and the Presidency* (Lexington, MA: Heath, 1977).

Aaron, Henry J., 101–2
Adler, James, 43
adult education, 119
Advisory Committee on Teacher Training
    for Project Head Start, 99–100
African Americans, in poverty in 1964, 6
Agnew, Spiro, 137
Agricultural Act of 1954, 14
Alinsky, Saul, 96
Allen, James E. Jr., 54
American Independent Party, 138–39
antiwar demonstrators, 138
Appalachian poverty, 6
Arden House Conference on the Preschool
    Environment of Socially Disadvantaged
    Children, 1962, 11
Ayers, William, 81

baby boom, 6
Bain, George, 73
Baker, Donald M., 97–98
Baldwin, Bird T., 9
Bank Street College of Education, 28, 55
Barger, Dixie, 127
Beatty, Barbara, 2
Bell, David E., 18

Berry, Theodore M., 66–67
Biber, Barbara, 55, 69
Bipartisan Citizen's Committee for Federal
    Aid for Public Elementary and Sec-
    ondary Education, 23
Bloom, Benjamin S., 10–11, 145
Bohen, Fred, 130
Boone, Richard, 72, 130, 148
Boutin, Bernie, 62–63
Brademas, John, 84
Bronfenbrenner, Urie, 3, 75; call for a longi-
    tudinal, random-assigned study of Head
    Start, 105; Task Force on Early Child-
    hood Development, 110, 117; testimony
    before House on Economic Opportunity
    Act of 1964, 46, 68, 80, 148, 169n64; work
    on assessment instrument, 102
Brooks, J. Deton Jr., 91
Brown, Dyke, 29
Bruner, Jerome S., 71, 74, 110, 149, 175n62
Bundy, McGeorge, 28
Bureau of Education, 13
Bureau of Elementary and Secondary Edu-
    cation (BESE), 115
Bureau of the Budget: favored summer
    Head Start programs, 104; 1963 omnibus

Bureau of the Budget (*continued*)
education bill, 23; opposition to a separate education bill, 40–41; questions about OEO, 64; task force to address issues raised in Vocational Education Amendments of 1968, 135
Bush, George W., 1
busing, 119

"Calendar Wednesday" procedure, 21
Califano, Joseph A. Jr., 63, 64, 65, 108, 109, 110, 128, 136
campus protests, 128
Cannon, William B., 37–38, 39, 42, 44, 54
Capron, William M., 32, 36–37, 38, 41
Carpenter, Liz, 74
Carter, Lisle, 108, 109
Catholic Church, opposition to the public-school-only federal aid, 19, 20
Caudill, Harry, *Night Comes to the Cumberlands*, 6
Celebrezze, Anthony, 33, 40, 41, 53, 153
child-benefit approach, 80
child development: changing views of, 9–11, 145–46; "critical period," 11; growing interest in from 1964, 148
Child Development Group of Mississippi (CDGM), 96, 97, 98–99, 150, 182n49, 182n53
Child Development Task Force of 1967, 117–18
Children's Bureau, 8
child-teacher ratio, 78
Child Welfare League of America, 133–34
Citizens Crusade Against Poverty (CCAP), 98, 120, 130
Civil Rights Act of 1964, 79
Clark, Joseph S. Jr., 16, 120, 126, 131
Cloward, Richard A., 27, 29, 30
Cohen, Wilbur, 41, 82, 129, 178n112; call for interagency coordinating committee for preschool and day care programs, 128; and Kennedy's education agenda, 18; little initial interest in preschool education, 50; opposition to creation of new agencies, 38, 40; recommendations for placement of education within HEW, 53; and

transfer of Head Start from OEO, 131, 132, 136, 153
college protests, 137
college student financial aid, during Eisenhower administration, 15
community action agencies (CAAs), 66, 67, 68; opposition to privileging of Head Start, 96, 107; preschools, 72
Community Action Program (CAP), 38, 58, 60, 64; controversy about control of, 66; funding of community action agencies, 67; funding of national emphasis programs, 67; funds, 124; largest component of OEO, 48, 66, 67; legislative requirement of "maximum feasible participation," 95, 120; major source of experimental funding for Head Start, 104–5; regional decentralization, 65
Community Commissions for Children, 113
Community Facilities Act of 1941 (the Lanham Act), 8, 13
compensatory preschool programs, 51
Congress of the Confederation, 12
Conway, Jack T., 46–47, 62, 66
Cooke, Robert E., 72, 74, 76, 92, 106, 110, 148, 149
Cooke Head Start Planning Committee, 2, 74–78, 148, 176n73; concern over OEO administration of Head Start, 107–8; disagreements about the initial scope of Head Start, 75–76; emphasis on medical, social, and nutritional services, 99; insufficient attention to obtaining high-quality teachers, 77; lack of emphasis on educational component of Head Start, 89, 99, 106; opposed evaluations of Head Start, 102; reluctance to challenge administration on Head Start, 149–50
Cooperative Research Program, 14
Council for Urban Affairs, 141
Council of Economic Advisers (CEA), 31; desire to keep education projects within the War on Poverty package, 41; investigation of nature of American poverty, 146; planning of war on poverty, 36, 37, 40
Craig, Lillian, 120
Curtis, Thomas, 81

Daley, Richard, 138
day care: growth of day nurseries in late nineteenth and early twentieth centuries, 7, 8; postwar, 9
Delaney, James J., 20
delegate agencies, 99
Dellenback, John R., 128
Democratic Convention of 1968, 138
Democrats: denounced GOP's targeting of Title I funds to early childhood education at the expense of older children, 149; 1964 platform, 57–58; sweep of the 1958 midterm elections, 15
Department of Education, 13
desegregation of schools, 119
Deutsch, Martin, 46, 50, 51, 52, 78, 104, 149, 150
Devans, Edward, 72–73
The Devil Has Slippery Shoes (Greenberg), 182n49, 182n53
disadvantaged children, experimental programs designed to enrich intellectual experience, 11
Division of Compensatory Education (DCE), 115
Dodge, Philip, 70
Dominick, Peter H., 126, 128–36, 153
Dufresne, Art, 127

early childhood development. See child development
Early Childhood Development Task Force of 1966, 110–13; call for a broad approach to help disadvantaged children, 112–13; call for federal-level Office for Children, 113; call for more emphasis on education component of Head Start, 155
Economic Opportunity Act of 1964, 45–49, 58, 60, 119, 147–48; drafting of, 44–45
Economic Opportunity Council, 63
Economic Report of the President, 1964, 40
education, early federal involvement in, 8, 12–14. See also federal aid to education; preschool programs
"Educational Improvement in Low Income Areas," 41–42
Education Initiative Act, 81, 149
Eisenberg, Leon, 103

Eisenhower administration: educational involvement, 14–15; endorsement of classroom construction assistance, 14; extension of GI educational Benefits to Korean War veterans, 15; national conference on juvenile delinquency, 29; research and development funding, 15
elections: of 1960, education in, 15–17; of 1964, education and poverty in, 57–59
Elementary and Secondary Education Act (ESEA) of 1965, 3, 59, 60, 69, 119; amendment permitting use of Title I funds for preschool programs, 83; confusion about whether Title I monies could be used for preschool programs, 82; House debates on, 82–86; passage of, 79–86; Senate hearings, 85
Elliot, Emerson J., 54, 110, 115
Erlenborn, John N., 128
Eurich, Alvin, 162n34
Evans, John, 105

Family Assistance Plan (FAP), 141
federal aid to education: constitutional and political opposition to for K-12 education, 80, 146; debates about funding for preschools during the ESEA passage, 80–86; early, 8, 12–14; federal college housing loan program, 18
Federal Emergency Relief Administration (FERA), 8; adult education and nursery school programs, 13
Feldman, Myer (Mike), 18, 71
Finch, Robert H., 142
fixed-IQ orthodoxy, 9–10
Folsom, Marion, 91
Ford Foundation, 2; and early childhood education, 26–28; Great Cities Schools Program, 11; and the Kennedy administration, 28–31; key role in funding urban preschool programs, 31, 146; role in federal juvenile delinquency program, 30
Frelinghuysen, Peter Jr., 47, 68
Friday, William, 115
Friday Task Force on Education, 115
Froebel, Friedrich, 9
Froomkin, Joseph, 114

Gaither, James C., 66, 95, 133, 136

Gardner, John W., 54, 90, 162n34

Gardner Task Force on Early Childhood Development: exploration of early childhood education, 54–57, 69; report to the White House, 56–57, 113, 148

General Accounting Office (GAO), study of OEO's efficiency and effectiveness, 142

George Peabody's Teachers' College, 70

Getzels, J. W., 90

Gibbons, Sam M., 125

GI Bill of Rights, 14

Goldwater, Barry M., 20, 48, 49, 57, 58, 136, 137

Goodell, Charles E., 46, 81, 121, 122, 124, 125, 148

Goodenough, Florence, 10

Goodlad, John, 55, 69, 110

Goodwin, Richard, 54

Gordon, Edmund W., 39, 102, 103, 105, 110

Gordon, Kermit, 38

Gorham, William, 117

Gorham Task Force on Child Development, 117–18, 128

Gray, Susan, 70, 110

Gray Areas Program, 26, 27, 28, 30

Great Cities School Improvement Program, 26, 27

Great Depression, 8

Great Society, 1, 3, 128

Green, Edith, 25, 125, 130, 132, 133

Greenberg, Polly, 71, 89, 97, 102; *The Devil Has Slippery Shoes*, 182n49, 182n53

Hackett, David, 29, 30

Hamilton, Ann, 43

Harding, Bertrand M., 63, 131, 132, 136

Harrington, Michael, 44; *The Other America: Poverty in the United States*, 6–7, 32, 158n10

Head Start. *See* Project Head Start

Head Start: The Inside Story of America's Most Successful Educational Experiment (Zigler and Muenchow), 2

Head Start Planning Committee. *See* Cooke Head Start Planning Committee

Health, Education, and Welfare (HEW), Department of: battle to lead the anti-poverty program, 41; call for preschool programs to be placed in Office of Education, 82; Office of Child Development (OCD), 142, 153; Office of Juvenile Delinquency, 30; oversight of the Office of Education, 13; support for early childhood education, 56–57, 69

Hebb, Donald O., *The Organization of Behavior*, 10

Heineman Task Force on Government Organization, 64

Heller, Walter, 32, 33, 34, 36, 37, 39, 43, 45

Higher Education Facilities Act of 1963, 57

Hobbes, Nicholas, 117

Housing and Urban Development (HUD), Department of, 64

Hovde, Frederick, 162n34

Hovde Education Task Force, 162n34, 162n42

Howe, Harold, 111, 127, 129, 136, 153, 154

Hughes, Sam, 39

Humphrey, Hubert H., 57; addressed issue of preschool education, 139; education recommendations, 139; 1960 presidential race, 16; 1968 presidential race, 138, 140; *War on Poverty*, 58–59

Hunt, J. McVicker, 115; *Intelligence and Experiences*, 10–11; on IQ, 145; Task Force on Early Child Development, 110, 117

Hunter, David, 29

Hymes, James L. Jr., 73, 77

illiteracy rates, 13

impact aid, 13, 14, 21, 162n43

"Improving the Opportunities and Achievements of the Children of the Poor," 75, 76–77, 149

income: growth of real per capita during the 1960s, 6; personal per capita, from 1950 to 1970, 6

Institute for Developmental Studies, 28

Interagency Task Force on Education of 1965, 108–10

IQ, view of as fixed at birth, 9–10, 145

Jacobs, Andrew, 85

Javits, Jacob K., 49

Jeffrey, Julie Roy, 44–45
Job Corps, 42, 44, 49, 64, 65, 67, 123
job training programs, 44
Johnson, Lady Bird, 74, 88, 103
Johnson, Lyndon Baines: adoption of Kennedy's commitment to fight poverty, 147; advocate for public education throughout his career, 52; announcement that he would not run for reelection, 128; endorsement of war on poverty, 35–36; final State of the Union Address, 140–41; 1960 presidential race, 16
Johnson, Paul B., 97
Johnson administration: announcement of Project Head Start, 73–74; announcement of year-round Head Start programs, 104; call for "a national war on poverty," 45; creation of eleven task forces, 110, 117; decision not to reorganize OEO, 65; disadvantaged student assistance, 79–80; Education Task Force, 54–57; emphasis on role of local citizens in planning and implementing CAP's antipoverty initiatives, 66; exaggeration of effects of eight-week Head Start program, 181n17; fear that Republicans and southern Democrats would dismantle antipoverty programs, 125; fear that Shriver might help Robert Kennedy seek the presidency in 1968, 64; follow-through program for Head Start, 113–14; funding of War on Poverty, 65, 88; funding of year-round Head Start programs, 93; "Great Society" speech, 54; interagency group to coordinate preschools and day care services, 128; interest in early childhood education, 49–52; low-quality, underfunded early childhood education projects, 154–55; placement of OEO within the Executive Office, 61; planning the war on poverty, 36–40; postponing of major education initiatives in 1964, 52–54; PPB system, 101; "President's Report to the Nation on Poverty," 88; signing of Economic Opportunity Act, 60–61; signing of ESEA, 86

Jones, Jim, 132
Joseph P. Kennedy Jr. Foundation, 69, 175n50
Juvenile Delinquency and Youth Offenses Control Act of 1961, 29–30
juvenile delinquency programs, 26, 29

Kelly, William Jr., 43–44
Kennedy, Edward, 120
Kennedy, John Fitzgerald: involvement in education during tenure in Congress, 17, 25; perspective on domestic poverty, 6, 32; 1960 presidential race, 16; 1963 State of the Union Address, 24; Why England Slept, 17. See also Kennedy administration
Kennedy, Robert F., 126; broad view of Head Start, 189n30; endorsement of War on Poverty, 167n24; head of committee on Juvenile Delinquency and Youth Crime, 29; hearings on Economic Opportunity Act, 45; Johnson and, 64, 65; on need for preschool education programs, 30; 1968 presidential race, 137–38; opposition to new agencies, 38; support for increased OEO funding, 120; support for preschool programs in ESEA, 82; support for transferring OEO's education programs to Office of Education, 83
Kennedy, Rosemary, 69
Kennedy administration: attempts to deal with poverty and education, 2, 12, 19; beginning of war on poverty, 31–34; cabinet, 18; Education Task Force, 18; endorsement of across-the-board tax cuts, 31; failure to enact federal school-aid legislation in 1961 and 1962, 146; interagency task force on poverty, 33; juvenile delinquency concerns, 29; and K-12 education, 17–22; limitation of federal funding for elementary and secondary schools to public schools, 19; 1962 education agenda, 21–22; 1963 education bills, 22–26; 1963 education message to Congress, 24
Keppel, Francis: growing support for preschool education, 51, 52, 68, 148, 153; and Interagency Task Force on Education, 54, 108–9, 139, 162n34

Kerr, Clark, 54
kindergarten, incorporation into public
    school systems, 9
King, Martin Luther Jr., 138
Kleiner, Harold, 133
Kravitz, Sanford, 104
Krock, Arthur, 17

Lampman, Robert J., 32, 40
land-grant colleges, 13
Landrum, Phil, 47
Lanham Act, 8, 13
Legal Services, 67
Levin, Harry, 51–52, 68–69, 148
Levin, Thomas, 96–97
Levine, Robert, 105
Levitan, Sar, 61, 103
Lewin, Kurt, 10
Lewis, Oscar, 110
Library Services and Construction Act of
    1964, 57
Lodge, Henry, 15
Loney, Katherine Deadrich, 86
Loomis, Henry, 108, 109

Macdonald, Dwight, 32
Manatos, Mike, 132
Marland, Sidney P., 54
Marris, Peter, 27
Mary Holmes Junior College, 97
McAndrews, Lawrence J., 20
McCarthy, Eugene, 138
McNamara, Patrick, 19
media endorsement of Project Head Start,
    73–74
"Memorandum of Understanding between
    the Office of Economic Opportunity
    and the Department of Health, Educa-
    tion Welfare Relative to the Adminis-
    tration of the Head Start Program
    under a Delegation of Authority,"
    130
Miller, William E., 57
minimum wage, 119
Mississippi Action for Progress (MAP), 98
Mississippi Freedom Democratic Party
    (MFDP), 97

Mississippi Head Start program, 3, 182n49,
    182n53; controversy, 97–99
Mobilization for Youth, 29, 30
Moorhead, William S., 51
Morrill Act, 13
Morse, Wayne L., 19, 25, 79, 85, 131, 132, 153
mothers' pension programs, 7
Moyers, Bill, 41, 63, 71, 108
Moynihan, Daniel Patrick, 44, 141
Muenchow, Susan, 2, 180n3
Murphy, George, 126, 130

National Advisory Council on Economic
    Opportunity, 63
National Catholic Welfare Conference, 25
National Defense Education Act (NDEA) of
    1958, 14, 18, 19; reauthorization, 21, 54
National Education Association (NEA), 13,
    79
National School Lunch program, 14
National Science Foundation, 14
Neighborhood Youth Corps, 64, 65, 67, 123,
    124
New Frontiers of the Kennedy Administration,
    18
"A New Look at Pre-School Education, Pres-
    ent and Future," 122
New York Mobilization for Youth program,
    29
Niemeyer, John, 73, 98
Nixon, Richard M., 15, 137, 140, 153; and
    preschool education, 139; 1960 presiden-
    tial race, 16–17; shaping of 1960 GOP
    platform to endorse federal aid for ele-
    mentary and secondary school construc-
    tion, 16
Nixon administration: move of Head Start
    into Office of Child Development in
    HEW, 153; on OEO's role, 141–42; special
    administrative study of Head Start, 142;
    transition to, 140–41
Northwest Ordinance, 13
nursery schools, geared toward middle-class
    families, 7

Office of Child Development (OCD), 142,
    153

Office of Economic Opportunity (OEO), 3, 40; advisory board, 63; annual revamping by Congress, 107; beginning of focus on early childhood education, 68–73; description of Head Start to Congress, 99; did not welcome criticism of Head Start, 104; efforts to create Head Start programs for summer of 1965, 87–90; estimated average cost per student for Head Start, 79; and Follow Through Program, 3, 115; founding of, 60–68; funding for new national assessment, 106; growing criticism of, 95–97; Information Center, 63–64; information packet for Head Start applicants, 88–89; as an innovative agency, 101; lack of adequate internal coordination, 63; mandate to coordinate the War on Poverty, 65, 101; mission to help disadvantaged youngsters, 56; neglect of preschools' educational component, 89; Office of Civil Rights, 64; Office of Congressional Relations, 64; Office of General Counsel, 64; Office of Inspection, 64; Office of Public Affairs, 64; Office of Research, Planning, Programs, and Evaluation, 63, 105; organizational plan, 61; participation in legislative affairs, 133; poor administration of antipoverty programs, 131; pressure to transfer some of its programs to other federal agencies, 64; reauthorization, 123; refusal to allow local transfers of monies from summer to full-year Head Start projects, 94; regional offices, 65; staff offices, 63–64
Office of Education (OE): contributions in initiating and developing Head Start, 71–72; insistence that it was the best location for Head Start, 135–36; transfer to HEW, 13; willingness to work with states and local communities to improve K-3 education, 154
Office of Programs for Education of the Disadvantaged (OPED), contributions to development of Head Start, 71–72
Ohio University, 106
Ohlin, Lloyd E., 27, 29, 30

omnibus 1963 education bill, 23, 24–25, 146
Omwake, Eveline, 99–100
Opportunity Crusade, 123, 125
Orton, Richard E., 133, 135–36
Osborn, Keith, 77
The Other America: Poverty in the United States (Harrington), 6–7, 32, 158n10

Peace Corps, 42
Perkins, Carl D., 79, 82, 83, 134
personal per capita income, from 1950 to 1970, 6
Planning-Programming-Budgeting (PPB) system, 101–2
post–World War II prosperity, 5–6
poverty: African Americans in 1964, 6; Appalachian, 6; discovery of, 5–7, 146; Kennedy administration and, 2, 31–34; in 1964, 6
Poverty Task Force, 43–45, 46
Powell, Adam Clayton, 19, 21, 25, 45, 120, 162n46
"Pre-School Plan for Republicans," 80
preschool programs: amendment to ESEA permitting use of Title I funds for, 83; under community action agencies, 72; compensatory, 51; debates about funding for during the ESEA passage, 80–86; Ford Foundation funding of, 31, 146; Francis Keppel and, 51, 52, 68, 148, 153; Hubert Humphrey and, 139; Richard Nixon and, 139; Robert Kennedy and, 30; Sargent Shriver and, 68, 69, 124–25; teacher qualifications, 85; White House preschool initiative, 73–74
President's Committee on Juvenile Delinquency and Youth Crime, 29, 146
President's Panel on Mental Retardation, 70, 73
private sector, interest in early childhood education programs during the late 1950s and early 1960s, 26
Project Head Start: challenges faced by in second half of the 1960s, 3; child-teacher ratio, 78; disadvantaged backgrounds of children, 94; efforts to create, 3; estimated average cost per student, 79;

Project Head Start (*continued*)
evaluating, 100–105; Follow Through
Program, 3, 64, 65, 113–17, 126, 152, 155;
funding for research and evaluation, 103;
hiring of nonspecialist paraprofessionals,
95, 99–100; information packet for applicants, 88–89; jobs for adults, 92; Johnson
administration and, 73–74, 104, 113–14,
181n17; lack of mandatory or recommended preschool curriculum, 99; literature on origins of, 1–2; local assessment
studies, 103; national evaluation of, 105–
8; 1965 launch of, 87–90; 1965 summer
program, 91–93; and the 1968 election,
136–40; and Office of Education, 71–72,
135–36; organization of, 78–79; paraprofessionals, 95; public enthusiasm for
summer programs, 103; receipt of CAP
monies, 67; research committee, 105;
studies of long-term effects, 151; substitute teachers, 151; teachers' salaries, 79;
transfer to HEW, 141–43; uneven program quality, 99–100; volunteers, 95;
year-round programs, 93–95, 151. *See also*
Office of Economic Opportunity
(OEO); Shriver, Sargent
*Project Head Start: A Legacy of the War on
Poverty*, 2
Prouty, Winston L., 49, 124, 134
Public Works Administration, school construction assistance, 13

Quie, Albert H., 148; amendment to transfer Head Start and Upward Bound
from OEO to OE, 128; call for legislation to improve training of preschool
teachers, 68; early childhood substitute
for Title I, 83–84, 179n121; Education
Initiative Act, 149; and ESEA, 91, 125;
"Opportunity Crusade," 123, 125; plans
for developing preschools, 46; Republican Task Force on Education, 122; request of federal funds for teachers of
disadvantaged children, 80; support for
broader public school services for K-3
students, 154; support for Head Start,
121

Reagan, Ronald, 137
real per capita personal income, growth during the 1960s, 6
Rein, Martin, 27
Reinert, Paul C., 54
Republican Party: alternative education legislation to ESEA, 81–84, 149; 1966 antipoverty alternative, 125; attacks on the
Johnson administration's education and
poverty programs, 116; attempts to transfer Head Start from OEO, 121–25, 126–
28, 152; initial championing of early
childhood education, 148; 1964 platform,
57; Opportunity Crusade, 123, 125; proposal to increase Head Start support, 123
Republican Task Force on Education, 122–23
Ribicoff, Abraham, 18, 21, 22
Richmond, Julius, 78, 91, 96, 97, 101, 102
Riesman, David, 54
Robinson, Wade, 71
Rockefeller, Nelson, 15, 57, 137
Romney, George, 137
rural loans, 64

Saltzman, Henry, 27
Samuels, Howard, 91
Sanders, Barefoot, 132
Sarge: The Life and Times of Sargent Shriver
(Stossel), 2, 157n7
"Saturday Club," 32
Schlei, Norbert A., 44, 62, 68
Schlesinger, Arthur, 34
Schnapper, M. B., 162n34
school desegregation, 119
Schultze, Charles L., 38, 44, 93–94
Scranton, William W., 57
segregated schools, debate about funding
for, 20
Servicemen's Readjustment Act (GI Bill of
Rights), 13
Sesame Street, 28
Shepoiser, L. H., 91
Shriver, Eunice Kennedy, 69–70
Shriver, Sargent, 2, 3, 49, 58, 74; administra-
tive strengths and weaknesses, 62; ap-
pointment as director of OEO, 61;
appointment as director of War on

Poverty, 147; arguments against combining Head Start with early childhood education programs under Title I of ESEA, 122; and assessment of Head Start, 103; and Boutin, 62–63; bringing together of existing and proposed programs, 43; citation of local studies testifying to the success of Head Start, 103; and community action programs, 96, 126–27, 153, 168n35; as director of the Peace Corps, 61–62; and Early Childhood Development Task Force, 111; emphasis on educational aspects of early childhood education, 74; endorsement of ambitious plan to begin summer Head Start programs, 149; exploration of preschool education, 68; on jobs created by Head Start, 92, 151; and Johnson, 64; launching of Head Start, 88; opposition to efforts to transfer Head Start from OEO, 96, 153; opposition to GOP and OE efforts to designate Title I monies for preschools, 124–25; opposition to higher percentage of CAP funds to Head Start, 121; opposition to increase in number of Head Start children in full-year programs at the expense of the summer program, 94; original conception of Head Start as an educational program, 106; on Project Head Start as greatest success of the War on Poverty, 121; recruitment of Julius Richman, 78; relationship with members of Head Start Planning Committee, 75; resignation as director of the Peace Corps, 172n5; sympathetic to the idea of preschool education, 69; termination of CDGM contracts, 98; testimony on OEO bill, 45–46; and Theodore Berry, 67; used popularity of Head Start to offset increasingly negative attitudes toward OEO, 95–96; and War on Poverty, 42–45
Silber, John, 85
Silberman, Charles E., 50, 51, 52, 148
Sizer, Ted, 104
Smith, Howard W., 48
Smith Hughes Act of 1917, 13

Snyder, Richard, 116
Sorensen, Theodore, 18, 23, 33–34, 37
Spellman, Francis, 18–19
Sputnik, 5, 14
Stein, Annie, 103
Stennis, John, 97, 98
Stoddard, George, 10
Stone, Jeanette, 165n115
Stossel, Scott, *Sarge: The Life and Times of Sargent Shriver*, 2, 157n7
Sugarman, Jule M., 69, 127, 128, 148; cost per child estimate for Head Start, 150; as deputy director of CAP, 89; as deputy director of Head Start, 78–79; endorsing the Children's Bureau as a possible home for Head Start, 129–30; on funding of Mississippi Head Start, 99; and Head Start Planning Committee, 72–73, 98, 107–8; on OEO management, 61; suggestion that Head Start remain with OEO, 129
Sullivan, J. Graham, 133
Survey Ordinance of 1785, 12–13
Symington, Stuart, 16

Taft, Robert A., 13
task-oriented curriculum model, 114
tax credits, 81
Teacher Corps, 120
teachers' salaries, debate over in 1960 presidential race, 16
Terman, Lewis M., 10
Thackery, Russell, 162n34
"Toward Excellent Education for All Americans," 139
Tower, John, 48, 49
Truman administration, increase in federal aid to education, 14
Tyler, Ralph W., 54

United States Congress: attempts to transfer Head Start from the OEO to HEW, 106, 120–36; "conservative voting alliance," 124; Eighty-ninth, 79, 119; 1967 legislation on Economic Opportunity Act and OEO, 125; and 1963 omnibus education bill, 24–25; Ninetieth, 115, 152; question-

United States Congress (*continued*)
ing of administration of OEO programs,
120; resistance to requests for federal aid
for public education during late nine-
teenth and early twentieth centuries, 13
United States House of Representatives: debates on Elementary and Secondary
Education Act of 1965, 82–86; General
Education Subcommittee and Kennedy
administration's aid-to-education bill, 20;
Rules Committee block of Kennedy administration's aid-to-education bill, 20;
Rules Committee scuttled most federal
school aid initiatives, 14
—Committee on Education and Labor: Ad
Hoc Subcommittee on the War on
Poverty Program, 45, 120–21; Economic
Opportunity Act of 1964, 47; ESEA debates, 82; and Kennedy administration's
aid-to-education bill, 20; minority response to the *Committee Report on the Elementary and Secondary Education Act of
1965*, 81–82
United States Senate: amendment to transfer Head Start from OEO to the Office
of Education, 130–32; Labor and Public
Welfare Committee hearings on reauthorizing EOA, 125; Labor and Public
Welfare Committee Select Subcommittee on Poverty, 48
—Committee on Labor and Public Welfare,
85; and Kennedy administration's school-
aid bill, 19; Report on the Economic Opportunity Act of 1964, 48–49
University of Chicago Research Conference
on the Education of the Culturally Deprived, 1964, 11
University of Iowa Child Welfare Research
Station, 9
Upward Bound, 67
Urban Job Corps centers, 43
urban redevelopment, 26
urban riots, 115, 137

Valentine, Jeanette, 2, 104
Vice President's Task Force on Education, 139
Vietnam War: cost pressures, 65, 116, 118,
124, 128, 147; public frustration regarding,
115, 137
Vocational Education Act of 1963, 57, 153
Vocational Education Amendments of 1968,
130, 134
volunteers, 95
Volunteers in Service to America (VISTA),
44, 64

Wallace, George C., 138, 139, 140
War on Poverty: Community Action Program (CAP), 38–39; Council of Eco-
nomic Advisers planning, 36, 37, 40, 41;
debates about in 1966, 120–21; debating
education's role in, 40–42; House of
Representatives Subcommittee on, 120–
21; Johnson administration and, 35–40,
45, 65, 88, 147; OEO coordination of,
65, 101; reauthorization, 116; Robert
Kennedy and, 167n24; Sargent Shriver
and, 42–45, 147. *See also* Shriver, Sargent
Weeks, Christopher, 68
Wegman, Myron, 177n82, 177n92, 184n81
Weikart, David P., 114–15
Weisbrod, Burton, 36–37
Wellman, Beth, 10
Westinghouse Learning Corporation evalu-
ation of Head Start, 106–7, 153
White, Theodore, 58
White House Conference on Children: 1909,
7; 1965, 181n18
White House Conference on Education,
90–91
White House preschool initiative, 73–74
White House Task Force on Urban Prob-
lems, 64
Willis, Benjamin, 162n34
Wirtz, Willard, 38, 41, 43, 44, 136
Wolff, Max, 103
women, entry into the labor force during
World War II, 8
Works Progress Administration (WPA),
public nursery schools, 8
Wright, Stephen J., 54

Yarborough, Ralph, 85
Yarmolinsky, Adam, 44, 49, 62

Ylvisaker, Paul N., 26, 27, 28
Youth Employment Act, 37

Zacharias, Jerrold R., 54
Zigler, Edward, 2, 75–78, 100, 104, 150, 180n3;
    acknowledgment of overall ineffective-
    ness of Head Start, 184n93; called for a
    longitudinal, random-assigned study of

Head Start, 105; as director of Office of
Child Development, 106; on 1965 Head
Start programs, 92–93; warning about
exaggerated and unrealistic expectations
for Head Start and Follow Through,
116–17
Zwick, Charles, 136